P.F.M. FONTAINE

THE LIGHT AND THE DARK

A CULTURAL HISTORY OF DUALISM

VOLUME XII

J.C. GIEBEN, PUBLISHER
AMSTERDAM

THE LIGHT AND THE DARK

P.F.M. FONTAINE

THE LIGHT AND THE DARK
A CULTURAL HISTORY OF DUALISM

VOLUME XII

DUALISM IN ROMAN HISTORY III

THE CHRISTIAN CHURCH IN CONFLICT
WITH THE ROMAN EMPIRE AND WITH JUDAISM

J.C. GIEBEN, PUBLISHER
AMSTERDAM 1997

To my friend Dr. Evert M. Janssen,
historian, critical mind,
author of fine books, Burckhardt expert

No part of this book may be translated or reproduced in any form, by print, photoprint, microfilm, or any other means, without written permission from the publisher.

© by P.F.M. Fontaine / ISBN 90 5063 357 9 / Printed in The Netherlands

"For all things are called
light and darkness"

Parmenides

CONTENTS

Preface		xv
I	THE CHRISTIANS IN CONFLICT WITH ROME	1
	PART I INTRODUCTORY	1
1.	The first expansion of Christianity	1
2.	Non-Christian evidence for the presence of Christians	2
	PART II PAGAN AUTHORS ON CHRISTIANS	3
1.	A historian's opinion	3
2.	A governor's opinion	4
3.	'Atheism'	4
4.	Alleged scandalous behaviour	5
5.	The portrait of an 'atheist'	7
6.	An emperor's opinion	7
7.	A satirist's opinion	7
8.	A doctor's opinion	8
9.	'Philosophy'	8
10.	The opinion of Celsus	9
	a. A stupid sort of people	10
	b. Silly doctrines	11
	c. The Christian rejection of Judaism	12
	d. The Christian rejection of the imperial cult	12
	e. The old and the new	13
11.	A philosopher's opinion	13
	a. Criticism of the Book of Daniel	14
	b. Criticism of the New Testament	15
	c. Porphyry's main objection	15
	PART III THE EMPIRE AND THE CHURCH IN OPPOSITION	17
1.	The Roman attitude to alien religions	17
	a. An eminently religious people	17
	b. Abhorrence of foreign religions	18
	c. An action against the Bacchics	19

	d.	The Christians treated worse than others	19
	e.	Problems of the state with Christians	20
	f.	Christian doctrine at variance with the imperial ideology	21
2.	What the Christians thought of the Empire		22
	a.	The fundamental position	22
	b.	Paul's ruling	23
	c.	A fiercely anti-Roman book	24
	d.	The two realms of Hermas	25
	e.	More critical sounds	26
	f.	Was the end near?	26
3.	Two great authors averse of the Empire		27
	a.	'The Caesar imitating Satan'	27
	b.	The devil at work	28
4.	Frustrated expectations		29
5.	Politics of accomodation		29
	a.	The Empire not the work of the devil	30
	b.	'Honour the Emperor'	30
	c.	Resistance unallowed	31
	d.	Keeping a low profile	31
	e.	The future of the Empire	32
6.	A tale of two cities		33
	a.	Why Augustine wrote the City of God	33
	b.	Cities with a difference	34
	c.	All these wars ...	35
	d.	Why an Empire?	36
	e.	The fundamental difference between the two cities	37
	f.	Is the Christian Empire a better one?	38
	g.	Cain and Abel as ancestors	38
	h.	The parallel course of the two cities	39
	j.	The inhabitants of the heavenly city	39
	k.	Assessment	40

	PART IV WAR ON THE CHURCH	41
1.	A state in the state?	41
2.	The 'ten persecutions'	43
3.	Why the Church waspersecuted	44
4.	Popular outbursts against the Christians	44
5.	Official policy	45
6.	Nero's anti-Christian action	46
7.	Domitian the competitor	47
6.	The policy of the Antonini	49
	a. Trajan's ruling	49

	b.	Hadrian's moderation	49
	c.	No change in the official policy during the reign of Antoninus Pius	50
	d.	New problems under Marcus Aurelius	51
	e.	A confused situation under Commodus	52
9.	The policy of the Severi		52
	a.	Their attitude to Christianity	52
	b.	A baneful edict	53
	c.	The victims	53
10.	Steady growth of Christianity		54
11.	The religious position of the Severi		55
12.	A 'barbarian' on the throne		56
13.	The persecution of Decius		57
	a.	Decius' religious policy	57
	b.	The first general decree	58
	c.	Victims	58
	d.	Apostasy	59
	e.	Disorganization of the Church	59
14.	The persecution of Valerian		60
	a.	Valerian's religious policy	60
	b.	The First Edict	61
	c.	The Second Edict	61
15.	The Great Persecution		63
	a.	Diocletian's motivation	64
	b.	The action against the Christians	65
	c.	The persecution petering out	66
16.	The pacification policy of Constantine the Great		68
17.	All quiet on the Christian front?		69
18.	The last revival of paganism		70
	a.	Julian's Christian youth	70
	b.	The rupture with the Church	71
	c.	On his way to the throne	73
	d.	Julian's book against he Christian faith	74
	e.	His own creed	75
	f.	The decree on education	76
	g.	The offensive against the Christians	77
	h.	The end	78
19.	Conclusion		78
Notes to Chapter 1			79

II	JUDAISM AND CHRISTIANITY: A DUALISTIC RELATIONSHIP?	95
	PART I PRELIMINARIES	95
1.	My credentials	95
2.	Clarification of terms	98
3.	The Jewish heritage of the Church	98
4.	What exactly is Judaism?	100
5.	Where did Jesus himself belong?	103
6.	Why Jesus had to be done away with and who were responsible	104
7.	Jesus' conflict with the Pharisees	106
8.	A drastic change after A.D. 70	107
9.	The miracle of the survival of the Jewish nation	108
10.	Who are 'the Jews' of the New Testament?	109
	a. Books without any Jews	110
	b. Paul's Letter to the Romans	110
	c. 'The Jews' in the Gospels	111
	d. 'The Jews' in Acts	112
	e. The Jewish anti-Christianism of the first century A.D.	114
	f. John again	115
11.	Where Jews and Christians disagreed	116
	a. Jesus as the Messiah	117
	b. Jesus' divinity	117
	c. Ideas of redemption	118
	d. The Christian rejection of Mosaic Law	119
	e. Paul the great enemy	120
12.	The Jewish predicament	120
13.	An ethic nation	122
14.	A sore spot: the question of proselytism	124
	a. What is a proselyte?	124
	b. The 'God-fearers'	125
	c. Modern views of Jewish proselytism	125
	d. Proselytes and proselytism	126
	e. The lack of evidence	127
	f. Was the great number of Diaspora Jews the result of proselytism?	128
15.	Christian anti-Judaism compared with that of pagans and Gnostics	130
	PART II CHRISTIAN AUTHORS ON JEWS AND JUDAISM	132
1.	The Christian authors of the first hundred years	132
	a. The Letters of Clement	132

	b.	Ignatius of Antioch	132
	c.	The Didache	134
	d.	The Epistle of Barnabas	135
	e.	The Pastor of Hermas and the Martyrdom of Polycarp	136
	f.	The Letter to Diognetus	137
	g.	Conclusion	137
2.		Christian authors of the late second century	137
	a.	Justin the Martyr	137
	b.	Melito's paschal homily	141
	c.	Irenaeus of Lyons	143
	d.	The first 'Adversus Judaeos'	144
	e.	What Theophilus had to say to Autolycus	145
	f.	Minucius Felix and his 'Octavius'	146
3.		Fathers of the third century	147
	a.	Clement of Alexandria	147
	b.	Tertullian	149
	c.	Origen	152
	d.	Successors of Origen	157
	e.	Hippolytus	157
	f.	The Didascalia	159
	g.	Cyprian	160
4.		Fathers and Councils of the fourth century	161
	a.	The canons of the Elvira synod	161
	b.	Eusebius	162
	c.	Lactantius	164
	d.	The Council of Nicaea	165
	e.	Silvester I	167
	f.	Aphrahat	168
	g.	Hilary of Poitiers	168
	h.	John Chrysostom	169
	j.	Synods of the second half of the fourth century	178
5.		Fathers of the late fourth and the fifth centuries	179
	a.	Ambrose	179
	b.	Augustine	180
		PART III STATE LEGISLATION REGARDING JEWRY	181
1.		Judaism as a religio licita	181
2.		Measures of Constantine the Great	181
3.		Sharpening of the legislation under the sons of Constantine	182
4.		Benevolent measures of Valentinianus I	182
5.		The policy of Theodosius I the Great	182
	a.	Legislation	182

	b.	The Kallinikon incident	183
6.		Legislation after Kallinikon	185
7.		Attacks on synagogues	185
8.		Legislation with regard to synagogues	187
9.		The general attitude of the imperial authorities	188
10.		The abolishment of the Jewish patriarchate	188
11.		An overall view	189
	a.	Why synagogues were attacked	189
	b.	Jewish retaliations	190
	c.	Conclusion	190

PART IV ASSESSMENT 192

1.		Problems of the early Church	192
	a.	Internal problems	192
	b.	External problems	192
2.		The attitude of the Fathers regarding Jews and Judaism	193
3.		The main points of the Jewish-Christian debate	195
4.		The problem of judaizing	197
5.		Was the Jewish-Christian relationship dualistic?	199
6.		Patristic neurosis	201
7.		A personal note	203
		Notes to Chapter II	204

III JUDAIZING AS A SEED OF DISRUPTION 225

1.		Why this chapter	225
2.		About terminology	225
3.		The model community	226
4.		Messianic Jewish Christians	227
5.		The Ebionites	227
	a.	Their name	228
	b.	The Pseudo-Clementines, a source for Ebionism	228
	c.	The Jerusalemite community and Ebionism	229
	d.	Liturgy and organisation of the Ebionite Church	230
	e.	The Ebionites and the Old Testament	231
	f.	The dualistic Ebionite theology	231
	g.	About Eve	232
	h.	The situation of mankind	234
	j.	The true prophet: Ebionite Christology	234
	k.	The problem of Evil	235
	l.	Was the Ebionite ideology Gnostic?	236
	m.	The spread of Ebionism	237

n.	The orthodox Church and Ebionism	238
o.	Ebionism and Islam	238
6.	The Elkasaites	239
7.	The Judaizers	240
Notes to Chapter III		241
Bibliography		247
General Index		263

PREFACE

Everyone of the twelve volumes can be read independently of the others, but I may expect of nobody that he or she will read all those volumes from beginning to end. Therefore, I join to this volume a Manual. On the premise that not everyone will feel inclined to read the work in toto, at least I can guide scholars and other interested readers to their fields of study and interest. In the Manual these field are tabulated, with reference to the corresponding volumes, chapters, and sections.

However, with this much conceded to the overburdened reader, allow me to state that the series forms a whole, with all the parts interconnecting and interrelating. It has one all-comprising and over-arching theme, that of dualism. I hope that reviewers will realize this. For it has already happened more than once that they restrict themselves to their own field of study and leave the rest alone, as though it was not written at all. It has occurred several times in the past that I am confronted with misunderstandings about my main subject, dualism. It seems to be very hard for scholars to realize that unbridgeable oppositions can occur outside the fields of religion and history. I must, therefore, ask reviewers to take cognizance of those parts of the series where I explain what, in my opinion, dualism is (and, equally important, what it is not). I have written enough about it for not being misunderstood on this point. I refer the reader to the Prefaces of Vols. I, VI, IX, and XI, to the Afterword of Vol. I, and to Vol. IV, Ch. IV.4. Throughout this volume I use the same definition of dualism as in all former ones. There is dualism when we are confronted with two utterly opposed conceptions, systems, principles, groups or kinds of people, or even worlds, without any intermediate terms between them. They cannot be reduced to each other; in some cases the one is even dependent on the other. The opposites are considered to be of a different quality - so much so that one of them is always seen as distinctly inferior and hence must be neglected or destroyed.

"You couldn't have done it without me", is a popular saying nowadays. There are four persons who are fully entitled to say this to me. Dr. J.R. Dove, a native English speaker and an emeritus professor of English and American literature in the University of Oulu in Finland, corrected my English for the twelfth time in succession as carefully and courteously as ever. Somewhere my oldest daughter, Dr. Resianne Smidt van Gelder-Fontaine, a philosopher, found the time to read this volume chapter by chapter and provide me with many a useful comment, especially on Chapter II on the subject matter of which she is an expert. My dear wife Anneke painstakingly corrected the one-but-last version on typing errors. I must point out that the responsibility for all that this book contains lies with me, for its scholarly contents, the English, the typography, and the lay-out. The fourth person to be grateful to is my publisher, J.C. Gieben; without him nobody would ever see my text.

Vol. XIII will describe the conflict between orthodoxy and heterodoxy in the ancient Church.

P.F.M. Fontaine
Amsterdam NL

MANUAL

This manual is destined for those readers who do not want to read the whole work, but, instead, want to see what is said in it about the subject(s) they are interested in.

I   ON DUALISM AS SUCH

    Prefaces of Vols. I, VI, IX, XI,
    the Afterword of Vol. I,
    Vol. IV, Ch. IV.4

II   PERIODS AND CIVILIZATIONS

    1. Greece
       Vol. I Archaic and early classical periods
       Vol. II and III Fifth and fourth centuries B.C.
       Vol. VI The Hellenistic world
    2. Egypt
       Vol. IV, Ch. I
    3. Mesopotamia and Anatolia
       Vol. IV, Ch. III
    4. Israel
       Vol. IV, Ch. II
    5. Iran
       Vol. IV, Ch. IV, Vol. V, Ch. I
    6. India
       Vol. V, Ch. II
    7. China
       Vol. V, Ch. III
    8. Roman history
       Vols. X, XI, XII

III   POLITICAL HISTORY

    1. Greece
       Vol. II
       Vol. VI, Chs. I and II
    2. Rome

XVIII

       Vol. X
       Vol. XI, Chs. I, II, III, IV
  3. Egypt
       Vol. IV, Ch. I.1-4
  4. Mesopotamia and Anatolia
       Vol. IV, Ch. III.1-9.
  5. Israel
       Vol. IV, Ch. II.14
       Vol. VI, Ch. II.11
  6. Iran
       Vol. IV, Ch. IV.1-3
       Vol. V, Ch. I.1-3
  7. India
       Vol. V, Ch. II.1-11
  8. China
       Vol. V, Ch. III.1-5

IV   SOCIAL HISTORY

  1. Greece
       Vol. II, Ch. III.3
       Vol. II, Ch. IV.4
  2. India
       Vol. V, Ch. II.13-15
Since esoteric religious movements are socially distinct from the rest of the population, we may subsume these too under this heading :
  3. The Pythagoreans
       Vol. I, Ch. I
  4. Eleusinian mysteries and Orphics
       Vol. I, Ch. IV
  5. Yoga
       Vol. V, Ch. II.21
  6. Jainism
       Vol. V, Ch. II.22
  7. Dao
       Vol. V, Ch. III.25
  8. The Essenes
       Vol. VIII, Ch. V
  9. Almost all Gnostic movements
       Vol. VII, Ch. III, Vols. VIII and IX
  10. The subjected peoples of the Roman Empire
       Vol. XI, Ch. IV
  11. The Jews of the Roman Empire
       Vol. XI, Ch. V
  12. The Greeks of the Roman Empire
       Vol. XI, Ch. VI
  13. The Christians of the Roman Empire
       Vol. XII, Ch. II

V. HISTORY OF RELIGIONS

1. Pythagoreanism
   Vol. I, Ch. I
2. The Olympian religion
   Vol. I, Ch. IV.1-8
3. The Eleusinian mysteries
   Vol. I, Ch. IV.8
4. The cult of Dionysus
   Vol. I, Ch. IV.9
5. Orphism
   Vol. I, Ch. IV.10
6. Greek shamanism
   Vol. I, Ch. IV.11
7. Egyptian religion
   Vol. IV, Ch. I.5-7
8. The religion of Israel
   Vol. IV, Ch. II
   Vol. VII, Ch. VI
9. Religions of the Middle East
   Vol. IV, Ch. III.10
10. Iranian religion
    Vol. IV, Ch. IV.4-12
    Vol. V, Ch. I.4-5
11. Mazdakism
    Vol. V, Ch. I, Appendix
12. The New Testament
    Vol. VII, Ch. IV
13. The Essenes
    Vol. VII, Ch. V
14. Hermetism
    Vol. VIII, Ch. II
15. The Veda
    Vol. V, Ch. II.17
16. Brahmanism
    Vol. V, Ch. II.18-19
17. Hinduism
    Vol. V, Ch. II.20
18. Yoga
    Vol. V, Ch. II.21
19. Jainism
    Vol. V, Ch. II.22
20. Buddhism
    Vol. V, Ch. II.23
21. Confucianism
    Vol. V, CH. III.16-21, 23-24
22. Mohism
    Vol. V, Ch. III.22
23. Daoism

Vol. V, Ch. III.25
24. The Gnosis
   Vol. VI, Ch.IV
   Vol. VII, Chs. I-III
   Vol. VIII, Chs. III-IX
   Vol. IX
25. The Christian religion
   Vol. XII

VI PHILOSOPHY

1. Pythagoreanism
   Vol. I, Ch. I
2. Ionic and Eleatic philosophy
   Vol. I, Ch. II
3. Sophists and Socrates
   Vol. III, Ch. II
4. Plato and Aristotle
   Vol. III, Ch. III
5. Hellenistic philosophy
   Vol. VI, Ch. III
6. Indian philosophy
   Vol. V, Ch. II.16
7. Chinese philosophy
   Vol. V, Ch. III.15
8. The philosophy of Philo
   Vol. VIII, Ch. I

VII LITERATURE

1. Greek epics and lyrics
   Vol. I, Ch. III
2. Greek tragedy and comedy
   Vol. III, Ch. I

VIII HISTORIOGRAPHY

1. Greek historiography
   Vol. III, Ch. III.1
2. Old Testament
   Vol. IV, Ch. II.1-6
3. New Testament
   Vol. VII, Ch. IV.1-2.

CHAPTER I

THE CHRISTIANS IN CONFLICT WITH ROME

PART I INTRODUCTORY

1. The first expansion of Christianity

The Christian Church was founded on the first Pentecost day after the death of Jesus; the year is not exactly known but it must have been A.D. 30 or thereabout. The events took place in Jerusalem where the apostles had returned after Jesus' ascension; with a number of other adherents, among them Mary, the mother of Jesus, they were assembled in the 'room upstairs', the 'cenaculum', the location of which is unknown. Inspired and encouraged by the Holy Spirit, the apostles left the building, and Peter, their spokesman, began to preach to the crowd that had come together in front of the building. These people were Jews and proselytes who were celebrating the Pentecost festival and came from the whole eastern half of the Roman Empire. On that first day a considerable number of them allowed themselves to be baptized [1]. The fact that many of these converts came from far away may mean that 'the word', as the New Testament often calls the new creed, was now being carried into distant regions.

The Church gained converts in all Palestine, even in Samaria [2]. Soon enough, even before Paul's conversion, we hear of a Christian community at Damascus in Syria [3]. Later the faith spread to Phoenicia and Antioch; it was in this city that the 'Christians' were first given that name [4]. It was the converted Pharisee Saul, the apostle Paul, who on his extended missionary journeys, brought the faith to Cyprus, to all Asia Minor, and to Macedonia and Greece. In these regions he founded a great many Christian communities. He stayed for a long time in Corinth, the great harbour town. The communities of Rome and Alexandria were not founded by Paul. In these first decades Christianity was mainly a creed of city dwellers; the countryside remained largely pagan [5].

2. Non-Christian evidence for the presence of Christians

There exists very little non-Christian evidence for the presence of Christians in the Roman Empire in the first decades after the foundation of the Church [6]. We find a text in Flavius Josephus which would be of the greatest importance if only it were authentic. We read it in his 'Jewish Antiquities' which date from A.D. 93/94. This text is worth quoting in full. "About this time there lived Jesus, a wise man, if one ought to call him a man. For he was one who wrought surprising feats and was a teacher of such people as accept the truth gladly. He won over many of the Jews and many of the Greeks. He was the Messiah. When Pilate, hearing him accused by the men of the highest standing amongst us, had condemned him to be crucified, those who in the first place had come to love him did not give up their affection for him. On the third day he appeared to them restored to life, for the prophets of God had prophesied these and countless other marvellous things about him. And the tribe of the Christians, so called after him, has still to this day not disappeared" [7].

This text has long been read as an authentic statement about Jesus Christ and his adherents. It was even seen as a proof that Josephus himself was 'christianizing'. However, beginning with the sixteenth-century Renaissance scholar Scaliger, the text has been subjected to severe criticism; nowadays it is generally thought to be an intercalation by a Christian hand [8]. But there is another text in Josephus, one about James, which is generally considered authentic and in which the name of Jesus Christ is mentioned. "(Ananus, the High Priest) convened before him the judges of the Sanhedrin and brought before him a man named James, the brother of Jesus who was called the Christ, and certain others. He accused them of having transgressed the Law and delivered them up to be stoned" [9].

A passage in Suetonius would be very revealing for the early presence of Christians in Rome, if only it was not so confusing. It is the rendering of an edict by the Emperor Claudius issued in A.D. 49. "Since the Jews constantly made disturbance at the instigation of Chrestos, he expelled them from Rome" [10]. A cryptic passage! Is 'Chrestos' the misspelled name of Jesus Christ and were the Jews of Rome at loggerheads over the question whether or not Jesus was the promised Messiah? In fact, both Tertullian in A.D. 197 [11] and Lactantius in A.D. 310 [12] accused the pagans of being too stupid to know how the words 'Christianus' and 'Christus' should be spelled. If Suetonius really thought that his 'Chrestos' was identical with Jesus Christ, he must have assumed that Jesus was still alive in A.D. 49. But to quote Stephen Benko, "it is almost impossible that Suetonius writing in the first part of the second century would confuse the founder of the Christian movement with a local troublemaker, 'Chrestos'" [13]. If this is correct, then Chrestos was only a Roman Jew with an axe to grind - which axe remains unknown.

There is more substance in a Suetonius text referring to the next reign, that of Nero (54-68) in which it is said that "punishment was inflicted on the Christians, a class of men given to a new and mischievous superstition" [14]. It is not only the words 'superstitio malefica' which show that the author held the Christians in deep contempt; this is also made clear by his placing this phrase between the prohibition of the sale of cooked viand in the taverns and measures against unruly chariot drivers and pantomime actors. This leads us to the next part of this chapter.

PART II PAGAN AUTHORS ON CHRISTIANS

1. A historian's opinion

It is well-known that Tacitus in his 'Annals', written in the first decade of the second century, was the one to describe what kind of punishment, referred to by Suetonius, was inflicted on the Christians who were accused of having started a disastrous fire in Rome. They were nailed to crosses and set on fire as torches. In this famous 'testimonium Taciteum' [15], its author states that the Christians "were hated because of their crimes". He found their creed a 'destructive superstition' which had begun in Judaea, 'the origin of this evil', in consequence of Christ's teaching, and had now surfaced in Rome, "where all atrocious and shameful things flow together from all over the world". This distinguished historian thought as unfavourably of Christians as he thought of Jews; both religions he found 'superstitious'. Since the terms used by Tacitus to castigate both creeds are identical, it is by no means unthinkable that Tacitus considered the Christians to be a particularly obnoxious Jewish sect [16].

2. A governor's opinion

A short time later, around A.D. 112, Pliny the Younger, then governor of Bithynia, wrote to the Emperor Trajan on the subject of Christians and how they should be treated. What witnesses told him of Christian creed and practice seemed innocent enough. "They use to come together on a certain day before daylight to sing a song with responses to Christ as a god, to bind themselves mutually by a solemn oath not to commit any crime, but to avoid theft, robbery, adultery, not to break a trust or deposit when they are called for it. After these practices it is their custom to separate and then come together again to take food but of an ordinary and harmless kind (the 'agapê' is meant. Had Pliny heard rumours of the ritual murder of a child?)." But then this haughty Roman sums up the findings of his interrogations in this way : "I found nothing but a depraved and excessive superstition" [17].

3. 'Atheism'

The customary confusion between Judaism and Christianity is probably also to be found in the measures taken by the Emperor Domitian against his cousin Flavius Clemens, a consul, and his wife Flavia Domitilla. The man was executed, the woman banished. The charge against them was 'atheism', " a charge on which many others who had drifted into Jewish ways were condemned" [18]. Since Judaism was a 'religio licita', it is more probable that the couple were Christians - the more so because the owner of an early Christian cemetery in Rome, the 'coemeterium Domitillae', was a Flavia Domitilla who without any doubt belonged to the Flavian family [19].

The charge of 'atheism' accompanied that of 'superstition'. This does not mean that the Christians were supposed to acknowledge no god at all, but rather that they did not venerate the imperial supreme godhead. When Polycarp, the aged bishop of Smyrna, in A.D. 156 stood before his judges, he was greeted by the populace with shouts of 'Away with the atheists!' [20]. In the Paedagogicum of the imperial slaves on the Palatine hill a crude drawing was found on one of its walls, dating from the first half of the third century and representing a crucified slave with the head of an ass; another slave is kneeling down in adoration before him; the subscription says : "Alexamenos adores his god" [21].

The old legend that the Jews venerated an ass's head is here transferred to the Christians. This clearly implies that the artist was aware that Jesus was a god and that he had undergone the death of a slave. The artist, furthermore, obviously considered the Christian faith a repulsive superstition. In all probability a slave himself, he held it in deep contempt, as a religion fit for slaves.

During the second century a Roman philosopher, called Crescens, of whom hardly anything is known, repeatedly attacked the Christians in public on the same ground, namely that they were impious and atheists [22].

4. Alleged scandalous behaviour

Rumours were current about the scandalous behaviour of Christians during their sacred meetings. The Roman rhetor M. Cornelius Fronto (ca. 100-165), no mean person since he was the tutor of the later Emperor Marcus Aurelius, is probably the source of a story which we find in 'Octavius', a work by the early Christian author Minucius Felix (first half of the third century). "On the day appointed they (the Christians) gather at a banquet with all their children, sisters, and mothers, people of either sex and every age. There, after full feasting, when the blood is heated, and drink has inflamed the passions of incestuous lust, a dog which has been tied to a lamp is tempted by a morsel thrown beyond the range of his tether to bound forward with a rush. The tale-telling light is upset and extinguished, and in the shameful dark lustful embraces are indiscriminately exchanged; and all alike, if not in act, yet by complicity, are involved in incest" [23]. As Frend remarks, "what was believed by Fronto was readily believed by the less educated and enlightened populace in the capital" [24]. It should be noted that in the opinion of the ancients incest was a most heinous sexual crime and liable to capital punishment.

Minucius Felix introduces, apart from the Christian apologist Octavius Januarius, a friend of his, and then a pagan spokesman, Q. Caecilius Januarius. This man too accuses the Christians of impiety and of disdaining the imperial religion, and he does so in the strongest terms. They form 'an impious assembly', and 'a profane conspiracy'; "they despise the temples as dead-houses, they laugh at sacred things, ... (they) rage against the gods". They come, indeed, from the lowest rank of society, 'from its lowest dregs', and are 'men of a reprobate, unlawful, and desperate faction'. Almost out of breath Caecilius rants on. Once again he relates the story of the adoration of the ass's head, while even worse, "some say that they worship the virilia of their pontiff and priest". The story of the Black Mass has a very early origin! Rather unexpectedly sobering up, the speaker confesses that he does not know whether these things are true or false. All the same, theirs is 'a certain religion of lust', for they call one another 'brother and sister' which points to promiscuity and incest.

They are people who love secrecy and for good reason [25]. Secret and closed as the nocturnal meetings might be, Caecilius proved, nevertheless, well-informed about what happened there, especially when a convert was initiated. "An infant covered with meal ... is slain by the young pupil, who has been urged on as if to inflict harmless blows on the surface of the meal, with dark and secret wounds ... They lick up its blood; eagerly they divide its limbs. By this victim they are pledged together; with this consciousness they are covenanted to mutual silence." It will be evident that this is a crazy travesty of the Eucharist. The conclusion of the indignant Caecilius is : "Surely this confederacy ought to be rooted out and execrated" [26]. These reports show what the Roman public thought of the Christians and their practices.

5. The portrait of an 'atheist'

The North African author Lucius Apuleius leaves us in his 'Apology', written about A.D. 160 [27], the portrait of an 'atheist', a certain Aemilianus, in all probability a Christian. There is in his description a note of genuine surprise at the fact that somebody could really be an 'atheist'. "This fellow Aemilianus thinks it a good jest to mock at things divine ... To this day he has never prayed to any god or frequented any temple, while if he chances to pass any shrine, he regards it as a crime to raise his hand to his lips in token of reverence. He has never given first fruits of the crops or vines or flocks to any of the gods of the farmer who feed him and cloth him; his farm has no shrine, no holy place, no grave. Those who have been on his property say they saw there not one stone on which offering of oil has been made, not one bough where wreaths have been hung" [28].

6. An emperor's opinion

Christianity was not foremost in the mind of the philosopher-emperor Marcus Aurelius (161-180); in his Meditations he referred only once to Christians. What he had to say of them was not flattering. He found them a race distinguished by 'obstinate opposition'; their readiness to die for their faith was not the result 'of a reasoned and dignified decision' - by which he meant that it was sheer folly [29].

7. A satirist's opinion

Lucianus, a satirist who wrote in Greek and whose life spanned almost the whole of the second century A.D., had no high opinion of Christians either.

'Poor wretches', he called them, stupid enough to think they were immortal and would live on forever, although there is no definite evidence for such doctrines. Their Christ he dubbed 'that crucified sophist' [30]. Benko writes that he was "not really interested in Christianity and certainly not interested enough to make a study of their teachings and observe their morals ... The Christians are on the periphery of his horizon ... We cannot even be sure that he knew the difference between Judaism and Christianity" [31]. This would have been equally true of countless educated Greeks and Romans. Like so many pagans Lucianus considered that Christians should be put on a par with 'atheists' [32].

8. A doctor's opinion

A contemporary of Lucianus, and like him a Greek, was Galenus, a native of Pergamum and a medical doctor of great repute. He arrived in Rome in A.D. 162 and died there in 199. At that time there had been a Christian community in the capital, although not a large one, for more than a century. Galenus was better acquainted with Christian doctrine than most of his fellow-scholars. However, he too did not yet fully realize that Judaism and Christianity were two different religions [33]. But in contrast to most authors of the early Roman Empire he had some praise to spare for the Christians. He wrote of their contempt of death, of their self-discipline and self-control in matters of food and drink, of their keen pursuit of justice, and their abstaining from cohabitation. For these reasons he was prepared to call them 'philosophers', although they drew their faith from parables (and miracles) which he obviously did not consider really philosophical [34]. "This is not to say", says Wilken, "that he agreed with Christian teaching, or even that he thought it philosophically interesting" [35].

9. 'Philosophy'

In this period 'philosophy' had come to mean 'way of life' rather than 'system of thought'. When Galenus no longer spoke of Christianity as a 'superstition' but as a 'school', to be compared with other schools like the Stoa or Epicureanism, this may mean that this learned man sought to situate the new religion in the main stream of Graeco-Roman thinking.

This line of thought seems to have been popular with some Christians too. Justin the Martyr described his conversion to Christianity as one to philosophy; in his eyes Christian philosophy was the 'only sure and profitable one' [36]. This idea was expounded at some length by another convert, Athenagoras, himself a philosopher (originally a pagan one). In, probably, A.D. 177, he presented a 'plea for the Christians' to Marcus Aurelius and his co-emperor Commodus. Whether he did this in person is an open question. In it he rebuts the charges brought against the Christians of cannibalistic meals and incestuous licence, but what really spurred him on was the wish to show that they were no atheists.

When we consider that this came from a Christian, it cannot help striking us as a very curious treatise. The names of Jesus Christ and of the apostles are never mentioned; the author never speaks either of baptism or of the Eucharist nor of bishops and priests. The Old and the New Testaments are indeed quoted or alluded to. But it is hardly credible that Athenagoras should have thought that the rulers or, indeed, the general public to whom his plea was, in the last resort, destined, were sufficiently acquainted with the liturgy and the hierarchy of the Church. Instead, the treatise is deeply steeped in Hellenistic scholarly and literary lore. The names of Homer and Plato, to quote only two of his frames of reference, constantly pass before our eyes. According to him, the Christian tenets are wholly in accordance with the doctrine of the ancient thinkers. In this way Athenagoras tried to make Christian doctrine fashionable and palatable to the pagan mind [37]. It does not seem that Marcus Aurelius came under his spell.

10. The opinion of Celsus

Until the last quarter of the second century Graeco-Roman authors were not sufficiently interested in Christianity to occupy themselves intensely with it. But around 178-180 one Celsus wrote a whole book against the Christians.

Of this author next to nothing is known except that he was a philosopher. Origen thought he was an Epicurean; however, "he is closest to the Platonists, but his own philosophical stance is eclectic" [38]. His book, called 'Alêthos logos' = True doctrine, is lost. But some eighty years later the Christian apologist Origen took upon himself the task of refuting him in a voluminous work in eight books, called 'Contra Celsum'. This proves that Origen thought that Celsus's book could be influential with the general public. Now Origen had the laudable habit of quoting the opinions of his opponent literally and extensively; he does this so often that we have a fairly good idea of what Celsus had to say. The pagan's main aim seems to have been to defend the time-honoured Roman cult against an emerging oriental religion like Christianity. Although he is not above prejudice, he proves himself reasonably well acquainted with the doctrine he is attacking; he was knowledgeable with the Bible.

a. A stupid sort of people

Celsus does not show any sympathy with the Christian Church. Quite the contrary! This prompts him often enough to express himself in satirical terms. One of his lines of attack is that the Christians were a low sort of people, stupid and uneducated, even enemies of a good education. Only the lower classes felt attracted to it; they even have a predilection for crimimals, for the ones whom they use to call 'sinners'. What they teach is vulgar and interesting to the vulgar alone. They "make arrogant announcements about matters of which they know nothing" [39], i.e. against philosophical tenets of respected authors.

Their own teachers are 'persons of the most rustic and uninstructed character' who in any case are sensible enough to keep their peace when in the presence of more intelligent people. But if these Christian teachers are only fullers and leather workers [40], how then, asks Celsus, is it possible that they succeed in winning over people to their faith? This is to be explained in this way that they pretend to know a lot about the divine, and this is a source of wonder to the rabble [41]. They threaten with doom and damnation and at the same time they offer the means to escape perdition and be saved [42]. They also use magic, conjure up demons, and intone incantations [43]. Christians, in consequence, are not only stupid but dangerous. Jesus, the founder of their sect, was a sorcerer; Celsus did not deny that he worked miracles, but he performed them by means of magic [44]. As a magician he was trained in Egypt where he grew up and worked as a labourer (there is no warrant for these statements in the Gospels) [45].

b. Silly doctrines

Having put the Christians firmly in their place socially 'as a society that consists of intellectually low level people', Celsus turns his attention to their doctrines which are to him 'an inadequate philosophical-theological system' [46]. In his attack on the Old Testament he took Judaism too in his stride. This book, he claims, is a collection of fables that are at once stupid and inconsistent [47]. For instance, how could God make man in his image when he has no human form himself [48]? The alleged anthropomorphism of the book is downright blasphemous [49]. Some of its stories are simply repellent. He knows that Jews and Christians are sometimes trying to escape from these problems by offering allegorical explanations [50], but this kind of exegesis is a blind alley. He does not deny that there are valuable ideas in the Old Testament, but they are also to be found, and better worded, in Greek authors [51].

The intensity of Celsus's artillery barrage grows when the approaches the New Testament. Jesus the Son of God? Out of the question! Jesus was the son of a Roman soldier, by the name of Panthera, and a poor (married) country woman [52] - a story that has always remained popular. In order to camouflage this shameful fact, Jesus fabricated the story of a virgin birth himself [53]. Anyhow, he was entirely human, all too human, for he was a 'pestilent fellow' [54] and a 'great liar' [55]. The men who formed his company came from the dregs of society, and he lived the life of tramps with them [56]. That Jesus rose from the grave is a piece of utter nonsense. People who believe such things are out of their mind [57].

c. The Christian rejection of Judaism

A curious element in Celsus's polemics is his charge that the Christians had abandoned Judaism. "What was wrong with you" - Celsus puts these words into the mouth of a Jew - "that you left the law of our fathers ... and have deserted us for another law and another life?" [58]. Benko calls this view "a mixed blessing, because on the one hand it put Christians under the protective umbrella which the Roman authorities extended to Jews; on the other hand it also included the Christians in that contempt which the Romans reserved for Jewish superstition" [59]. But Celsus found that Christians had no right to this official protection since they had allowed themselves to be deluded by Jesus [60].

d. The Christian rejection of the imperial cult

Celsus is extremely critical of the Christian attitude to the Graeco-Roman public religion. Christians, is his opinion, should "help the emperor with all their might, and cooperate with him in what is right, and fight for him and be fellow-soldiers if he presses for this, and fellow-generals with him" [61]. But this is exactly what they are not doing. Christians shun military service and do not accept public service [62]. They keep themselves aloof from all that is authentically Roman; they "wall themselves off and break away from the rest of mankind" which is 'seditious' [63]. In the days of Celsus many enlightened people had come to the belief that there was only one supreme divinity; it did not concern Celsus at all how he was named, Zeus or Adonai or Amon [64]. He was quite content that the Christians should have their own supreme godhead. But what did not please him was that they made Jesus into a second supreme godhead [65]. "Christian worship of Jesus set up a rival God whose followers created an independent and factious group within the body politic" [66]. Or should we rather say : without the body politic?

e. The old and the new

Christianity was new, brandnew. But real wisdom, in the opinion of the ancients, was old. Even Judaism was entitled to some measure of respect because of its antiquity. Christianity could not claim this respect. The great problem for Celsus, as the spokesman of the Roman educated class, was that Christianity presented him with an insoluble riddle. In the ancient world religion was always part of the life of a nation or tribe. One could think here of Greek polis religion, each polis having its own type of cult, of the Roman Empire with its imperial cult of Jupiter Capitolinus, of the Celtic and Germanic religions, each with its own divinities, and even of Judaism which was the religion of the Jewish ethnos.

But the Christians formed no ethnos, no nation or people of their own; they were not 'national'. They were not bound together by ties of consanguinity, by political allegiance, or by a common history. Their ideology contradicted all that was essential in the life of ancient political and national entities. This severing of the bond between the nation and religion could, in Celsus's opinion, only have the direst consequences. If their ideology prevailed, there would be "nothing to prevent the Emperor from being abandoned, alone and deserted, while earthly things would come under the power of the most lawless and savage barbarians" [67]. It is for this reason that pagan Romans viewed the Christians and their religion with so much disgust, abhorrence, and apprehension, that their attitude must be called dualistic.

11. A philosopher's opinion

A century after Celsus wrote, Christian doctrine was again subjected to a critical appraisal by a philosopher. Times had changed then. Could Celsus still have hoped that Christianity would go away, in the third century such a hope had proved idle. Porphyry, the philosopher in question, was a Greek speaking Phoenician from Tyre who lived from 233 to 305. Most scholars assume that he wrote a book against the Christians, to which we must add the objections contained in his 'Philosophy from oracles', this last work being a spirited defense of the Roman religion. Both works are lost, alas; we have to be content with fragments, to be culled from the books of other ancient authors. Coming from such an erudite man, Porphyry's attack made a deep impression on the Christians; their best minds, Eusebius, Methodius, Apollinarius (who wrote a work in thirty books against him which is also lost), Jerome and Augustine, all took up the pen in order to refute him [68].

a. Criticism of the Book of Daniel

In one field Porphyry certainly won the day. His critical assessment of the Book of Daniel has become common ground among scholars, whether they be Christian or not. In the first centuries (and even long afterwards) it was generally believed that the Book of Daniel was a genuine prophecy written in the sixth century B.C. It foretold that after the Babylonian Empire there would follow three others, Median, Persian, and Graeco-Macedonian, of which the Syrian kingdom of the Seleucid monarchy would be a branch. We saw already that Christian authors combined the Median and Persian Empires into one, in order to create room for the Roman Empire.

But Porphyry was of another opinion. He "wrote his twelfth book against the prophecy of Daniel, denying that it was composed by the person to whom it is ascribed in its title, but rather by some individual living in Judaea at the time of Antiochus (IV) who was surnamed Epiphanes. He furthermore alleged that Daniel did not foretell the future so much as related the past, and lastly that whatever he (Daniel) spoke of until the time of Antiochus contained authentic history, whereas anything he may have conjectured beyond this point was false as he would not have known the future" [69]. The upshot of the philosopher's criticism was that the Book of Daniel is not a prophecy but an historical account; as a prophetical announcement it was a 'vaticinium ex eventu', a 'prophecy' after the events had happened.

What Porphyry overlooked, however, and what Jerome reproached him with is that not all 'Daniel' is historical description, meant to put a heart into the Jews during the Seleucid persecution. Jerome agreed with Porphyry that by no means all of Daniel is prophecy. But he rightly contended that there is also genuine prophecy in it. There is the prediction of the eternal kingdom that will be established when all earthly kingdoms will have been destroyed [70] - an element that is often neglected even by Christian interpreters. And then there is the apocalyptic foretelling of the final wars and the triumph of the just [71].

b. Criticism of the New Testament

There can be no doubt that Porphyry was equally critical about the New Testament, but our information about his opinions in this field is scanty. Wilken thinks that Augustine had Porphyry in mind when he spoke of pagan critics who said that the Gospel authors had doctored the facts of Jesus' life [72]. They "had claimed for their master more than he really was", that he was, for instance, the Son of God or the Word of God, and even that he was God. That Jesus was the wisest of men these critics did not deny, but he should not be worshipped as divine [73]. It is in any case something Porphyry could underwrite.

The philosopher showed himself very keen on the inconsistencies to be found in the Gospels, in the discrepancies, for instance, between the genealogical trees of Matthew and Luke and between the infancy gospels of these two authors. He also took pleasure in commenting on the quarrels between the disciples and on the disagreement between Peter and Paul on the subject of circumcision. The backdrop to this criticism seems to have been that, according to Porphyry, the Church from its very first days had been torn asunder by strife and disunity. Why put your trust in such infantile, quarrelsome, and unreliable men as the apostles [74]?

c. Porphyry's main objection

As I said, although Porphyry had no high idea of Christianity, he was convinced that it had come to stay. It would be advisable, therefore, to assign it a place in the Graeco-Roman religion, as far as this was possible. In common with so many other great minds of the time, Porphyry did not equate the Olympian deities with what was highest and most venerable in religion. Above them rose another god, a first god who "is incorporeal, immovable, and invisible, and is in need of nothing external to himself ... We should venerate him in profound silence with a pure soul, and with pure conceptions about him" [75]. This must not be taken to mean that our philosopher was a monotheist. His 'high god' was the highest but not the only one; there were also the Olympian deities, the daimones, the stars, and still more.

More than one Christian apologist had contended that the supreme being of so many Hellenistic philosophers was none other than the God of the Christians. Only to quote Augustine : the God of the Christians "is the God whom Porphyry, the most learned of philosophers, although the fiercest enemy of the Christians, acknowledged to be a great God" [76]. But Porphyry himself was not at all ready to assume that pagans and Christians adored the same supreme being. His "strategy was to sever the link between Christianity and Hellenism by showing that the Christians had abandoned the worship of this God in favour of the worship of Christ" [77]. So, if Christianity deserved a place in the Graeco-Roman religious system, it was far below that of the beliefs of the philosophers.

By their belief that Jesus is God, the Christians are 'polluted and contaminated and entangled in error ... This they worship because truth is a stranger to them" [78]. Certainly Jesus was an outstanding wise man who worshipped the supreme being and taught others to do the same. But he should not be worshipped as God. What he really taught has, however, been distorted and misrepresented by his disciples. This reproach of Porphyry is well expounded by Arnobius who writes that the pagans say : "The gods are hostile to you because you maintain that a man, born of a human being, ... was God" [79]. This 'hostility of the gods' put the Christians outside the main stream of ancient religion and made them liable to persecution.

"In a more sophisticated form, Porphyry has restated the same arguments that were implicit in the second century, when Christianity was called a superstition" [80]. The difference with a man like Celsus, however, is that, in the opinion of Porphyry, the original doctrine, that of Jesus himself, was not at fault, for he venerated the supreme being. It was his disciples who had perverted the message, and since the faithful choose to believe them rather than Jesus, they had to pay the price for this [81].

PART III THE EMPIRE AND THE CHURCH IN OPPOSITION

1. The Roman attitude to alien religions

a. An eminently religious people

Generally speaking, the Roman attitude towards foreign, non-Roman religions was not benevolent. The terms used to denote them were 'superstition' and 'atheism'. The religions of the Celts, the Germanic tribes, the Egyptians, the Jews, the Christians, were all equally repellent to them. Even the strange habits of the Greeks, like the Bacchanalia, were not for them : 'no ecstatic transports, ... no bacchanals or secret mysteries ..., nor any other mummery of this kind'. Instead "in all their words and actions with respect to the gods a reverence is shown (by the Romans), such as is seen among neither Greeks nor barbarians" [82].

These last words show that the Romans thought of themselves as an eminently religious people; they ascribed their successes in the conduct of their wars and the expansion of their Empire to their reverence for their gods, their 'pietas', their piety. As everywhere in the ancient world, public life and religion were closely interwoven. King Numa Popilius had judged it above all necessary to implant 'the fear of the gods' in the hearts of the people [83]. In this way, thought Cicero, he had laid 'the foundation of our state' no less than Romulus had done [84]. Disappearance of the piety towards the gods, he added, would spell the end of the fabric of the state, of loyalty, of social unity, and of justice itself [85]. Since the Romans had always scrupulously stuck to their religion, without neglecting any detail of it, their "fathers had been able to build this great republic" [86].

b. Abhorrence of foreign religions

No wonder, then, that the Romans kept foreign religions and cults at more than an arm's length; they drew a dualistic distance between 'religion' and 'superstition'. "Religion has been distinguished from superstition, not only by philosophy but by our ancestors ... Hence 'superstitious' and 'religious' came to be terms of censure and approval respectively" [87]. But what exactly is the difference? Cicero explains it to us : "Superstition implies a groundless fear of the gods; religion consists in piously worshipping them" [88]. Plutarch makes it clear that "the superstitious man enjoys no world in common with the rest of mankind" [89]; such a person stands apart. Philosophers and statesmen agree that "the majesty of God is associated with goodness, magnanimity, kindliness, and solicitude" [90]. A superstitious person, by contrast, "assumes that the gods are rash, faithless, fickle, vengeful, cruel, and easily offended" for which reason "he will hate and fear them" [91]. Plutarch accentuates the dualism in the opposition between religion and superstition by downgrading the last as 'antagonistic' and 'contradictory' [92].

All this does not necessarily mean that the Roman state automatically harassed and persecuted members of non-Roman religions. As long as their tenets and practices did not present a danger to the state, the authorities left them in peace. It was the state which decided whether or not a religion or cult was 'licit' [93]. "No one shall have gods to himself, either new gods or alien gods, unless recognized by the state." What people did in private or thought in foro interno did not concern the state; "privately they shall worship those gods whose worship they have duly received from their ancestors" [94]. But let them stay out of the public domain with their rites and sacrifices [95]!

Roman magistrates were always extremely vigilant in keeping public religion unpolluted by foreign trash. "How often ... has the task been assigned to the magistrates of forbidding the introduction of foreign cults, of excluding dabblers in sacrifices and fortune-tellers from the forum, the circus and the city, of searching out and burning books of prophecies, and of annulling every system of sacrifice except that performed in the Roman way" [96]. The characteristics of such dubious religions were 'nocturnal rites, orgies and ritual murders' [97].

c. An action against the Bacchics

The Roman state was prepared to defend itself and the religion upon which it was based against polluting influences. The Christians were by no means the only ones to suffer from persecution. Frend cites an action against adherents of the Bacchus cult as a case in point. In 186 B.C. the Senate swooped down on them; they were accused of holding nightly meetings. Feeling threatened, many attempted to escape but were caught; some committed suicide. The authorities persecuted what they called the conspiracy throughout all Italy; in all more than seven thousand men and women were involved, and "more were killed than thrown into prison". "The task was entrusted to the consuls of destroying all forms of Bacchic worship, first at Rome and then throughout Italy ... For the future it was then provided by a senatusconsultum (senatorial decree) that there should be no Bacchanalia in Rome or elsewhere" [98]. However, the Bacchus cult was ancient and for that reason entitled to some respect; the gods, Frend pointed out, might have been offended if it had been abolished altogether [99]. Therefore, ancient altars and images were to be spared, which means, obviously, that the cult was not eradicated root and branch. But it was kept tightly under control. The city praetor permitted meetings as long as no more than one hundred persons attended and five priests celebrated [100]. For the next two centuries, the Bacchanals "remained the by-word for a dangerous and disorderly cult in both the Roman and Greek worlds" [101].

d. The Christians treated worse than others

The Christians began with a disadvantage most other unpopular cults did not have : since theirs was not an ancient religion, the authorities and public saw no reason to respect it. A second drawback was that the animosity against the Jews devolved upon them too since, for a long time, the authorities did not distinguish sharply between Judaism and Christianity. But this was at the same time an advantage because Judaism, although not popular, was a 'religio licita' under the cover of which the Christians could find shelter. The Romans had their problems with the Jews as a 'rebellious people' but they did not persecute them for religious reasons.

Slowly but certainly the state became aware of the fact that Christians were no Jews; from the reign of Domitian (81-96) it began to understand them as a separate religious entity, and one towards which they were not prepared to practise their usual tolerance in religious matters. Why, asks Marta Sordi, did Rome make an exception in the case of Christianity [102]? The same question was asked by ancient Christian authors. Athenagoras, for example, admitted that the Roman Empire tolerated all religions with their cults and practices, even if it found them ridiculous [103], for all the citizens of the Empire enjoy equality before the law [104]. However, the Christians, and they alone, are excluded from this tolerance and this equality; they are subject to abuse, bad treatment, and persecution by the crowds [105].

e. Problems of the state with Christians

A first problem for the authorities with the Christians was that they could not treat them as a nation, an 'ethnos', as they did the Jews. There were Christians in every tribe, nation, and language group. This made them elusive which contributed to the nervosity of the authorities about them; authorities do not relish situations which they cannot effectively control. Furthermore, in the eyes of the state the Christians were a 'conspiracy' given to secrecy and nocturnal meetings. This made the authorities still more nervous. But perhaps the state might have chosen to neglect them and leave them to their own devices - after all, Pliny reported to Trajan that there was nothing criminal in them -, if the problem of the emperor cult had not been there.

The refusal of the Christians to pay homage to the Emperor by burning incense before his statue hit at the core of Roman religiosity, for in the person of the ruler heaven and earth hung together. He was the guarantor that the

Empire was forever under the benevolent protection of the godhead. Tolerant the Romans might be, but this was more than they were prepared to endure. Perhaps the Roman irritation over the Christian 'non possumus' was only the tip of the iceberg. In itself it was no strange idea to the Christians that the ruler should enjoy the special protection of the supernatural world. As Marta Sordi writes, the conflict between Rome and Christianity was not of a political order [106]. Christians were quite ready to recognize the Emperor as their lawful ruler, just as they were prepared to obey the laws of the state and behave themselves as law-abiding citizens. There have been Jewish insurrections but there never was a Christian rising. Sordi is of the opinion that the refusal to perform the cult ceremony was not the main cause for the persecutions but only the pretext for them. The real conflict was one of a religious and ideological character [107].

f. Christian doctrine at variance with the imperial ideology

What the Christians purported to bring about was an absolute 'novum', a totally new ordering of the world, with a new understanding of what 'divine' meant and with a new ethics; we shall have to come back to this. The Romans, authorities, intellectuals, and pagan public of all ranks alike, sensed in this, vaguely at first and then ever more clearly, a dire threat to all that was Roman. For the world had already been ordered, in the form of the Empire; no new order was necessary, quite the contrary, it was dangerous.

When Pilate asked Jesus whether he really was a king, the answer was that he was a king indeed, but that his kingdom was 'not of this world' [108]. Since John's Gospel was written at a late date, around A.D. 100, this passage may have had the function of proving to the authorities that the Church was not a political organization. For, as Nock states, "Christianity gave special cause for fear because of its teaching on the Kingdom of God" [109]. Several decades later, Justin the Martyr quoted the same words of Jesus with the same intention, adding : "You, having heard that we expect a kingdom, have formed the uncritical impression that we mean a kingdom in the human sense" [110].

Denying the time-honoured customs, the traditions of the fathers, was treason, and, says Sordi, this "became the root of all objections and all attacks on Christianity" [111]. A dualistic duel between the imperial ideology and the Christian doctrine was at hand in which only one of the two could survive. To quote Nock again, "with these facts in view we can see that no concession could be expected by the Christians. The Jewish reluctance to worship the Emperor seemed queer, but the Christian dangerous" [112]. When Tertullian around 200 asked to extend the general freedom of conscience to the Christians and to allow them to adore the God of their own choice and not to oblige them to venerate gods they would not recognize [113], he was asking for the impossible. It would have turned the whole fabric of the Roman Empire upside down [114].

2. What the Christians thought of the Empire

a. The fundamental position

So much for the Roman attitude with regard to Christianity. Now the reverse of the coin : how did the Christians react to that pagan Empire? We find a first (and fundamental) answer in a word of Jesus himself. Some Pharisees showed him a coin destined for tribute-money asking him : "Master, is it permissible to pay tax to the Emperor?". This, of course, was a catch question. If Jesus had said 'yes', they would have stigmatized him as a traitor to the Jewish cause; had he said no, they would have branded him as a Zealot, a dangerous rebel. But Jesus answered neither 'yes' nor 'no'. He said : "Give onto Caesar what is of Caesar, and onto God what is of God" [115].

First of all, Jesus makes it clear here that he is no Zealot, for a Zealot would have asserted that it was blasphemy to pay tax to that pagan. Jesus acknowledges the actual political situation, namely that Judaea belonged to a Roman province. He does not say that this is an ideal situation, but there is no way of changing it. If paying tax to the Roman state was part of this situation, so be it. But when all is said and done, Jesus makes a distinction between the two spheres, the secular one and the divine. Without any doubt there is an anti-Roman attitude underlying this, because to the Romans their Empire was secular and divine at the same time, with the Emperor participating in both spheres. The background is the notion that the secular power should not intrude upon the sphere of the divine. This distinction, made by Jesus, might under circumstances give rise to a dualistic opposition.

b. Paul's ruling

Christians, thought Paul, who was a Roman citizen himself, are obliged to pay the taxes demanded by the state and had to live orderly and civilized lives. Since they were, whether they liked it or not, subjects of the Empire, they should obey its laws without making trouble. He declared categorically that "every soul must submit to the supreme authorities". He founded this duty of civil obedience on the fact that "there is no authority but by act of God, and the existing authorities are instituted by him", that is, even the pagan authorities. "Consequently. who rebels against authority is resisting a divine institution ... It is an obligation imposed not merely by fear of retribution but by conscience; that is also why you pay taxes. The authorities are in God's service and to these duties devote their energies" [116].

He said this when writing to the Romans; in that letter he was explicit about the civic duties of Christians. Everyone should be obedient to the powers that be. The apostle does not discuss the question whether or not a pagan government was legitimate. The simple answer is that it was, for all power comes from God; the powers that be are instituted by God. In consequence, he who resists them resists God. When the government punishes evil-doers, it acts as God's servant [117]. When Paul wrote this about A.D. 58, he was of course acquainted with the spirit of rebellion in Judaea. He also knew that the authorities did not distinguish as yet between Jews and Christians. He obviously wanted his Christians to keep a low profile and to remain law-abiding subjects, in order not to get implicated in the problems the Jews would inevitably have.

The First Letter to Timothy urges the faithful to pray 'for sovereigns and all in high office that we may lead a tranquil and quiet life in full observance of religion and high standards of morality" [118]. It is curious that the Emperor himself is not mentioned in this context. The First Letter of Clement contains such a prayer, saying that "you, Lord, gave them the power to rule through your lofty and indescribable power, so that we acknowledge the glory and honour that is given to them by you" [119].

c. A fiercely anti-Roman book

Towards the end of the first century A.D. the situation had changed dramatically. The Christians too had drawn the fire of the state; the first rounds of persecution had taken place. It was under these circumstances and during the reign of the Emperor Domitian (81-96) that the Book of Revelation was written, a book that in Volume VII I characterized as a fiercely anti-Roman book [120]; the opposition is so fierce that we may call it dualistic. The book is not directed against individual Romans, not even against the occupation of the Holy Land, but against the Roman Empire itself. This is seen as an utterly un-Christian, utterly pagan power. For the Christians it is all or nothing : either they must perish or the Empire. Actually the author never speaks of 'the Empire'; it is always 'the beast' or 'Babylon'. It is portrayed as 'a great fiery dragon with seven heads and ten horns' [121]. This monster may be interpreted as Satan, the Antichrist, and the politico-religious Roman power rolled into one. No other earthly realm is summoned up to destroy and replace it; obviously all kingdoms are equally bad in the judgment of the author. All "the kings of the earth have committed fornication with her (the great harlot of Babylon = Rome) and wallowed in her luxury" [122]. What is really standing over against all earthly kingdoms is the celestial realm of the Lamb (the Son of Man), also called 'the New Jerusalem'. Underneath one senses a polemic against politics as such, in particular against power politics (in which Rome excelled) [123].

d. The two realms of Hermas

In the 'Pastor' of Hermas, a little book, written in the period between A.D. 120 and 150, we see the distinction I already mentioned growing into dualism. Frend mentions scholars who suppose that the author was a convert from Essenianism. If this is correct, it does not come as a surprise since in Essenian doctrine the two realms, the secular and the divine, could not be opposed more sharply [124]. But it could also have been that he was influenced by the Book of Daniel which is equally antagonistic to political power [125], or by the Book of Revelation. According to Frend, "the Shepherd sheds light on ideas circulating among Christians drawn from the petit-bourgeoisie in Rome" [126]. For Hermas too, the world, that is the Empire, and the People of God stand in opposition to each other. This opposition is purely dualistic, for there is no link between the two realms [127]. The apocalyptic vision is in fact not wanting : "The heathen shall be burnt because they did not know their creator" [128].

The People of God - the Christians, the Church - has in Hermas's vision its abode in Heaven; its protecting angel is Michael. Its law is God's law given to all the world and preached until the end of the earth. Here the Church enters into competition with the Empire which equally gave its laws to all nations. It is God "who put the law into the hearts of those who believe" [129]; it is not the Empire. Just as Augustine did centuries later, the author portrayed the Church and the Empire as two 'cities' - cities that are fundamentally different and far apart. The servants of God - the Christians - are living 'in a strange country'. The ruler of that other city, the Emperor, will say to them : "I do not wish you to dwell in my city, but you go out from this city, because you do not use my law". And he will put before them the choice : "Either use my law or go out from my country". Clearly a Christian existence and the life of a law-abiding subject of the Empire are incompatible. "Whenever the master of this city (the Emperor) wishes to expel you for resisting his law, you may go out from his city, and depart to your own city, and joyfully follow your own law suffering no harm" [130].

e. More cricital sounds

The anonymous author of the Epistle of Barnabas, of uncertain date but written in one of the decades around A.D. 100, is equally critical of Roman rule. "The worker of evil himself is in power", he states ruefully [131]. Referring to the Book of Daniel, this author too uses an apocalyptic image, that of the Beast, wicked and powerful and fiercer than all the beasts of the sea; "the final stumbling block is at hand". Therefore, "let us hate the error of this present time, that we may be loved in that which is to come" [132]. Here again we find two irreconcilable modes of existence.

The author of the Second Letter of Clement, probably written around A.D. 150, sees the Church as not belonging to the present and as having existed right from the beginning, even 'created before the sun and the moon' - something the Roman Empire could not say of itself [133]. Once again we meet the apocalyptic element. The Day of Judgment is near; "the whole earth shall be as lead melting in the fire" [134].

3. Was the end near?

The expectations of a catastrophic end of the Roman Empire were not only figments of the Christian mind. In the night of July 18/19, A.D. 67, a fire broke out in Rome; in the sweltering heat of the summer-night the flames spread with incredible rapidity. It was only days later that the last flames could be extinguished. Of almost 80 % of the town only smouldering ruins remained. Soon enough there was a rumour current that the fire was started expressly and that the incendiary's name was Nero; he was suspected of wanting to dispose of the city centre for his own ends, as, for instance, that of holding the 'Neronia' there, his own brand of games [135]. But since his own new buildings on the Palatine went up in flames too, it is not probable that the catastrophe was his work (he was not even in Rome then). It is well-known that the Emperor, wishing to exculpate himself, put the blame on the Christians; I shall have to come back to this, because it led to the first persecution.

What is important in this context is that the Christians rejoiced in the disaster; they thought, or they hoped, that Rome would be destroyed and that this would inaugurate the end of the world. They believed, as Michael Grant writes, that "the second coming of the Messiah would be accompanied by a general conflagration". The same author quotes a letter of bishop Dionysius of Corinth to Soter, the bishop of Rome, to this effect : "Beloved, think it not strange concerning the fiery trial which is to try you" [136]. Since this letter was written ca. A.D. 170, this proves that the idea that the end was near had a long life. Doubtless, says Karlhorst, "there was a connection between the apocalyptic beliefs of the Christians and the fire" [137].

3. Two great authors averse of the Empire

a. 'The Caesar imitating Satan'

Hippolytus, an ecclesiastical author who lived from ca. 170 to 235/236, harked back to the prophecy of the four Beasts, the four realms, in the Book of Daniel; the fourth of these realms is the Roman Empire, that is in Hippolytus's opinion, for the author of the Book of Daniel was not aware of it. The prophet also wrote of a great and blasphemous statue (of Nebukadnessar) that is filling the earth but that will be swept away by a stone. Was he thinking here of the statue of the Emperor in front of which incense was burnt? In the Church Father's commentary this stone is God who will sit in judgment over the world [138]. For the Son of God will come with his armies of angels and overthrow all the kingdoms of this world; he will disperse them as dust. The straw, that is the atheists and the impious, he will burn in the inextinguishable fire. Then the Kingdom will be given to the Saints of the Most High [139].

This picture of coming events is at the same time apocalyptic to the core and thoroughly dualistic. Hippolytus takes the same distance from political power as the Books of Daniel and of Revelation : all worldy power stands condemned. Of the Roman Empire, "which is now reigning over us", he speaks in dualistic terms. Through his apostles the Lord will convoke all nations and tongues and make them into a people of faithful Christians, giving to them a new name. But the Caesar, 'imitating the Satan', also calls men together 'the best born men equipping them for war and giving them the name of Romans'. "The men of this world, called up by an earthly king take the name of Romans; those who believe in the king of heaven take the name of Christians and bear on their foreheads the sign that puts death in flight (= the sign of the cross)" [140].

b. The devil at work

If Hippolytus was of the opinion that the devil had something to do with Roman rule, he found his contemporary Origen at his side. In the introduction of his book against the pagan scholar Celsus, Origen expressed himself forcefully on this point. "Under the tyranny of him whom they call devil and lie, they (the Christians) form associations in defiance of the laws laid by the devil, against the devil, but for the salvation of others whom they can persuade to withdraw themselves from what is as a law of Scyths (= the most barbarous of all barbarians) and of the tyrant (= the Emperor)" [141]. Celsus had written that "all that is on earth is given to the Emperor, and all that we receive in this life we receive from him". Of course, this sounded like blasphemy in the ears of his opponent. No, he retorts, we deny this absolutely. "What we receive we receive from God and his Providence, eatable fruits, bread and wine and olive oil" [142]. With these words he rejects the prevailing idea that the Emperor was divine.

Both Hippolytus and Origen had their problems with the established Church; for this reason they may perhaps not count as the authentic voices of orthodox Christianity. For some time already a change in the attitude of the Christians with regard to the Empire was discernible. We have to go somewhat back in time to detect this.

4. Frustated expectations

The fire of Rome did not spell the end of the world, not even of the eternal city itself. Quite the contrary! The town was rebuilt and became more beautiful than before, the true 'caput mundi'. Soon enough the first difficult decades of the Empire belonged to the past; the second century A.D. became its best stabilized and most prosperous era, the 'halcyonic days' of the ancient world [143]. The apocalyptic perspective became ever more vague. An existential crisis in the Christian community was the result. Some Christians got impatient and asked when the prophecies would be fulfilled. "We have heard this already in the days of our fathers, and see, we have got old, and nothing of all this has happened" [144].

The Christians of the first century of the Church should have known better than to believe that the Second Coming was near at hand. Had not Jesus himself, speaking of the end, warned his disciples : "About that day hour no one knows, not even the angels in Heaven, not even the Son; only the Father" [145], and he added that "the Son of man will come when you least expect him" [146]. Since the early Christians were eagerly expecting him, their very fervour should have told them that the event was not near. It seems that in particular the first Christians firmly believed that the end might arrive any moment; oracles and prophetic utterances were alarming them. But Paul admonished them to keep their heads cool. The great day was not near, he wrote to the Thessalonians; the events that would precede the second Coming had not yet taken place [147].

5. Politics of accomodation

That early Christian authors, beginning with the Book of Revelation, took a fiercely anti-political line is easily explainable. They did not always see that the authorities, as Paul wanted them to believe, were acting on their behalf and for their welfare. On the contrary, they became subject to discrimination and much harassment and were openly persecuted as enemies of the Empire. But be this as it may, the Second Coming did not take place, and the Empire continued its course. For better and worse the Christians had to live with and in the Empire. And so were inaugurated what I would call 'the politics of accomodation'. At the end of the second century A.D. Christian authors began to take a more positive view of the Empire and of politics in general.

a. The Empire not the work of the devil

The first to do this was Irenaeus, a bishop of Lyons, who died as a victim of persecution around 202. He referred expressly to Paul when he wrote that one had to obey the authorities, quoting him verbally. Irenaeus presented a kind of theory of the origin of worldly power, namely that people who had no knowledge of God should at least fear one another - and this fear was implanted into them by God himself -, so that they would obey the law and experience some degree of justice.

Irenaeus squarely opposed the opinion of others that all power, that of Rome included, was the work of the devil. "Earthly dominion has been established by God for the benefit of the heathen, not by the devil, for the devil does not wish that the heathen live in peace" [148]. It is, however, evident that the Empire was 'second choice' for Irenaeus, a temporary measure to preserve the pagans from general anarchy and lawlessness. A Christian Empire would be something quite different. This author avoids mentioning the Emperor himself.

b. 'Honour the Emperor'

Writing in the first decades of the third century, Tertullian assured the opponents of Christianity that Christians were nobody's enemy, and above all not of the Emperor whom they should love and fear and honour and, indeed, wish all every good to him, and, in addition, to the whole Roman Empire. For "as long as the world will exist, for so long will the Empire exist". The Christians, he wrote, are quite ready to offer sacrifices for the well-being of the ruler, but such sacrifices should only be offered to God. Tertullian, so much is evident, rejects the veneration of the statue of the Emperor. The idea of revenging themselves - the author is referring to the persecutions - is entirely foreign to Christians [149]. Quoting Jesus' saying that one has to give to the Emperor what is of the Emperor, he asks (rhetorically) what is 'of the Emperor'. Why, money, of course. One has to pay one's taxes [150].

c. Resistance unallowed

Even Hippolytus who shows no enthusiasm for the Empire considered resistance to the authorities impermissible; he quoted Paul to this effect [151]. In this he found Origen on his side who also exhorted the faithful to obedience and submission, even when their rulers were tyrannical and brutal and led unworthy lives [152]. The Christian authorities of these times were all convinced that the faithful should not provoke the authorities by acts of rebellion or of open or secret resistance. Origen, no friend of the Empire, summarizes this by stating that "the Church of God should undertake nothing inimical against the princes and powerful of this world, but should promote the work of justice and piety by a quiet and tranquil life" [153].

d. Keeping a low profile

The general tactics of the Christians in these difficult times seem to have been to keep as low a profile as possible and to prove by every means that they were perfect citizens. Justin the Martyr even assured the Emperor that he had no better and more trustworthy subjects than the Christians [154]. Athenagoras, in his petition to the highest rulers, said that the Christians prayed for the Empire that it might expand so much that the whole world would become subject to it; this would be advantageous for the Christians who would then be able to lead a quiet and peaceful life and obey the commandments from above [155].

There is a touch of servility in this which is easily explained by the always precarious and sometimes dangerous position in which the Christians found themselves. Tertullian seems to have felt that they could be reproached for fawning upon the rulers. "Are we only flattering the Emperor and are our good wishes no more than lies, in the hope that we might escape the violence?". But no, he answers himself, we are dead serious, even when we are praying for those who persecute us! We know quite well that, when the Empire is convulsed, we too, with all others, will suffer from the evil consequences [156]. We have arrived here at the other end of the spectrum : the Empire that once was Satan's private domain has now become a conditio sine qua non for the welfare of the Christians, persecutions or no persecutions. This is one of the very rare instances of a dualistic opposition being overcome.

e. The future of the Empire

Tertullian may be seen as a connecting link between negative and positive visions of the Empire. Although he has a low opinion of it, he does not believe that it is the domain of the Antichrist. But as soon as the deathknell for the Empire has sounded, the Antichrist will appear [157].

In the last decades of the second century Melito was bishop of Sardes. In A.D. 170 he addressed an apology for the Christians to the Emperor Marcus Aurelius of which only fragments survive. The bishop begins with stating that the Empire had had a new and auspicious beginning under Augustus, and that in the same time Christianity began to flourish. Obviously the God of the Christians had taken the Empire under his protection, the proof of which is that since the days of the first Emperor it did not come to any harm [158].

Origen did not see much in the Empire, but he was convinced that - and history put him in the right - it would eventually become a Christian realm. This would even be its apogee, for then it would be invincible; it would no longer be necessary to conduct war - in this, however, history gave him the lie [159].

Two Christian authors, Tertullian and Lactantius, saw in the Roman Empire the last of the great realms [160]. Lactantius, a North African writer, who lived from ca. 250 to ca. 323, digressed extensively about this [161]. He hesitates to say it, but "the Roman name that now governs the world ... will disappear from the earth; the mastery will return to Asia; the East will rule again, and the West will be its slave". Nobody should be surprised when the Roman Empire, in spite of its great power and its mighty rulers, breaks down one day, for it is the work of mortals and mortal itself. The same fate has befallen all other realms of history. The Sibylline Books foretell that Rome will perish.

This is a remarkable utterance! Lactantius does not rejoice in the idea of the end of Rome which he finds inevitable. The curious thing is that he rekindles the old East-West dualism, that of 'Europe' and 'Asia' in which one of the two must be subject to the other. Since the idea of Empire came from the East and since Rome was the only western Empire ever, the mastery would necessarily return to the East. The spectre of the imminent fall of Rome fills him with the greatest apprehension. It is the end of the world for him; it will cause untold misery. Tertullian is more optimistic. The Christian faith is constantly expanding; the coming ruler of the world will be Christ. All realms of history have remained confined within limits, but the name of Christ will reign everywhere [162].

The attentive reader will by now have detected the mechanism by means of which the Christians were able to overcome their original radical rejection of Roman rule. They came to accept the Empire, but never really in its pagan form; they could accomodate themselves to it only on the condition that it would once become a Christian Empire or that it would be succeeded by the supreme and world-wide rule of Christ.

6. A tale of two cities

a. Why Augustine wrote the City of God

Christianity had been recognized as a religio licita already for a century and it had been the official imperial religion for some decades when Saint Augustine made the final, most authoritative, and highly consequential assessment of the relationship of the political and spiritual domains. At the end of the year 395 or in the beginning of 396 he had become bishop of

Hippo, near Carthage in North Africa. Although his diocese asked much of his time and energy, he nevertheless found enough spare hours to write extensively, amongst other works his famous autobiography, the 'Confessions', which he completed in or about 400. He was fifty-nine when he wrote the first lines of his magnum opus, 'The City of God against the pagans', and seventy-two when he has completed his enormous task in 426. Four years later he died; when he lay on his death-bed, the Vandals were beleaguering Hippo. Saint Augustine lived in the declining years of the Roman Empire, and he knew this. In 410 the Visigoths had sacked Rome - a town that in exactly eight hundred years had seen no foreign enemy within its walls. This event deeply shocked and frightened the whole Roman world. Was the end near?

For centuries it had been common ground among the heathen that the calamities which befell Rome should be blamed on the Christians. The fact that they did not venerate the gods was the cause of all that went wrong. Augustine himself states that the pagans, "attempting to attribute this visitation (= the sack of Rome) to the Christian religion, began more sharply and more bitterly than usual to blaspheme the true God. Burning with the zeal of God's house, I decided to write against their blasphemies and errors the books of the City of God" [163]. It must be remarked at the outset that this huge book is neither an attack on the Roman Empire nor a defense of it, but fundamentally an apology for the Christian faith. This faith is treated here in its relation to outward and secular events. It is for this reason that Augustine did not write of one city but of two, the City of God and the earthly city. He often goes out of his way to discuss a great many questions, which seem to us at the best side-issues with regard to his main theme, questions, for instance, of moral theology, for example why it is not permitted to commit suicide, or in Book V the long diatribe against astrology, one of his favourite subjects.

b. Cities with a difference

Already in the Preface to Book I the author makes it clear that the City of God stands much higher than the earthly city. "Our city is raised above all earthly heights, not raised by the devices of human arrogance, but by grace divine". He finds this arrogance in that famous line by Virgil stating that it was Rome's task 'to spare the fallen and subdue the proud' [164] which he calls 'the inflated fancy of a proud spirit'. In this Preface he does not mention the name of Rome, but he is evidently speaking of it when he refers to "that earthly city which, when it seeks for mastery, though the nations are its slaves, has as its own mastery that very lust of mastery" [165].

Augustine's criticism of the Roman way of life is long and sharp. Their gods are powerless and present no rules for right living, their government is corrupt, their stage plays are obscene, their behaviour is often utterly immoral. And they learned this immoral conduct from their own gods! "These stories of enticement and crime on the part of these gods, these infamous deeds that the gods either criminally or shamefully committed or that were even more shamefully presented to the ears and eyes of the people, in these the whole city was schooled" [166]. Over against this unholy city stands the wholesome city of Christianity.

c. All these wars ...

Augustine also criticizes the warlike spirit of the Romans. They aver that it was necessary to wage wars in uninterrupted succession, or else "the Roman domain could never have spread so wide or its fame been so gloriously broadcasted. Isn't that a relevant argument! Why should it have been necessary to be so turbulent in order to be a great empire? ... Did the end, the extension of their domain, justify the course that was taken?" [167].

The author had a lot to say on the unjust wars fought by Rome and on the civil discord prevailing in the state since the end of the Second Punic War until the days of Augustus. Ironically, he calls it 'a matter of great refinement' that by senatorial decree a Concordia temple had been erected on the spot where the most bloody fights of the civil wars had taken place and "where so many citizens of all ranks" had fallen. A temple of Discord would have been more apt, but obviously Rome did not know the difference between Concord and Discord [168]. Augustine does not believe that "men are happy who always live amongst the disasters of war. It matters not whether the blood shed was that of fellow-citizens or of enemies; in any case it is the blood of men. The dark shadow of fear and the lust of blood are always with them" [169].

d. Why an Empire?

"Is it proper for good men to find pleasure in the extent of their dominion?" - which is tantamount to the question whether imperialistic and conquering Romans really were good men. The answer of the author is somewhat ambiguous. He adopts here the well-known thesis, so dear to imperialists of all times, that Rome was sometimes provoked into war by her neighbours. But "the history of men would have been happier and all kingdoms would have been small, enjoying harmony with their neighbours", if no wars had been fought, just or unjust. "Waging war and extending their dominion over conquered nations is in the eyes of the wicked a gift of fortune but in the eyes of the good it is a necessary evil" [170].

When all is said and done, there was an Empire indeed, and a very big one at that! However, the Romans should not think that their gods had helped them to it. Augustine does not say that God gave it to them, but "they could by no means have gained it against the will of God. If they had ... worshipped the one God with purity of faith and conduct, they would have had a better kingdom here below, whatever its size, and would have received an eternal kingdom hereafter, whether they had any kingdom here or not" [171]. With regard to the salvation of souls the Roman imperial success did not count at all.

Now the great question is : "for what reason God willed that the Roman Empire should be so great and so lasting?" [172]. Its existence is not the result of the chance of fate or the position of the stars [173]. It is God's Providence by which the whole world and all mankind in it are ruled. But since the

Roman Empire could not have existed without the favour of God, there must be some reason why he "deigned to help them to enlarge their Empire" [174]. It even seems that, in Augustine's view, God wanted to create an equitable distribution of power in the world, for "when splendid Empires had long been known in the East, God willed that an Empire of the West should arise, later in time, but more splendid for its extent and greatness" [175].

e. The fundamental difference between the two cities

Augustine found the urge which drove the Romans forward on the path of empire-building generous and selfless and even serving the welfare of the world. "To overcome the grievous vices of the nations he (God) granted supremacy to men who for the sake of honour, praise and glory served the country in which they were not seeking their own glory, and did not hesitate to prefer her safety to their own." The author acknowledges that love of praise is a vice, but we should not expect too much of pagans. "Men who do not obtain the gift of the Holy Spirit and bridle their baser passions by pious faith and love of intelligible beauty (= God), at any rate live better because of their desire for human praise and glory. While these men are not saints, to be sure, they are less vile" [176].

Of course, the Romans, as the heathen that they are, are not entitled 'to eternal life with the angels in the eternal city'. But their reward they will have, and thus "they will have no complaint against the justice of the supreme and true God". This reward is that "they were honoured amongst all other nations; they imposed the laws of their Empire upon many nations; and today they enjoy the glory conferred by literature and historical writing amongst all nations" [177]. Although the Romans remain consigned to the earth, there is a link between their earthly city and the heavenly one for which the saints - the Christians - are destined. For the Empire "was also destined for the benefit of the citizens of the eternal city while they are pilgrims here". The diligence the pagans display for the sake of human glory is an example for the Christians who must exert themselves for the sake of eternal life [178].

However, in spite of this link, there remains a fundamental difference between the two cities. "The city in which the Christians have the promise of reigning is as far removed from this Rome as heaven is from earth, eternal life from temporal joys, solid glory from hollow praise, the company of angels from that of mortals, and the light of him who made the sun and the moon from the light of the sun and the moon" [179].

f. Is the Christian Empire a better one?

The question is whether the Empire, with Christianity for some time already as its state religion, was better off than when it was still pagan. Not with regard to politics, thinks the author : the Christian Emperors do not reign longer and are not luckier in their wars than their heathen predecessors. But we may call them happy if they are good Christians, reign justly, and worship God. Augustine obviously had his doubts about the behaviour of certain Christian Emperors since he writes : "Christians Emperors <u>of this sort</u> (my underlining) we declare happy" [180]. He found much to praise in Constantine the Great and Theodosius I, while keeping a prudent silence on the intervening rulers [181].

g. Cain and Abel as ancestors

It is only after an enormously long disquisition on the differences between Christian and pagan philosophy and theology and on the creation of heaven and earth and all that they contain, that Augustine rather unexpectedly returns to the subject of the two cities. They have been created by two different kinds of love. The earthly city is the result of the love of self, 'carried even to the point of contempt of God'; the heavenly city is the product of the love of God, 'carried even to the point of contempt of self' [182]. Just as there are two opposed cities, there are two entirely different branches of the human race, by which he means "two societies of human beings, of which one is predestined to reign eternally with God and the other to undergo eternal punishment". The ancestor of the first city is Abel, of the second Cain. When

Genesis 4:17 says that Cain founded a city while Abel founded none, this should be taken to mean that his city exists only 'above' [183].

Augustine does not deny that the earthly city has its own goods, but on the whole it is characterized by litigations and warfare [184]. The author does not miss the opportunity of mentioning that the foundation of Rome - to him the earthly city par excellence - was accompanied by a fratricide, because Romulus slew his brother Remus. This crime shows "how the earthly city is divided against itself". The slaying of Abel by Cain demonstrates that "there is enmity between the two cities themselves", since Abel was a citizen of the higher one [185].

h. The parallel courses of the two cities

The author then proceeds to describe "the origin, progress and appointed ends of the two cities, the one of God and the other of this world in which the former resides as an alien, so far as mankind is concerned" [186]. In the Books XVI and XVII the course of the City of God is traced as it became apparent through the historical events related in the Old Testament. In Book XVIII the progress of 'the society of mortal men' is studied which, "no matter how great the variety of environment, yet retained in a way some bond of fellowship, as being of one and the same origin" [187]. We read of the kingdoms of the Assyrians and the Egyptians, of the state of the Athenians, of the fate of Troy, and then of the foundation of Rome. This book ends with the biblical prophecies of the coming of Christ.

j. The inhabitants of the heavenly city

It will be evident that the people of Israel were the inhabitants of the heavenly city before the birth of Christ. The question is whether there were non-Jews who belonged to the fellowship of the City of God - a question that is not without importance for the debate on the thesis of 'extra ecclesiam nulla salus'. "To be sure, there was no other people especially called the people of God. Nevertheless, they (the Jews) cannot deny that among other peoples too there have been certain men who belonged not by earthly but by heavenly fellowship to the company of true Israelites who are citizens of the country that is above." Augustine cites Job as an example [188]. Just as pagans can be Jews in a spiritual sense of the word, the heavenly city (now the Church), going its way as a stranger on earth, "summons citizens from all peoples, and gathers an alien society of all languages, caring naught what difference there may be in manners, laws and institutions" [189].

k. Assessment

We have gathered enough materials now for assessing with sufficient precision what Augustine's attitude was with regard to the Roman Empire. We should never forget that this bishop of Hippo was a citizen of the Empire, subject to its laws; although a North African, a Punic, he was a master of the imperial language. He lived and worked in the context of this Empire and followed its vicissitudes with growing anxiety. The first thing that strikes the eye is that it did not make much difference to him whether the Empire was either pagan or Christian. Neither the pagan Empire nor the Christian one was the City of God; the conversion of Constantine the Great and Theodosius' making Christianity the state religion had not changed it into the heavenly city. It was and remained an earthly city, a purely political and human institution and as such the successor of the older eastern Empires.

The heavenly city possessed no political organization and found its citizens everywhere and among all nations; basically, it was a spiritual companionship. Although having its real abode 'above', on earth it had its embodiment first in the people of Israel, then in the Christian Church. It should be noted that Augustine nowhere says that the privileges of Israel were taken away from it. Doubtless, there are some links between the two cities, if only because a Christian has to live within the earthly city. But the differences between the two realms are great, so great that they are downright dualistic. It is even radical dualism, since the heavenly city is in no way dependent on the earthly one. The dualism becomes apparent in the author's frequent use of oppositions : founded by Abel - founded by Cain, chararacterized by love of God - characterized by love of self, to exist eternally - destined for destruction. I don't believe that Augustine was a great friend of political institutions in general; at best he found them necessary evils. Although moderate and generally dispassionate in tone, he places himself in the anti-political line of Daniel and the Book of Revelation.

IV WAR ON THE CHURCH

1. A state in the state?

We shall have to study the relation between the Empire and the Christian Church somewhat more carefully. Are we allowed to call the Christian community a 'state in the state'? Christopher Dawson, while stating in as many words that it was not a state in the state, nevertheless comes in his description very close to this concept with his words that the Church was 'at least an ultimate and autonomous society'. This means that, principally and fundamentally, the Church had nothing to do with the Empire. Different from it and in many respects in opposition to it, the Church had its own leadership, its own jurisdiction and its own laws. It addressed all those who felt dissatisfied with the existing order and prevailing culture which they found empty and immoral. We should not primarily think here of a movement of political or economic protest; the causes of the discontent which brought people into the Church lay much deeper; it was, as Dawson writes, 'a protest against the spiritual ideals of the ancient world and its whole social ethos' [190].

A later scholar, Paul Karlhorst, went a step further; in his opinion the Christian Church was a 'state in the state' indeed, and as such it was an 'anti-state'. The Church had not only its own leadership and organization, but no less an economic, juridical, and administrative structure of its own so that it comprised and regulated the whole life of its members. "It fulfilled all the conditions that are put nowadays to a state" [191]. The only thing that failed was international recognition [192]. And as a 'state' the Church was 'the true state, the community of God' [193]. The Christian could not participate in pagan associations since these were placed under the aegis of some pagan divinity; they could not assume military or civil duties since these meant veneration of the Emperor. They had (later) to found their own schools since the existing schools (there were only private ones) were all based on pagan philosophy. They needed their own prayer-houses and their own cemeteries [194].

What the Christian community really made into an 'anti-state' was that it had its own ethos and its own social attitude. It was not so much that the pagan Empire had no ethos at all. It certainly had one. But the idea behind all imperial legislation was the assumption that law-giving, regulation of public life, would ipso facto lead to a well-ordered society of law-abiding citizens. The Empire turned out laws and decrees on the assembly line. But those who issued these well-intentioned decrees belied them by their own conduct. The general public knew of the scandalous luxury, the squandering of money, the immorality of high society, and of the cruelty and callousness of official policy. Thus why bother about being law-abiding yourself?

Although the Church had its own moral laws and stipulations, it was not believed that they would of themselves create a holier life and a better world. Its real ethos was not of a political, administrative, or juridical order; it was basically spiritual. Its foundation was the two great commandments : to love God from the depth of your heart, and your neighbour like yourself [195]. To sum up in the words of Dawson : "the idea of citizenship, which was the fundamental idea of the classical culture, was transferred by Christianity to the spiritual order. In the existing order the Christians were peregrini - strangers and foreigners; their true citizenship was in the Kingdom of God, and even in the present world their most vital social relationship was found in their membership of the Church, not in that of city and Empire" [196].

The situation of the Christians in the Empire was, in fact, an anomaly. Peter Brown has expressed this admirably, speaking of 'the disturbing feature of third-century Christianity'. "It offered a community which, in symbolic form, clearly accepted the breakdown of the equipoise on which the traditional pagan community had rested. Its initiation was conceived of as producing men shorn of the complexities of their earthly identity. Its ethos produced a more atomistic view of the person, who was less bound than previously to the ties of kinship, of neighborhood, and of region" [197]. We may add that it also slackened the ties that bound the citizen to the state.

2. The 'ten persecutions'

Already in primary school I learned that the Church had suffered ten persecutions from the reign of Nero until that of Constantine the Great. I did not know, and my teachers did not know it either, that this number 'ten' is a formalized number, used to equate the persecutions with the ten plagues of Egypt. Since the Church was 'the true Israel', it ought to have its own ten plagues. However, that there have been ten Egyptian plagues is in itself a formalized number, since ten (we have ten fingers to count on) stands for a 'multitude', a great many, as much as we can count. The equation 'ten plagues - ten persecutions' is mentioned by Augustine.

The ten persecutions he enumerates are those of the Emperors Nero, Domitian, Trajan, Antoninus Pius, Septimius Severus, Maximinus Thrax, Decius, Valerianus, Aurelianus, and Diocletian, all between 54 and 305. There will, however, according to popular Christian belief, be an eleventh one, to be inflicted by the Antichrist. Augustine has his doubts about this exact number of ten, for why not include the persecution by Julian? Valens (364-378), an Arian Emperor, he says, "laid waste the Catholic Church in the East in a great persecution". And what to think of recent events in Persia where the Christians were persecuted so fiercely that some fled over the border to Roman territory? Since he is by no means sure of there having been exactly ten persecutions, he is, in consequence, unable to equate them with the ten plagues of Egypt. There are people who match plagues and persecutions very precisely one by one, he writes not without irony, 'with far-fetched ingenuity'. "But I do not think that those events (the plagues) were prophetic symbols of the persecutions"; the equation is not the result of 'prophetic inspiration' but of a 'speculation of the human mind' [198].

3. Why the Church was persecuted

In the foregoing pages where I discussed the relationship of Church and Empire in the first centuries A.D., the reader will have found the fundamental reasons why state and public were inimical to the Christians and their creed. Karlhorst, in his very precise study, summarizes these reasons as follows. Juridically the Church was illegal and did not enjoy the privileges other cults received; the Christians were and remained outlawed outsiders. In practice the attitude of state and society regarding the Christians hovered between a contemptuous 'laissez faire' and active persecution, sometimes aiming at wholesale eradication. Although there were relatively quiet periods, on the whole the actions against the Christians until ca. 300 became steadily harder, perhaps because there were ever more of them. Karlhorst says that, at least at first, it was not really the state that organized the actions but the pagan public that indulged in pogroms. The Christians felt that a war was waged against them; they offered no resistance but did not give in either [199].

4. Popular outbursts against Christians

First of all popular outbursts against Christians must be mentioned. They were very numerous and occurred everywhere. The Christians were convenient scapegoats for everything that went wrong [200] : whatever happened, floods, droughts, pestilence, famine, invasions, the Christians were blamed for it. In this context we should keep in mind how cruel and bloodthirsty the Roman public, from high to low, was; people went to the amphitheatres to view how men, gladiators, fought another until one of them dropped dead. This was obviously an amusing pastime for an afternoon.

Tertullian depicts how fiercely the populace, the 'vulgus', could rage against the Christians. "Often the governor takes action against the Christians in the most cruel way, sometimes of his own accord, sometimes because of the laws. But equally often the vulgus arbitrarily takes matters into its own hands, bypassing the authorities, by stone throwing and arson. Like wild bacchics they don't even leave deceased Christians in peace, pulling the decaying corpses from the quiet of the tomb, hack them to pieces, and scatter them in all directions" [201].

A good instance of popular justice is what happened in Lyons (Lugdunum) in A.D. 177, 'one of the most terrible dramas in the history of the early Church' [202]. The amphitheatre there was in need of gladiators, preferably cheap ones; gladiator games were held so often that there was a dearth of such men. Now there existed a senatorial decree that allowed towns in Gallia to use men who were condemned to death as gladiators [203]. To condemn Christians to death would have a double advantage : one was to get rid of them, and the other was a supply of cheap gladiators. That they were not so thoroughly trained as professional fighters presented no problem in this case, since the condemned were destined to fight wild beasts. A howling multitude dragged quite a number of Christians before the judges and enjoyed the spectacle of seeing them die in the arena at the fangs and claws of panthers and tigers after a token resistance. One of them was a woman, Blandina. Those who had fallen were not buried but burned; their ashes were cast into the Rhône [204]. The authorities did nothing to prevent this lawless cruelty [205].

There was also no sign of the authorities during an anti-Christian pogrom in Alexandria in 248 which degenerated into downright lynch justice. When a poet had foretold calamities for the city, the populace threw itself on the Christians who got the blame for what had not yet happened. Individual Christians were maltreated; a certain Quinta was dragged through the whole town over the cobbles and finally stoned. Houses of the faithful were broken into and plundered, their possessions burned in the street. Pagan bands rambled through the streets singing blasphemous songs and forcing everyone who met them to tune in so that Christians had to stay indoors [206].

5. Official policy

The policy makers of the Empire were, in general, not very intent on persecuting the Christians. Not a few Emperors were religiously indifferent and sceptics. Although they loathed Christianity and found the faithful bigoted fanatics, they realized that a great persecution would cause a lot of unrest and trouble; at the same time they, and the judiciary, knew that, with regard to charges of treason, rebellion, fomenting unrest, and being the cause of natural calamities, the evidence against the Christians was more often than not extremely flimsy or even totally non-existent. Hence Karlhorst concludes that after Nero and until the middle of the third century the state on the whole remained passive, with the exception of isolated actions under Hadrian and Marcus Aurelius [207]. Trajan ordered that "no search should be made for these people (the Christians)". But when they were denounced and found guilty (= if they didn't retract), "they must be punished" [208]. Did this ruler realize that by this prescription he made the judiciary dependent on a despicable kind of person, the denunciator [209]?

6. Nero's anti-Christian action

With this in mind, it is easy to see that the first bout of persecution, that of Nero in A.D. 64, was something out of the ordinary; no later Emperor followed his example. Traditionaly the immediate cause is considered to be the enormous conflagration that reduced a great part of the capital. The wider context was, as Frend writes, that the authorities undertook an action against cults which they found harmful [210]. For Nero himself it was important to shift the blame for the fire that was laid at his door to the unpopular Christians. They were suspected of hatred against the human race rather than of arson, says Tacitus [211]; Momigliano concludes that "the persecution was directed against the Christians as Christians", rather than as incendiaries [212]. The alleged culprits were wrapped into the skins of animals and then torn apart by dogs or crucified in the gardens of Nero and kindled as torches to illuminate the night. Many found this treatment so cruel, according to Tacitus, that even those who held the Christians liable to heavy punishment felt pity for them [213].

7. Domitian the competitor of the Christian God

There followed three decades of quiet, but towards the end of Domitian's reign (81-96) the hatred against the Christians flared up again. He made victims amongst the Jews too. Anti-Judaism had been steadily growing since the Jewish War. There was a rumour current that 'masters coming from Judaea' would possess the world. Although Tacitus pointed out that this referred to Titus and Vespasian, the populace preferred to believe that the Jews were meant [214]. Eusebius quotes Hegesippus to the effect that Domitian was, 'like Herod, afraid of the coming of Christ'. He once questioned in person men who were descendants of David about 'the Christ and his kingdom, its nature, origin, and time of appearance'. The men in question, obviously Jewish Christians, assured him that this kingdom was not earthly, but 'heavenly and angelic' and would only come at the end of time whereupon the Emperor released them [215].

What made Domitian clamp down on Jews and Christians? First of all, he had a difficult and authoritarian character and was vain and revengeful. Opposition made him furious; in his later years his distrust degenerated into persecution mania. Bengtson calls his behaviour in the last period of his reign 'downright psychotic' [216]. He was also megalomaniac, the first Emperor to style himself 'dominus et deus' [217]; this title was not assigned to him by the Senate as in other cases. There can be no doubt that he was convinced of his own divinity. A telling example of this is that he recalled his divorced wife Domitia Longa to the 'pulvinar' [218]; now a 'pulvinar' is not just a nuptial bed but the divine couch, to be found only in temples, upon which the 'hieros gamos', the marriage of a deity and a mortal was consumated [219].

Domitian's idea of being a god had a double consequence. The first is that he was extremely strict in matters of religion, 'not the man to tolerate religious deviations'. Secondly, he was jealous of other gods, especially of a god who claimed to be just as supreme and universal as he thought himself to be. Therefore, "his profound hostility towards any form of religious unorthodoxy resulted in the punishment of any prominent citizen who lapsed too blatantly into an 'external religion'" [220], that is, Jewish proselytes and Christians.

Two Christian books of the period contain echoes of the difficulties the Christians experienced. The First Letter of Clement speaks of the 'misfortunes and reverses' of the Roman Christians [221]. The Book of Revelation is evidently written in a time of troubles; "it demonstrates beyond doubt that Christianity was engaged in a death battle with Imperial Rome" [222]. Eusebius relates that in these days its author called John was banished to the island of Patmos [223]. There is no saying how many victims Domitian's anti-Christian policy made, but it is certain that there were some. The Emperor even hit at his own family. I mentioned earlier how his cousin Flavius Clemens and his wife Flavia Domitilla, a granddaughter of Vespasian were arrested; both were accused of 'atheism' and of 'drifting into the practices of the Jews' [224]. Clemens was executed, Domitilla banished to the island of Pandateria. It has often been doubted that these two were Christians; rather, it is thought, they were proselytes [225]. But the expression 'drifting into Jewish ways' does not reveal very much since authorities and public had not yet wholly figured out the difference between Judaism and Christianity. Furthermore, it is improbable that Jews would be accused of being 'atheists' [226]. Eusebius says in as many words that the couple was condemned because they confessed the Christ [227]. Although Domitian did not launch a persecution in a grand style, what he did was enough for Tertullian to dub him 'half a Nero' [228].

One of the measures of Domitian, who needed money, was to collect the fiscus judaicus with the utmost severity. This tax had to be paid by ethnic Jews, circumcized and practising the Law. Although Christians were often thought to live like Jews, they were not circumcized, while it was evident that they did not follow the prescripts of the Law. Moreover, "they were disowned by those whose orthodoxy as Jews could not be doubted". That they were exempted from paying the Jewish tax made it clear that they were no Jews at all. This, as Frend remarks, increased 'the legal difference between Jews and Christians in the eyes of the authorities' which worked 'to the disadvantage of the Christians' [229].

8. The policy of the Antonini

a. Trajan's ruling

During the first Antonini the Christians, allowance made for occasional, local, and unauthorized popular outbursts against them, enjoyed a period of relative calm. The state had no clearly defined policy respecting them; this becomes apparent from that famous (and already quoted) letter of Trajan to Pliny in A.D. 112 in which the Emperor, questioned by the governor on the line to be followed, answered that there did not exist definite prescripts [230]. Christians should not be run to earth. Judges should not accept anonymous information, but if Christians were denounced, they had to be punished [231]. One might well ask what, in the absence of definite prescripts, was the legal title for these condemnations. To be a Christian was obviously enough. Tertullian found it 'a confused decision' : if the Christians were criminals, they should be tracked down, he found. But if they were not to be traced, they should not be condemned either [232].

b. Hadrian's moderation

The Emperor Hadrian established a less ambiguous juridical position. In a rescript of 124/125, destined for the proconsul of the province of Asia, Minicius Fundanus, he told him not to pay attention to denouncements, anonymous or not. Christians should only be condemned if it could be proved that they had done something specific against the law; obviously, to be a Christian was no longer enough. Hadrian even stipulated that persons who slanderoulsy accused others had to be punished themselves [233]. It is also possible that the tragic end of the Bar Kokhba revolt in A.D. 135 influenced the opinion of the authorities regarding the Christians in a favourable sense : it was evident that they had had no part in it [234]. However this may be, "to all intents and purposes, the Christians would be free from molestation except in quite extraordinary circumstances. Thus, in practice, "the rescript of Hadrian was the nearest to toleration the Christians were to attain before the end of Valerian's persecution in 260" [235]. The rescripts of Trajan and Hadrian remained for two centuries the legal basis for the treatment of the Christians by the state [236].

c. No change in official policy during the reign of Antoninus Pius

The new rule was not modified by Hadrian's successor Antoninus Pius (138-161). But it is possible, and even probable, that the lower authorities did not take it into account always and everywhere. Or else Justin the Martyr would not have protested to this Emperor around A.D. 150 that, in spite of the rescript, Christians continued to be condemned as Christians. Normally, he writes, the judges only condemn an accused on the basis of convincing proof, but for us, Christians, to be called by this name is sufficient. But the name is not enough, this is no crime. It is the conduct that counts, not the label [237]. Should it be found that this conduct is criminal, let justice be done. But as a Christian a person should go scotfree [238].

Justin mentions an incident of this kind. In Rome the city prefect Urbicus condemned three Christians to death soley because they were Christians. Similar injustices were being committed by the magistrates everywhere, adds the author. Somebody in Urbicus's court-room cried out : "What! This is a man who is not an adulterer, not a profligate, not a murderer, not a thief, not a rapist, a man, in short, who cannot be convicted of any crime; he only professes to be a Christian, and you condemn him! This judgment, Urbicus, does not conform to the intentions of the pious Emperor" [239].

It is because of incidents such as this one that Frend characterizes the period 135-165 as 'a false dawn'. "Christian communities remained illegal societies ... Always underlying periods of relative calm glowed fires of fear and hatred" [240]. Soon enough this 'false dawn' was followed by 'years of crisis', as Frend dubs the period 165-180 [241].

d. New problems under Marcus Aurelius

During the reign of the Emperor Marcus Aurelius (161-180) new problems arose. Was Hadrian's rescript rescinded? In his already mentioned petition to the Emperor and his son Commodus Athenagoras protests that, although the state tolerates the Christian religion, the mob attacks and denounces the faithful so that they have to suffer summarily and in an absolutely illegal and unjustified manner [242]. It was exactly in this period that the horrifying events at Lyons in 177, a disgrace to the Empire, took place. As Grégoire remarks, there was during the Antonine Emperors a sort of contradiction between official policy and the facts, with the result that, in practice, the situation of the Christians was not modified at all [243].

Somewhat earlier Melito, the bishop of Sardes, had also addressed a petition to the rulers. He wrote that everywhere in the province of Asia the Christians were being persecuted; evil-intentioned people tried to seize their possessions [244]. And he adds : "When this is done on your orders, it is right." But when it did not originate with him, "then we have to ask you urgently not to leave us in the lurch" [245]. Melito obviously doubted that Marcus Aurelius himself could have given order to persecute the Christians; it is also very much doubted nowadays.

But there are some 'sententiae' of this period that point in this direction, ordering the magistrates to proceed against thieves and robbers but also against sacrilegious and superstitious people [246]. Persons who are introducing new rites and unknown religions are to be punished with death [247]. There is a real possibility that the Christians are not meant here; nobody could say in about 180 that they were introducing a new religion. But it is quite conceivable that local magistrates felt entitled by these sententiae to act against people whom they themselves considered sacrilegious and superstitious, the Christians.

It is evident that the Christians preferred to believe that the Emperor had not instigated the measures against them. This is a well-known and time-honoured device : the benevolent sovereign is innocent; it is his bad advisers and the ill-intentioned lower magistrates who are really guilty. But we may well ask whether Marcus Aurelius was blameless. Would he have known nothing at all of what his magistrates were doing? Or did he prefer not to know? When Justin the Martyr stood trial in A.D. 167 - he was condemned to death -, his judge was Q. Iunius Rusticus, the praefectus urbis of Rome. This man was the leader of the Stoic school in the capital [248], and what is more important, a friend and confident of the philosopher-emperor [249]. Is it imaginable that nothing of this has reached the ears of his friend?

e. A confused situation under Commodus

The situation became still more confused and contradictory under Commodus (180-192), the last and the least sympathetic of the Antonines. Personally this Emperor was no outspoken enemy of the Christian Church; it is said that his court teemed with Christians. Marcia, the slave girl who became his wife, was a Christian; it is related that she obtained the release of Christian prisoners in Sardinia, one of them the future Pope Callistus I (217-222) [250]. But the pogroms continued. At Scillium in North Africa twelve Christians were executed in 180 on the orders of the proconsul [251].

9. The policy of the Severi

a. Their attitude to Christianity

The dynasty of the Severi (193-235) was of North African origin; these rulers were not deeply committed to the Roman public religion and were, mainly through their wives, not wholly unacquainted with Christianity [252]. The founder of this dynasty, Septimius Severus (193-211) had had to fight for the throne in a civil war [253] during which the Christians had taken his side. He remained grateful for this. Neither he nor his son Caracalla (211-217) hindered the Christians of the court in the observance of their religion.

b. A baneful edict

However benevolent the personal attitude of Septimius Severus may have been, in 202 he issued an edict that forbade conversions to both Judaism and Christianity; severe punishment was threatened in case of transgression of this rule [254]. Why did he do this? Were Jews and Christians getting too numerous to his taste? Or did he want to placate the other side? The Historia Augusta, our source in this respect, does not give his reasons. Was it the start of a persecution? Eusebius says it was : "Severus was stirring up persecution" [255]. Frend agrees : "The Severan persecution was the first world-wide move against the Christians" [256]. But Molthagen disagrees : although there were occasional proceedings against Christians, the Severan period is characterized by great tolerance [257]. Their respective positions are not so far apart as it seems. Frend states that the Severan edict hit "the relatively small class of Christian converts and was confined to major centres", but, he adds, "it provided a precedent for later official actions" [258]. Molthagen, on his part, says that the authorities here and there took action against Christians, for instance in Carthage and Alexandria [259]. It is possible that the state was not actually involved in these occurrences but that they were instigated by pagan and Jewish agitators [260]. The fact is that the victims we know by name were by no means of all of them recent converts; they were condemned as Christians, not as converts [261].

c. The victims

And victims there were. Clement of Alexandria saw with his own eyes how his co-religionists were 'roasted, impaled, and beheaded' [262]. Leonides, the father of Origen, was one of them [263]; his property was confiscated for the imperial treasury [264].

In Carthage many Christians were arrested, women among them, Perpetua, the twenty-two-year-old mother of a baby [265], and Felicitas, a young girl who was eight months pregnant [266] - obviously no reasons to spare them! The procurator, Hilarianus, questioned Perpetua : "Are you a

Christ?", and her answer was : "Yes, I am!". This sufficiently explains why they were condemned. Wild beasts would be their executors [267]. In the night before the execution the Christians were housed in the military prison of the town. The next day the little company courageously entered the arena, Perpetua psalm singing; she encouraged the others to remain steadfast. The men were set upon by a leopard, the women by a wild cow. The animal knocked them down but did not finish them. The public clamoured that the surviving victims should be brought to the middle of the arena in order to be able to enjoy the spectacle better. They kissed one another and were then stabbed to death by a young and nervous gladiator; the last one to fall was Perpetua [268].

10. Steady growth of Christianity

During the first decades of the third century the growth of Christianity became unstoppable. It was rapidly gaining ground in North Africa and penetrated into the West where it had been only weakly represented so far, but everywhere more in the towns than in the countryside. It was also winning converts in the higher circles of society. "Day by day you (the pagans) groan over the ever increasing number of Christians. Your constant cry is that the state is beset by us ... You grieve over it as a calamity, that every age, in short, every rank is passing over from you to us [269] ... We are filling all that is yours, cities, blocks of houses, citadels, townships, councils, even the army camps, the tribus and the decuriae, the palace, the Senate, the Forum" [270].

The faithful who had for so long celebrated their liturgy in private houses, now began to erect churches; they also acquired their own cemeteries. Molthagen, however, points out that, just as Christianity itself was tolerated but not more, its possessions were also tolerated but not more. That they factually existed did not mean that Christianity had now become a religio licita. But although only tolerated, the position of the bishops in the towns became ever more stronger, even vis-à-vis their management [271]. The reign of Caracalla (211-217), son and successor of Septimius Severus, was a period of religious peace, although there were local anti-Christian outbursts [272].

The calm continued during the reigns of the Emperors Elagabalus (217-222) and Alexander Severus (222-235); then even the local outbursts became rare [273]

11. The religious position of the Severi

The religious position of the Severi stood in a curious contrast to the official Roman cult. The god they adored was not Jupiter Capitolinus nor was it the supreme deity, the first Cause, of philosophically minded people; it was the sun, the Sol Invictus. They adhered to an oriental religion, with Syrian roots, just as they themselves were orientals rather than Romans. Elagabalus was a priest of this cult and remained so when Emperor. His real name was Varius Avitus and as Emperor Marcus Aurelius Antoninus, but he adopted the name of the Syrian god Elah-gabal, the god of the mountain. He was 'a pure Semite', says Grégoire [274].

His religion was a syncretistic one; he believed that "Roman polytheism would result, through this syncretism and by means of subordination, in the cult of the one and only supreme god (the sun god) of whom all other gods were symbols and aspects" [275]. In honour of this god the youth - for he was only fourteen when he ascended the throne - had two temples erected, one in a suburb but the other, the Eliogabalium, on the Palatine hill, next to the imperial palace. He decreed that "no god might be worshipped at Rome save only Elagabalus" [276]. Obviously, Jupiter Capitolinus had had his day. "Instructions were also issued to every magistrate or person conducting public sacrifices that the name of the new god should precede any of the others invoked by the officiating priest" [277].

The sacred emblems of the Roman cult, that of the Great Mother, the fire of Vesta, the Palladium, were brought over to the Eliogabalium. "He declared, furthermore, that the religions of the Jews and the Samaritans and the rites of the Christians must also be transferred to this place" [278]. If this statement is authentic, which is doubted by many scholars, but not by Marta Sordi who believes it to fit perfectly into the religious policy of Elagabalus [279], then this measure would imply a form of acknowledgement of the Christian religion.

However, the subordination of Christianity, its only serious competitor, to the sun cult would most certainly have led to a major clash. But the eighteen-year-old priest of the sun-god was murdered by his own praetorian guard in 222.

It is possibly because of Elagabalus' favouring of the Christians, even in the way he did it, that after his death there was an anti-Christian pogrom in Rome, the first ever in that city. A popular tumult broke out against the leaders of the Church in the city. The bishop, Callistus I (217-222), was thrown out of his window into a pool and then stoned; priests were killed and their corpses dragged through the streets of the town [280].

12. A 'barbarian' on the throne

With Maximinus Thrax (235-238) the first of the soldier-emperors came to the throne, the rulers who owed their position to their legions. He was a Thracian, a barbarian in the eyes of his subjects [281], a man who had been a shepherd and had then made a career in the army. Among his many enemies he counted also the Christians, or perhaps rather the Christians in the entourage of the Severi to whom he was bitterly inimical. "He immediately disposed of all the friends accompanying Alexander (Severus, 222-235) ... The entire serving staff, who had been with Alexander for many years, were dismissed from the court. Most of them were executed on suspicion of treason since Maximinus knew they had mourned the loss of Alexander" [282]. There must have been not a few Christians among them, because "the house of Alexander consisted for the most part of believers" [283].

It may seem that the new Emperor was not specifically aiming at Christians but at friends and relatives of his predecessor, whether they were Christians or not. But then he diverted his fire, for "he raised a persecution ordering the leaders of the Church to be executed for the teaching of the Gospel" [284]. What does this mean? Did he forbid the propagation of the Gospel? Or did he want to strike at the heart of Christianity itself? There seem to have been no death sentences. The bishop of Rome, Pontianus (230-235), together with his rival Hippolytus, was banished to the island of Sardinia where the unhealthy climate and the hard labour in the mines might make an execution superfluous [285]. But his successors on the Roman see, Anterus (235-236) and Fabianus (236-250), were left in peace by him [286].

More serious were the events in Cappadocia where Christianity was strong. It seems that the enemies of the Church in this province did not need orders from the Emperor to break loose. They were, as everywhere, twofold : "the Roman aristocracy who hated the Christians as potential revolutionaries, and the provincial mob who feared them as atheists responsible for natural disasters" [287]. Devastating earthquakes having occurred in Pontus and Cappadocia, scapegoats were needed and soon found. The governor of Cappadocia, Licinius Serenianus, turned out to be 'a bitter and terrible persecutor' [288]. A great many Christians fled the province to safer areas. Many churches went up in flames. There were arrests but no capital sentences. As bishop Firmilianus states expressly, the persecution remained restricted to Cappadocia.

13. The persecution of Decius

a. Decius's religious policy

The reign of Maximinus was short, only three years. A decade of quiet years under the Emperors Gordianus III (238-244) and Philippus Arabs (244-249) followed. But the sky darkened again when the city prefect of Rome, Decius, a Pannonian, ascended the throne for his short reign of two years (249-251). The new Emperor "raised a persecution against the churches", writes Eusebius, which he did "on account of his enmity against Philip" [289]. For Philip had befriended the Christians. But there was more to Decius's action than only this personal motive.

Decius's complete name was 'Imperator Caesar Caius Messius Quintus Decius Traianus (or Traianus Decius)'; he himself added that 'Traianus' (of whom he was no relative) to his family and personal appellatives. It will be clear what this meant. Trajan had been one of the greatest rulers of the Empire, a man intent upon the conservation of all that was authentically

Roman. Decius intended to do the same. As a Pannonian he considered himself a westerner, fundamentally different from these quaint easterners, the Syrians of the Severi dynasty, and from such uncouth barbarians like Maximinus the Thracian and Philip the Arabian, who had favoured strange oriental religions, the cult of the sun and the cult of Jesus of Nazareth. In every respect the old Roman discipline must be restored. For this reason he had an excellent press with pagan authors, but their Christain counterparts were far less enthusiastic. Restoration and confirmation of the official imperial cult was a natural part of his policy. A man like him could have no sympathy with Christianity.

b. The first general decree

At the end of 249 or in the beginning of 250 Decius issued an edict ordering to sacrifice to the gods of the Empire; libations should also be poured and it was obligatory to partake of the sacrificial meat. The literal text of this decree is lost so that we do not know whether it was imposed on all citizens or only on the Christians, in all probability the first. In practice it did not make much difference since for pagans such regulations never presented a problem. That it specifically aimed at Christians is shown by the fact that no Jews, who could not sacrifice either, were molested. Actually, it was an anti-Christian measure, and as such the first general decree against them ever. This means that now the imperial government fell in with the feelings that the multitude and the lower authorities had fostered against the Christians for two centuries already. Everyone who had fulfilled his or her duty of sacrificing and of partaking of the sacrificial meat received a certificate that he or she had done so, the so-called 'libellus', of which more than forty have been discovered as Egyptian papyri.

c. Victims

One of the first victims was Pope Fabianus. Decius took the trouble of trying him in person. Fabianus was put to death on January 21, 250. When the

Emperor heard he was dead, he said something revealing. "I would far rather receive news of a rival to the throne than see another bishop in Rome" [290]. This can hardly mean anything else than that he considered the supreme head of the Church a more dangerous competitor for the Empire than a political rival. This utterance lays bare the background of the persecution.

Other important clerics were caught and executed, the bishops of Antioch and Jerusalem for instance. In Caesarea Origen was in prison for three years and was so badly maltreated that he died of his wounds. Others, like the Church Father Cyprian in Carthage went into hiding in the countryside.

d. Apostasy

Since not everybody is built of reinforced concrete, many Christians, willingly or unwillingly, did what was asked of them, even to the point of denying that they were Christians. Even persons prominent in the life of the Church did not refuse to sacrifice. "Called by name, they approached the impure and unholy sacrifices, some pale and trembling, as if they were not for sacrificing but rather to be themselves the sacrifices and victims to the idols, so that the large crowd that stood around heaped mockery upon them, and it is evident that they were by nature cowards in everything, cowards both to die and to sacrifice. But others ran eagerly to the altars, affirming by their forwardness that they had not been Christians even formerly" [291]. In Smyrna even the bishop sacrificed [292]. In some towns it happened that the whole Christian community apostasized [293]. In Rome itself the pagans could relish the spectacle of Christians standing in a row on the Capitoline hill ready to sacrifice to Jupiter Capitolinus [294].

e. Disorganization of the Church

A terrible blow was thus dealt to the Church. Its normal life became totally disorganized; it may have seemed to the disheartened that the end had come. The vast number of those lapsed created quite a problem to the Church leaders : what to do with them when they asked to be integrated into ecclesiastical life again?

But there were also those who remained steadfast and who died for their faith. How many martyrs there were is difficult to say. Frend thinks, 'hundreds rather than thousands' all over the Empire, but enough to save the honour of the Church [295].

14. The persecution of Valerian

a. Valerian's religious policy

Then all of a sudden Decius died in 251. His successor Gallus (251-253) went on with the persecution for a short time, but from 252 onward the state became preoccupied with other problems, and the Christians were left in peace for the time being. The duration of the respite was only short, for the persecution was renewed by the Emperor Valerian (253-260). This caused a severe disappointment to the Christians, since the new ruler had the reputation of being well-disposed towards them [296]. It is hard to determine what made this ruler make such a volte-face.

The fact is that he could easily be acted upon by others. His family, the Licinii, came from Etruria [297], perhaps even from a priestly family [298] which may go some way to explain his religious fervour. The possessions of the Church may also have allured him [299]. It seems that Valerius Maximus, prefect of Rome in 255/256, directed the attention of the Emperor to the riches of the Church. An extremely wealthy family of Greek Christians had established itself in Rome and sustained there a great number of indigent co-religionists. Alerted by Maximus, the Emperor cited them before him and had them interrogated or perhaps even did so himself. "From where do these great riches come, these immense treasures you use for seducing the people?" [300]. After a long process, the 'Greek martyrs' were all send to their deaths. There was also a great Egyptian magician, Macrinius, who succeeded in getting a hold on the mind of the Emperor. This sinister man incited him against the

61

Christians whom he saw as the enemies of his practices; they should be slain and pursued [301].

b. The First Edict

The result was Valerian's First Edict of 257 [302]. The quintessence of the edict was that the clergy, for whom it was meant, were invited to sacrifice to 'the gods which preserve the Empire' [303]. The difference with the decree of Decius was that this sacrifice did not entail the abjuration of the Christian faith. If a Christian wanted to go on venerating Jesus Christ, let him or her do so. What Valerian counted on was the prevailing syncretism. Why should Christians make a problem of subordinating their peculiar faith to the general cult [304]? In the same edict the state extended its authority over the Christian cemeteries and forbade the faithful to come together there in order to hold their services (as was the custom).

Measures were taken against refractory clerics. Cyprian, the bishop of Carthage, was cited before the proconsul of the province of Africa, Aspasius Paternus. Asked why he refused to sacrifice, the bishop answered : "I am a Christian and a bishop. I acknowledge no other god than the one true God ... We pray to him day and night ..., also for the well-being of the Emperors (Valerian and his son and co-emperor Galienus)" [305]. This gives us an exact idea of the Christian stance : quite ready to obey and honour the Emperor but rejecting the syncretist solution. Cyprian was banished to a place some distance from Carthage. There were arrests in clerical circles, priests were severely beaten; a number of them were condemned to hard labour in the mines and badly treated. But for the time being there were no fatal victims.

c. The Second Edict

Valerian had far less success with his measure than Decius. He therefore decided to tighten his grip. In the summer of 259 the Second Edict followed. No longer was it aimed at the clergy alone. "Senators, viri egregii [306], and knights were to lose their dignities and be deprived of their property. If they still persisted in their Christianity, they would be executed. Matronae would lose their property and be banished. The civil servants would be reduced to slavery and sent in chains to work on the imperial estates" [307]. This time there were casualties and not a few.

The Emperor aimed at the leadership, clerical and lay, of the Christian community; he obviously hoped that Christianity would go away if only the common people were left to themselves [308]. Christian senators were deprived of their seats through a senatusconsultum, that is, by their pagan colleagues. As Allard states, "for the first time, the incomptability between the exercise of the Christian cult and the service of the state was declared" [309]. In the past many Christians could not reconcile it with their conscience to enter the public service, but the reverse, namely that the state could not appoint Christian officials, had never been stated.

Knowing what would be his fate, the head of the Church, Pope Sixtus II (257-258), had the corpses of Saints Peter and Paul transferred to the catacombs on the Via Appia, the first from the Vatican cemetery on the Via Cornelia, the second from the cemetery of Lucina on the Via Ostiensis; all Christian cemeteries and other properties were now being confiscated by the state. Sixtus was arrested by a military patrol just when he was preaching in a private subterranean chapel on the Via Appia. He and a number of his deacons were executed on August 6, 258 [310]. Later another deacon, Lawrence, who was in charge of the treasury of the Church, was ordered to deliver it to the authorities. When he refused, he was condemned to be burned alive. Put on a red-hot gridiron, he is reported to have said : "This side is done. Turn me!", and then : "Now you can taste" [311]. There were more victims in Rome [312], one of them being the famous scholar Hippolytus. Several ladies of Roman high society also suffered death.

Furthermore we hear of martyrs in Gaul, at Troyes for instance, and in Spain, among them the bishop of Tarragona, Fructuosus. When the governor of the province asked him : "Are you a bishop?" and the answer was : "I am", the magistrate retorted : "You were!" [313]. He and two deacons were burnt alive in the arena. In the province of Africa too there were a considerable number of victims. At Carthage Cyprian, the bishop, met the fate he had escaped seven years earlier. The passage of words between him and the proconsul Galerius Maximus presents in a nutshell the motivation behind the persecution and the dualistic distance between the two positions. "Are you Thascius Cyprianus? - I am - The Emperor orders you to sacrifice - I will not do it - You are living in sacrilege, you have gathered around you accomplices of your criminal conspiracy, you have made yourself the enemy of the gods of Rome and her holy laws, and of our pious and sacred Emperors. Your blood will restore the order ... Therefore, we order that Thascius Cyprianus will be put to death by the sword - Deo gratias!". The bishop was decapitated [314]. The persecuting rage reached Numidia in 259, where there were mass executions. Christians were also victimized in Palestine, Syria and Asia Minor. In Cappadocia even children were killed.

And then, all of a sudden, it ended. In June 260 Valerian was taken prisoner by the Persians, never to return [315]. He was succeeded by his son Gallienus (260-268) who "immediately by means of an edict put an end to the persecution against us" [316]. One of his reasons may have been, as Frend suggests, that, in spite of the vehemence displayed against the Church, it did not crumble away. Rome already had a new bishop and head of the Church, Dionysius (259-268) [317]. But still Christianity was not made a religio licita [318].

15. The Great Persecution

Decades of relative peace for the Christians followed. It seems that the Emperor Aurelian (270-275) intended a persecution against them, but nothing came of it since he was murdered by his staff [319]. The Emperors of the second half of the third century had so much work on their hands, mainly with restoring the lines of defense on the frontiers - and many of them had only short reigns -, that the Church enjoyed considerable freedom. Christianity was spreading ever farther, both socially and geographically. Many Christians may have thought that the pagan Empire would gradually change into a Christian one.

a. Diocletian's motivation

And then there was a flash of lightning from an apparently clear sky, the first anti-Christian edict of the Emperor Diocletian (284-305), promulgated on February 23, 303. Diocletian was a great ruler. For nineteen years he had been working very hard at the restoration of the imperial fabric, with so much success that one could speak of a 'new Empire'. He was a conservative in the literal sense, certainly in the field of religion where he wanted to preserve what was of old. And Christianity was not of old. He had no need of a new and alien god; he found that the imperial gods were the real rulers of the world. He himself was one of these gods. We should take into account that with Diocletian the most authoritarian period of the Empire began, the so-called 'Dominate' in which the ruler was 'dominus et deus' [320], officially acknowledged as such.

Frend puts the question why the Emperor "took nineteen years to make up his mind that the Christians were beyond the pale, and must forcibly be brought back" [321]. But there were signs of what was brewing. A bad accident occurred at some date between 295 and 300. In Teveste in North Africa (now Tebessa in Algeria) a Christian conscript, called Maxilianus, refused to serve as a soldier : "Non facio, non possum militare". He persisted even when he was threatened with death. Consequently, he was executed [322]. He lost his life, "not on the ground that he was a Christian, but that he had refused to take the oath of service" [323]. Now there exist no governments that are fond of conscientious objectors. It might be contagious. There were Christians serving in the imperial army, but were they to be trusted? Incidents with Christian soldiers had occurred. With another great war with Persia on the verge of breaking out, the Emperor preferred to be sure of his men.

Pressure on the Christian elements in the army was gradually stepped up. Soldiers who refused to sacrifice were dishonourably discharged; Eusebius reports that a few were executed [324]. And so "little by little persecution against us began" [325]. Lactantius presents an intriguing story about a sacrifice brought by the Emperor in person somewhere in the east, probably at Antioch in the winter of 299/300. Some slaves - Christians - who were assisting in the ceremony secretly made the sign of the cross on their foreheads 'in order to chase away the demons and to disturb the ritual'. It proved impossible to 'read' the intestines of the sacrificial animals. Then somebody said that this was because 'unholy persons' were present. This made Diocletian furious.

His co-emperor Galerius pressed him to take measures against the Christians, but Diocletian, already an old man, hesitated. He was not prepared, he said, to shed the blood of so many people. It would be sufficient to purge the court and the army of irreligious persons. Just as many other Christian authors, Lactantius tries to excuse the supreme ruler. When Diocletian's advisers kept telling him that the enemies of the gods and of the public cult should be destroyed, he sent at last an augur to the Apollo oracle at Milete; when the godhead there spoke of 'the enemy of the divine religion', the fate of the Christians was sealed [326]. Thus began the worst period the Church had ever experienced.

b. The action against the Christians

The above mentioned edict of February 303 decreed that all churches must be destroyed and all Christian scripture burnt. Christian magistrates and officials would lose their positions [327]. Still there were no death sentences. But twice in two weeks a fire broke out in the imperial palace at Nicomedia, the capital of Bithynia, where the Emperor was then staying; according to Lactantius the real incendiary was Galerius who threw the blame on the Christians; he wanted to stigmatize them as 'public enemies'. There now were fatal victims among the retinue of the Emperor; slaves of the household were drowned in the sea. The persecution spread rapidly further. Priests and deacons died at the stake. The prisons were full of arrested faithful, many of whom were tortured in the most cruel way [328].

Somewhat later a second edict was promulgated with the order that everywhere the ecclesiastical leaders must be arrested and thrown into prison; the prisoners became so full of clerics that there was no room left for ordinary criminals. Not only were the dioceses of Asia Minor severely hit but also those of Palestine, Egypt, and North Africa. Numerous people, male and female, old and young, lay and cleric, were confronted in the arenas with bears and leopards, with wild boars and bulls. The number of martyrs was high [329]. A third edict said that prisoners ready to sacrifice should be set free, but the others must be tortured. The order was duly executed : men, women, and children were torn, racked, scourged, crucified, even head downwards, drowned, quartered [330]. It was a great time for sadists! Eusebius speaks of a 'war' against the Christians [331], and Grégoire of 'a general offensive against Christianity' [332]. However, Diocletian's co-rulers in the West, Maximinianus and his Caesar, Constantius Chlorus, were lukewarm and did not harass their Christians very much [333]. The total number of victims in the years 303-305 is estimated at three thousand to three thousand five hundred [334].

c. The persecution petering out

And then, on May 1, 305, something totally unexpected happened : Diocletian, who was in bad health, announced in Nicomedia that he would retire into private life, the first Roman Emperor to do this. His Tetrarchy was followed by a second Tetrarchy [335]. A period of much confusion began. The senior Emperor was to be Constantius Chlorus, residing in the West, who, however, died in July 306 at York; his troops proclaimed Constantine (the Great), his illegitimate son, as his successor. In the East an obscure officer, Maximinus Daja, became Emperor, with as his second Galerius, who was really in command.

Maximinus was no admirer of Christianity either. He spoke of it as 'that accursed folly' and 'the baneful error', and of Christians as 'those unhallowed men'. It is a good and sensible thing to persecute them, he found. The great protector of the world was, in his eyes, Zeus, as ever; it was because of the benevolent gods that the earth yields its fruits. And if things went wrong, then this was the fault of the Christians. "If they persist in their accursed folly, let them be separated and driven far away from your city and neighbourhood (Maximinus was writing to the citizens of Tyre)" [336]. As Frend writes, "he aimed at the unification of his dominions through the common bond of religion, (but) his efforts came fifty years too late" [337].

In the spring of 306 Maximinus repeated the order that everyone was obliged to sacrifice [338]. This again caused some victims. Since death sentences obviously did not have the desired effect, in 307 torture was substituted for capital punishment. Eusebius brings blood-curdling descriptions of the brutalities perpetrated on Christians; many were condemned to hard labour in the copper-mines [339]

Meanwhile, public opinion got fed up with the constant terror exercized against colleagues, friends, neighbours, even relatives [340]. The anti-Christian mesures began to have a counter-productive effect, since the often very brave behaviour of the victims elicited amazement at their courage and even admiration [341]. Furthermore, the rulers had more to do with fighting one another than with persecuting the Christians. Early in 311 Galerius became fatally ill [342]. His recourse to his pagan gods did not help him, and he began to ask himself whether it was "for the cruel deeds he had perpetrated against the godly" that he had to suffer. Then "he openly confessed to the God of the universe" [343]; this does not signify at all that he now became a Christian, only that the Christian God was more powerful than his pagan deities.

The result of this 'conversion' was that he ordered that the persecution should stop. The official document in which the new policy was laid down is called the 'Palinode of Galerius' [344], dated April 30, 311; six days later Galerius died. The edict, after stating that the Christians only had themselves to blame for the persecution, stipulated that they now might live as Christians in security and rebuild their churches, provided that they did nothing contrary to public order. Did this mean that Christianity had now become a 'religio licita'? Not yet, it was rather a return to the abandoned policy of Trajan and Hadrian.

16. The pacification policy of Constantine the Great

Meanwhile the Empire was involved in a civil war the events of which need not be recounted here. Starting out from York in 306, Constantine conquered Gaul, crossed the Alps, and captured Milan in the spring of 312; from there he marched rapidly on Rome. There Maxentius, the co-emperor for Italy, stood ready with a large army to challenge his entry into the capital. Eusebius has the story that earlier, somewhere in Gaul, Constantine had a vision; this author assures us that the army saw it too. There was a blazing cross in the sky, and around it the words : 'in hic signo vinces', in this sign you wil be triumphant [345]. This may well be a legend, although Eusebius tells us that the Emperor confirmed it to him on oath.

Perhaps this story was needed to explain why Constantine, who had first been an adorer of the Sun-God Apollo, so suddenly accepted a Christian symbol. Whatever was the case, he did not become a professed Christian; he was only baptized on his death-bed. All the same, it was a kind of conversion. Was it sincere? Or was it a political move, made because this shrewd man felt that paganism was on the way out and that the future was to Christianity? Both theories have their adherents. We shall never know.

What in all probability is no legend is that just before the decisive battle against Maxentius, when he was still on the wrong side of the Tiber, Constantine adopted the Christ-monogram, the so-called 'labarum', as the emblem for his army; it was fixed to the shields [346]. The battle that followed was fought for the possession of the bridge on the Tiber, the Pons Milvius. Maxentius was defeated and was drowned in the river, when the bridge collapsed under the weight of his flying soldiers. On October 29, 312, Constantine triumphantly entered Rome. The Empire had a new and powerful ruler (313-337).

That the wind was now beginning to blow from another direction appears from a letter written by the new Emperor in the winter of 312/313 to Anulinus, the proconsul of the province of Africa in which he ordered him to harass the Christians no longer [347]. The idea that the Empire would suffer if its ancestral gods were not duly honoured was now completely reversed, because Constantine began by stating that the suspension of divine worship - and by this he meant the Christian cult! - "has brought great danger on public affairs". The Empire clearly now had another protective deity. In another letter to Caecilianus, the bishop of Carthage, he wrote that "certain persons of unstable mind are desirous of making the laity of the most holy and catholic Church" turn away ; this 'madness' should cease. If such things continued, the culprits should be brought before the judges [348]. This was really the other way round!

The definite turnabout came somewhat later, in 313. We need not go into the vexed problem whether the measure in question was taken by Constantine or by his co-emperor Licinius, whether it was laid down in a document commonly called 'the Edict of Milan' or wether it was issued in Nicomedia, and, finally, whether it really was an official document or only a new line of policy [349]. The decisive point is that a new policy was inaugurated which was extremely favourable for the Christians. It was decreed that the Christians would henceforward enjoy freedom of worship. No official should hinder them in this [350]. This meant nothing less than that, after two hundred and eighty years of a shadow existence, Christianity now became a 'religio licita', on a par with the official pagan cult (which was not abolished).

The persecution rage had spent itself. Public opinion had become disgusted with the incessant bloodshed and the horrible scenes of cruelty; even the butchers themselves had grown tired [351]. Lactantius writes that the pagans became curious what it was that made ordinary people so steadfast. The result was that there were ever more conversions [352]. It had become true, as Tertullian wrote in a famous phrase, that "the blood of the Christians is the seed (of the Church)" [353].

17. All quiet on the Christian front?

The common opinion is that the time of troubles was over, and that the Church, now enjoying undisturbed peace and quiet, would go from strength to strength. The Christians of the fourth century would not have shared this sentiment. They had so long been second-rate citizens, knowing that they might be victimized any moment, that they did not wholly trust the new situation. And there happened things indeed that made them feel uncomfortable.

In 322/323 Licinius, the co-emperor for the East, attempted to launch a persecution, but it remained abortive; there was no response, and nothing came of it. All the same, it will have put the Christians on the alert. Some later Emperors were either Arians or sympathetic to Arianism, which made them less than amiably disposed to the orthodox Church. Constantius II (co-emperor in 324, Emperor 337-361) sometimes took measures against orthodox bishops. In this period the great leader of the orthodox, Athanasius, bishop of Alexandria (328-373), was banished four times from his episcopal seat. Valens too, co-emperor for the East (364-378), was an Arian; he supported Arianism everywhere in his dominions; again some orthodox bishops were banished. In the West, Valentinianus II (375-392), who came to the throne as a young boy, was strongly influenced by his Arian mother Justina; this brought her into conflict with Ambrosius, the powerful bishop of Milan (374-397). Once he was even besieged in his own palace. Enough to give the orthodox Christians a permanent feeling of insecurity. But the period of the greatest anxiety for the Christians became the short reign of the Emperor Julian the Apostate (361-363).

18. The last revival of paganism

a. Julian's Christian youth

Julian the Apostate, born in 331, came to the throne when he was thirty years old, in 361, and reigned for nineteen months, until he fell far from home in 363, when fighting the Parthians. But short as his reign was, it became memorable. Since 313 Christianity was a religio licita, but not yet the official religion which it became in 391/392. Both his parents were Christians - his father was a half-brother of Constantine the Great -; their son was raised in the faith of his parents and later baptized as a Christian. He grew up as a motherless child, since his mother had died when he was still a baby [354].

Something horrible happened when he was only five years old. Constantine's son Constantius II, a suspicious man, feared to become the victim of a conspiracy in his own family. His hangmen killed Julian's elder brother and his father where they found them. It is related that the boy Julian was smuggled away to a church in the vicinity [355].

Julian's biographer Browning calls the now orphaned boy 'a traumatized child' [356]. Could the fact that the man who had ordered the murder of his father and brother was a fanatical Christian have had an influence on his later decision to leave the Church? Under able and sensible tutorship he made his early studies in Nicomedia (now Izmit), the birth-place of his mother [357], and later in Constantinople [358]. There was as yet no typical Christian education; a young student read the pagan authors, and Julian found much in them to admire. Intelligent and sensitive as he was, he absorbed a lot of learning. His temperament was religious with an inclination to mysticism. He grew up very lonely since the Emperor had all his contacts kept under strict surveillance.

When Julian was thirteen years old, he and his brother Gallus were ordered to move far deeper into the interior of Asia Minor, to rugged Cappadocia, where he was lodged on a royal estate called Macellum. It was a place of exile, but a gilded one [359]. Politically it was a banishment but intellectually not, since the inquisitive young man could dispose of the large library of a nearby bishop; this library contained the Christian authors as well as pagan philosophical works. Here he became acquainted with Neopythagoreanism and Neoplatonism. There were as yet no signs of a break with the Church. Quite the contrary! He was devout and was even ordained as lector [360].

b. The rupture with the Church

Diverse and contradictory influences were working on the gifted adolescent, that of Christian teaching and that of Neoplatonic philosophy with which he came into ever closer contact; on the personal level there was also his contempt for his cruel, bigoted and vulgar cousin the Emperor. The time was that of the great Arian controversy - Constantius II himself was an Arian -, a time that with its pamphleteering and intrigues did not present the best side of Christianity. The adolescent was subject to a crossfire of tendencies. In 351, when the ruler had thought it safer to make Gallus his co-emperor, the ban was lifted, Julian could move to Constantinople, for the first time a free man. Here he first studied rhetoric, which struck him as empty, and later philosophy, especially Neoplatonism. It was in this stage of his life that he began to take his distance from the Christian faith. This was not necessarily a consequence of his becoming steeped in Neoplatonism; many important and orthodox Christian authors were deeply influenced by it.

What Julian had missed in his young life was a caring and understanding father. Although well cared for and never maltreated, he was alone. Sex did not interest him; in this respect too he remained remarkably lonely, never having sought relations with girls, in spite of abounding opportunities. He was surely somewhat priggish, 'anaphroditos', as he said of himself. In Nicomedia, where he moved to in order to continue his studies, the twenty-year-old Julian found the man he needed, Maximus, a philosopher from Ephesus, a strange combination of scholar, magician, miracle-worker, and, above all, a Mithras-priest [361]. The influence of this man did not exactly strengthen the attachment of the prince to the Christian faith.

Julian had no mean idea of himself. Perhaps he found Christianity too common and, for his fervent temperament tending to mysticism, too down to earth. The Mithras-religion, one of those mystery religions that flourished in the Empire in this period, was for the elect and at the same time mystical and mysterious. Coming from Iran as it did, it showed distinct dualistic traits (I shall come back to this in Volume XII); Mithras is the servant of the light-god Ahura Mazda, and in consequence, the inveterate enemy of the god of Darkness, Ahriman. It is not inconceivable that this dualism appealed to a mind like that of Julian with his rigid character.

Another decidedly pagan influence in these years was the rhetor Libanius, a man who made no secret of his contempt for Christianity; he became a friend and confident of the Emperor. It must have been in this period of his life that Julian threw his Christian faith overboard. In his later years he studiously avoided mentioning his Christian youth; "let us vow these obscurities to oblivion" [362].

c. On his way to the throne

Meanwhile Julian's brother Gallus, the co-emperor, had got into such difficulties with the always suspicious Constantius that he was beheaded in 354. This was another heavy blow to Julian who doted on his brother. He himself was also for some time under a cloud and was summoned to Milan where he was under house arrest, but finally he was allowed to go to Athens in order to continue his studies. He always remembered his stay in this city with its myrtle lanes and its little house of Socrates with great pleasure [363]. It is possible, even probable that he became an initiate of the mysteries of Eleusis [364]. Anyhow, the distance between himself and his former faith became unbridgeable.

In August 354 a counter-emperor was proclaimed in Cologne. Nothing came of it, but Constantius, who was childless, was suddenly in a hurry to have a legitimate successor, and since Julian was his nearest male relative (and one who seemed utterly harmless), he summoned him to Milan where the young man was clad with the purple [365]. The still youthful and totally inexperienced lover of philosophy must now, with his headquarters in Paris, spend five years as a military commander, mainly to defend the Rhine frontier against the Franks and Alamanni. In February 360 his troops, who loved him just as much as they detested Constantius, proclaimed him as 'Augustus' = senior Emperor [366].

In August 361 he marched eastward with his devoted legions since no agreement with Constantius had proved possible. He followed the course of the Danube; in October he was in Serbia marching along the imperial highway to Constantinople. In Naissus (Nish) he halted to await reinforcements; here he received the unexpected news that Constantius II was dead [367]. There was nobody now to prevent Julian from entering the eastern capital where he arrived on December 11, 361; the new Emperor rode through the town 'as if he had descended from heaven', so sudden was his arrival [368]. What this meant is that the Empire now had, for the first time after half a century of Christian rulers, orthodox and Arian, a pagan one.

d. Julian's book against the Christian faith

The Emperor Julianus bears the surname 'Apostata', because he, although raised as a Christian, broke with the Church and became its enemy. What he really intended to realize was not so much the downfall of the Christian Church but rather the revival, the revitalization, of the pagan cult [369]. Being a scholar, he thought that a convincing treatise against the Christians (whom he persistently called 'Galilaeans') would be his best weapon. Therefore, he planned to write a book against 'that fellow from Palestine who claims to be a god and the son of God' [370], which task he performed in the winter of 362/363; he wrote it in the night, "when other people are usually more interested in matters of sex". Perhaps pious Christians, even puritanical ones, may have wished that he would have been somewhat more interested in amatory matters. But as it was, had not his official position forced him to marry, "he would have ended his days knowing nothing of sexual intercourse save by report" [371].

The book itself, that was called 'Contra Galilaeos' [372], is lost, but the fragments we still have and other utterances of his give us a fairly adequate idea of Julian's stance in religious matters. He reproached the Christians that they had abandoned the ancient and venerable cult of the gods; not he was the apostate, they were. And he qualified them as 'atheistic' and 'impious' and their cult as 'folly'. By the same token Christianity is an apostasy from Judaism. "Why did you not remain true to the religion of the Hebrews, to the Law that God gave them?" [373].

A second reproach is that Christianity, being neither ancient nor divine, is a human imposture, 'fabricated by perversity ..., catering to the stupid part of our souls that loves fables and infantile stories' [374]. Furthermore, Christians are 'adorers of death' because they venerate a dead man. Their faith is highly immoral too, since it forgives all faults and crimes by baptism and the sacrament of penitence. Summing up, he concludes that Christians must be mad or else possessed of demons [375].

They distort the monotheism of the Jews - he praised the Jews for adoring only one God - by proclaiming that Jesus too is God; Julian considers this as an invention of John. To him Christianity is a heresy of Judaism [376], only to be embraced by rootless people who permit themselves to be led astray by the infantile and silly elements in their Gospels. There is absolutely nothing divine in their doctrines [377]. This makes Julian speak of the Galilaean 'atheism', a mode of living and thinking for which there exist no 'divine models'; there is no place in the cosmic order for Christians [378].

Not that Julian had really much good to say of the Jewish faith. The Jews are inferior to the Greeks, and the Christians are inferior to the Jews, because they misinterpret Jewish theology [379]. Entirely in accordance with his Neoplatonist philosophy, Julian did not believe in a God creating ex nihilo; instead, a first, supreme and divine Cause expresses itself in emanations [380]. To these emanations belong the several gods of the nations [381] of whom the Jewish-Christian god is only one; he should have no pretension of being a universal god [382]. The Jews have contributed nothing at all to civilization; there is much good to be said of the moral quality of the Ten Commandments, but such precepts we find everywhere (with the exception of the Sabbath).

e. His own creed

Julian himself, in accordance with the Hellenistic philosophy of his days, believed in a supreme being who had created and who governed all that is; he is sometimes called Jupiter, sometimes he is the Sun-God. It seems that the Sun, or Mithra, was his favourite deity; Jupiter was rather the personification of the supreme godhead [383]. This does not make him into a monotheist; he believed in and honoured all the Olympian gods, and other divinities, most of whom figure in his letters and speeches; even the Egyptian gods Serapis and Isis are mentioned [384]. He sacrificed continuously to all these divinities.

Initially, Julian hoped to win over people of different opinions to his side by force of persuasion; it was all so rational and sensible what he had to propose, he thought. It was his intention to act as a doctor by "restoring health to the souls through making them acquainted with the true masters of heaven ... His friends were the friends of Zeus, and the enemies of Zeus were his enemies. Those whom he thought capable of conversion, instead of pushing them back, he attempted to win over, and finally, in spite of their initial resistance, he made them dance around the altars in chorus" [385]. But "bist Du nicht willig, so brauch' ich Gewalt" [386]. Those who stuck to their opinion that "there were no gods did not deserve an answer as though they were humans but, instead, blows as the wild beasts they were" [387].

f. The decree on education

For about a year the Christians could think that they had nothing to fear. But then, on June 11, 362, the blow fell. On that day Julian, who was then in Antioch, had a law on education promulgated. Henceforward everybody who desired a job in education would need an official certificate that he was of good morals [388]. Could anyone object? This depended on the question what was to be understood by 'good morals'. An imperial circular letter made this clear. Julian began by stating that the teaching of the classics should not have a purely philological character but rather lead to a healthy disposition of mind and to true beliefs of good and evil. Again nothing objectionable. But then it came.

The teachers should not think one way and teach differently. "Now that the gods have given us freedom it seems to me absurd for people to teach what they disapprove." This was directed at Christian teachers. "If they are real interpreters of the ancient classics ..., let them first imitate the ancients' piety towards the gods. If they, on the contrary, feel that these authors have erred with respect to these highly venerated beings, let them go to the churches of the Galileans and explain Matthew and Luke" [389]. This was unambiguous language : there was no longer room for Christians in education. Christian authors drew the inevitable conclusion that Christian pupils could no longer attend pagan schools (there were no others) [390], although the letter said that they should not be excluded.

There was, of course, an enormous outcry. Even a pagan like Ammianus Marcellinus found the measure 'inhumane and worthy to be buried in eternal silence' [391]. Many teachers, famous ones among them, retired; many parents no longer sent their children to school [392].

g. The offensive against the Christians

Meanwhile, the Emperor proceeded calmly on his road, reorganizing and revitalizing the pagan cult. "He seems to have come to the conclusion", writes Browning, "that what the gods wanted was a much more positive anti-Christian policy" [393]. If he did not expel the Christians from his army - which is doubted by some historians, because he needed them too much -, it can hardly be doubted that he expelled them from his praetorian guard [394].

To Atarbius, the governor of Syria, he wrote that, when there were two candidates for an office, a pagan and a Christian, "those who rever the gods should have absolute preference". But although there was a considerable amount of discrimination [395], there was as yet no bloody persecution. "I do not wish the Galileans to be put to death or beaten illegally, or to be maltreated in any way" [396]. He gave, however, the Christians a piece of his mind when he wrote to Eidikios, the prefect of Egypt, that he would prefer to see those godless Galileans radically exterminated [397]. And indeed, this episode did not end without some death sentences and a few outbursts of lynch justice. It was wholly in accordance with all this, on the eve of his departure for the Parthian front, he declared that he would on his return resume the war against Christianity with much greater vigour, and that he would extirpate even the name of this malevolent sect [398]. A revealing incident occurred in a town on the frontier of Palestine and Fenicia, Caesarea Panias [399], where a statue of Jesus Christ stood in the market-square. It was overturned by a pagan mob, dragged through the streets and hacked to pieces. The statue was replaced by one of the Emperor [400]. It was enough to make the Christians shiver.

h. The end

I have already dsecribed how Julian lost his life during the war against the Christians [401]. On June 27, 363, he died of a wound received in battle. Legend has it that his last words were : "You have triumphed, Galilean!" [402]. Although it is improbable that he did indeed say this, his friend Libanius in his funeral speech for the fallen Emperor sums up the results of his abortive attempt to subdue the Christians in these words. "A creed which we had until then laughed to scorn, which had declared such violent, unceasing war against you (sic), has won the day after all" [403].

19. Conclusion

I feel there can be no doubt that the relationship between state and Church in the first three centuries A.D. was dualistic, vehemently dualistic. The government, the leading intellectual lights, and the pagan public considered Christianity as hopelessly inferior, at variance with all that was noble, great, decent, and authentic in Roman life and society, with all that was truly Roman. There was not the slightest possibility of a modus vivendi. The general conviction was that this creed simply should not be; the sooner it disappeared, the better. For two centuries the state was ready to tolerate it, because its adherents were still only small in number, and also because the Christians were not rebellious. The conditions of this tolerance were harsh. Christians had to remain content with the fact that their creed was an illicit religion; they must lead a shadow existence, keep as low a profile as possible, and remain underground, often literally so, in the catacombs. They were not allowed to have prayer houses and to organize public meetings.

The general public, the populace, the mob, found it hard to stick to the official policy of toleration. In collusion with the local authorities, up to the provincial level, pogroms against the Christians were organized which resulted in many victims. The faithful could never and nowhere feel wholly safe; any time the fury of their co-citizens might turn against them. They knew they could not count on the protection of the government. Those in power were only too glad that the lower layers of society did the dirty work for them; it kept the Christians in check and showed them their place. Only when they became too numerous, the state took over and began bloody persecutions; terms like eradication and extermination then cropped up.

If there ever was a case that shows that dualism has its source in the mind, it was this. For as soon as there were Emperors who no longer thought that Christians were atheists and impious people, the persecutions ceased and Christianity became a religio licita.

NOTES TO CHAPTER VI

1. Acts 1.12-2.41.
2. Acts 9:31.
3. Acts 8:14 and 9:2.
4. Acts 11:19-26. Probably it were the heathen who called them thus, since the Jews dubbed them 'Galileans' or 'Nazarenes' (Acts 1:11 and 24:5), while the faithful gave themselves the names of 'the brethren' or 'the holy'.
5. The word 'pagan' comes from the Latin 'paganus'; a 'paganus' lives in a 'pagus', a peasant village or hamlet. We find a long and learned disquisition on the word 'paganus' in Grégoire, Persécutions 188-220, 'Paganus. Étude de sémantique et d'histoire'.
6. Herrmann, Chrestos, devotes many pages first to Philo (Ch. II) and next to Seneca (Ch. III) who may have been referring to Christians and Christianity, but if they did so, did it so obliquely that the references are hardly recognizable.
7. Jos., Ant. 18.63-64.
8. For all his peculiarities Josephus was an orthodox Jew in the Pharasaic line which makes it improbable that he would have seen Jesus as the Messiah. Then there is the curious anachronism that Jesus converted 'many Greeks'. We have also the testimony of Origen that Josephus did not believe in Jesus Christ, Contra Cels. 1.47. See Herrmann, Chrestos 97-98, and Louis Feldman in the Loeb Classical edition of the Antiquities 433, p. 63, note b. A passage in the Antiquities on John the Baptist is equally thought by some to have been interpolated and by others to be authentic.
9. Jos., Ant. 20.200.
10. Suet., Claudius 5.25.

11. Tert., Apolog. 3.5.
12. Lact., Div.Inst. 4.7.5.
13. Benko, Pagan Crit. 1059.
14. Suet., Nero 16.2.
15. Tac., Ann. 13.44.
16. Benko, Pagan crit. 1064.
17. Pliny, Ep. 10.96.
18. Dio 67.14.2.
19. CIL 6.948, 8942; see Streeter, The rise 255.
20. Martyrdom 3.2.
21. Olck s.v. 'Esel', PW VI (Stuttgart, 1909), 676.
22. Just.Mart., 2Apol.3.
23. Min.Felix, Oct. 9.6.
24. Frend, Martyrdom 252.
25. "They know one another by secret marks and insignia." When the Gospel is going to be read during Mass, Roman-Catholics use to sign themselves with three little crosses on forehead, mouth, and breast; it is said that this was the rapid sign of recognition among Christians in the days of persecution.
26. Min.Felix, Oct. 8.3-9.5.
27. Apuleius wrote this 'Apology', because he was accused of practising magic; he was on trial in one of the years 155-160, but was acquitted.
28. Apul. Apol. 56; the translation is Butler's (Oxford, 1909) which I found in Benko, Pagan crit. 1091.
29. Marc.Aur., Med. 11.3; some think the quoted words are a gloss on the ground that pagan authors preferably did not use the word 'christianus', Haines 383.
30. Lucianus, Passing of Peregrinus 13.
31. Benko, Pagan crit. 1096.
32. Lucianus, Alex. 25.4.
33. Galenus, De diff. 2.4 and 3.3.
34. Benko, Pagan crit. 1099 quotes this from an Arab source.
35. Wilken, Christians 73.
36. Just.Mart., Dial. with Trypho 8.

37. Athenagoras, Legatio passim (see Bibliography).
38. Wilken, Christians 95.
39. Orig., Contra Cels. 5.65.
40. Orig., Contra Cels. 3.55.
41. Orig., Contra Cels. 4.10.
42. Orig., Contra Cels. 9.11.
43. Orig., Contra Cels. 1.6 and 6.40-41.
44. Orig., Contra Cels. 1.6.
45. Orig., Contra Cels. 1.38.
46. Benko, Pagan crit. 1101.
47. Orig., Contra Cels. 4.50.
48. Orig., Contra Cels. 6.63.
49. Orig., Contra Cels. 6.61.
50. Orig., Contra Cels. 4.38 and 48.
51. Orig., Contra Cels. 6.1.
52. Orig., Contra Cels. 1.32.
53. Orig., Contra Cels. 1.28.
54. Orig., Contra Cels. 2.29.
55. Orig., Contra Cels. 2.7.
56. Orig., Contra Cels. 1.62 and 2.46.
57. Orig., Contra Cels. 8.48-49.
58. Orig., Contra Cels. 2.11.
59. Benko, Pagan crit. 1108.
60. Orig., Contra Cels. 2.11.
61. Orig., Contra Cels. 8.73.
62. Orig., Contra Cels. 8.75.
63. Orig., Contra Cels. 8.2.
64. Orig., Contra Cels. 5.41.
65. Orig., Contra Cels. 8.14-15.
66. Wilken, Christians 108.
67. Orig., Contra Cels. 8.68.

68. Much of what we know of Porphyry's writings is to be found in Eusebius' works; he could consult the books of his opponent in the well-stocked diocesan library at Caesarea in Palestine (Grant, Porphyry 184, presents a list of the philosophical works on its shelves).
69. Hier., Comm.Dan. prol.
70. Dan. 7.26-27.
71. Dan. 11.21-12.13. See for this passage Wilken, Christians 137-143.
72. Wilken, Christians 145.
73. August., De cons. 1.11.
74. See Wilken, Christians 144-147.
75. Porph., De abst. 2.37.1 and 2.34.2.
76. August., Civ.Dei 19.22.
77. Wilken, Christians 151.
78. August. quoting Porph. Civ.Dei 19.23.
79. Arnobius, Adv.nationes 1.36.
80. Wilken, Christians 156.
81. For a far longer treatment of Porphyry's anti-Christian treatise I refer the reader to the article of L. Vagany s.v. 'Porphyry', Dict.Théol.cath. 12.2., 2562-2590, Paris, 1935.
82. Dion.Hal. 2.19.2.
83. Livy 1.19.4.
84. Cic., De nat.deor. 3.5.
85. Cic., De nat.deor. 1.4.
86. Livy 6.41.9.
87. Cic., De nat.deor. 2.71-72.
88. Cic., De nat.deor. 1.117.
89. Plut., De superst. 166c.
90. Plut., De superst. 167e.
91. Plut., De superst. 170e.
92. Plut., De superst. 171f.
93. Sometimes foreign cults or elements of them were allowed and recognized by the Roman state. This task, and that of controlling and supervising them, was entrusted to a special priestly college, the 'quindecim viri sacris faciundis'.

94. Cic., De leg. 2.18.19.
95. Livy 25.1.12.
96. Livy 39.16.6.
97. Frend, Martyrdom 110.
98. Livy 39.16.10-17.8.
99. Frend, Martyrdom 111.
100. Livy 39.18.8-9.
101. Frend, Martyrdom 111.
102. Sordi, Cristianesimo 19.
103. Athenag., Legatio 1.1-11.
104. Athenag., Legatio 1.17-20.
105. Athenag., Legatio 1.21-40.
106. Sordi, Crist. 15.
107. Sordi, Crits. 15.
108. Jo. 18:33-37.
109. Nock, Conversion 128.
110. Just.Mart., 1Apol.11.
111. Sordi, Crist. 12.
112. Nock, Conversion 228.
113. Tert., Apol. 24.5.
114. Why didn't the Romans give the Christians the privileged position the Jews had? Theirs was a 'religio licita'; they were even exempted from the obligation to burn incense for the Emperor. The reason is that the Jews formed an ethnos' which could be kept strictly under control; the Christians were no ethnos and were to be found everywhere wich made it far harder to keep an eye on them. Furthermore, the Christians were a rapidly expanding community getting ever more numerous. The concessions the Romans had given the Jews were not offered out of love but for a political reason. The authorities were ready to go to some length in order to prevent new Jewish rebellions. They had no similar reason for freeing the Christians from the obligation to burn incense. Finally, we should not forget that the Jews had to pay homage to the supreme ruler indeed, albeit indirectly, for they paid the hated 'fiscus judaicus', the temple tax, that was destined for the sanctuary of Jupiter Capitolinus. It would have presented a far greater administrative problem to collect such a tax, a 'fiscus christianus', from the Christians.
115. Mt. 22:15-22; Mc. 12:13-17; Lc. 20:20-26.

116. Rom. 13.1-6.
117. Rom. 13.1-7.
118. 1Tim. 2.2.
119. 1Clem. 61.1.
120. Vol. VII, Ch. IV.5e.
121. Ap. 12:3.
122. Ap. 18:9.
123. In this passage I am repeating myself more or less verbatim from Vol. VII, Ch. IV.5d-e.
124. See Vol. VII, Ch. V.9.
125. See Vol. IV, Ch. II.7.
126. Frend, Martyrdom 195.
127. See Vol. VII, Ch. IV.5d.
128. Hermas, Pastor Sim. 4.4.
129. Hermas, Pastor 8.3.2-3.
130. Hermas, Pastor, Sim. 1.1-6.
131. Barn. 2.1.
132. Barn. 4.1-5.
133. 2Clem. 12.1-2.
134. 2Clem. 16.3.
135. Suet., Nero 29.
136. Eus., HE 2.25; Grant, Nero 160.
137. Karlhorst, Von Nero 45.
138. Hipp., De Christo 27-28, and Comm.Dan.2.12.2-7.
139. Hipp., Comm.Dan. 4.10.1-4.
140. Hipp., Comm.Dan. 4.9.2-3.
141. Origen, Contra Cels. 1.1.
142. Orig., Contra Cels. 8.67.
143. Karlhorst, Von Nero 48.
144. 1Clem. 23.
145. Mt. 24:36.
146. Mt. 24:44.

147. 2Thess. 2.1-3.
148. Ir., Adv.haer. 5.24.2. I refer the reader to an excellent collection of texts called 'Das frühe Christentum' (see Bibliography).
149. Tert., Ad scap. 2.6-10.
150. Tert., De idol. 15.3.
151. Hipp., Comm.Dan. 3.23.
152. Orig., Contra Cels. 8.65.
153. Orig., Comm. in Ep. ad Rom. 9.29.
154. Just.Mart., 1Ap. 12.1.
155. 'κεκελευσμένα; Athenag., Leg. 37.
156. Tert., Apol. 31.
157. Tert., De resurr. carnis 24.17-18. Richard Klein, Frühe Christ., 439, note 63, comments that Tert. describes the Empire as 'status' - which is exceptional - and not as 'res publica' - which is common -, because the last term expresses the Roman political doctrine from which he distances himself.
158. Eus., HE 4.27.7-8.
159. Orig., Contra Cels. 8.69-70.
160. Tert., Ad nat. 2.17.18-19.
161. Lact., Div.Inst. 7.15.
162. Tert., Contra Jud. 7.7-9.
163. Aug., Retractationes 2.69.
164. Virgil, Aeneid 6.853.
165. Aug., Civ.Dei, 1 Preface.
166. Aug., Civ.Dei 2.27.
167. Aug., Civ.Dei 2.10.
168. Aug., Civ.Dei 3.25.
169. Aug., Civ.Dei 4.3.
170. Aug., Civ.Dei 4.15.
171. Aug., Civ.Dei 4.28.
172. Aug., Civ.Dei 5 Praef.
173. Aug., Civ.Dei 5.1.
174. Aug., Civ.Dei 5.12.

175. Aug., Civ.Dei 5.13.
176. Aug., Civ.Dei 5.13.
177. Aug., Civ.Dei 5.15.
178. Aug., Civ.Dei 5.16.
179. Aug., Civ.Dei 5.17.
180. Auug., Civ.Dei 5.25-26.
181. Aug., Civ.Dei 5.25-26.
182. Aug., Civ.Dei 14.28.
183. Aug., Civ.Dei 15.1.
184. Aug., Civ.Dei 15.2.
185. Aug., Civ.Dei 15.5.
186. Aug., Civ.Dei 18.1.
187. Aug., Civ.Dei 18.2.
188. Aug., Civ.Dei 18.47.
189. Aug., Civ.Dei 19.17.
190. Dawson, Making 20/21.
191. Karlhorst, Von Nero 55.
192. Karlhorst, Von Nero 52, note 1.
193. Karlhorst, Von Nero 53/54.
194. Karlhorst, Von Nero 53/54. The reader will find a detailed overview of the fields in which the Christians distanced themselves from pagan society in Schäfke, Widerstand (see Bibliography).
195. Mt. 22:37-38; Lc. 10:25-28; Mc. 12:28-34.
196. Dawson, Making 20.
197. Brown, The Making 74.
198. Aug., Civ.Dei 18.52.
199. Karlhorst, Von Nero 118/119.
200. Pliny, Ep. 10.97.
201. Tert., Apol. 37.2.
202. Frend, Martyrdom 1.
203. CIL II.6278.
204. Eus., HE 5.1-61; see Karlhorst, Von Nero 130/131.

205. This whole affair is extensively treated and placed into a wide context by Jean Colin, L'empire des Antonins et les martyrs gaulois de 177. Antiquitas Reihe 1, Abhandlungen zur alten Geschichte, Bd. 10. Bonn, 1964. See also Frend, Martyrdom, Ch. I, The Martyrs of Lyons.

206. Bishop Dionysius of Alexandria relates these events in a letter to bishop Fabius of Antioch, Eus., HE 6.41.1-9.

207. Karlhorst, Von Nero 132/133.

208. Pliny, Ep. 10.97.

209. We saw that in 177 in Lyons one could do without them; Christians were tracked down there.

210. Frend, Martyrdom 163.

211. Tacitus is in fact the only author to connect the fire and the persecution with each other; neither Tertullian nor Eusebius or Jerome do the same. See Keresztes, Rome. Aufstieg 23.1, 256.

212. Momigliano, Nero, CAH X (1934), 725 and 887, note 8.

213. Tac., Ann. 15.44.2-5.

214. Suet., Vesp. 4.9; Tacitus, Hist. 5.13.

215. Eus., HE 3.20.1-5.

216. Bengtson, Flavier 181.

217. Suet., Dom. 13.4.

218. Suet., Dom. 13.1.

219. Bengtson, Flavier 185/186.

220. Frend, Martyrdom 212/213.

221. 1Clem. 1.1.

222. Keresztes, Rome 271.

223. Eus., HE 3.18.1; Ap. 1.1.

224. Dio 67.14.1-2; Eus., HE 3.18.4.

225. Keresztes, Rome 264-269; Frend, Martyrdom 214-217.

226. Bengtson, Flavier 237/238.

227. Eus., HE 3.18.4.

228. Tert., Apol. 5.4.

229. Frend, Martyrdom 213.

230. "aliquid, quod certam formam habeat".

231. Pliny, Ep. 10.97.

232. Tert., Apol. 2.8.
233. Eus., HE 4.9.1-3.
234. Frühe Christ. 325.
235. Frend, Martyrdom 225.
236. Freudenberger, Verhalten 241.
237. Just.Mart., 1Apol. 4.1 and 3-6.
238. Just. Mart., 1Apol. 7.4.
239. Just. Mart., 2Apol. 2.16.
240. Frend, Martyrdom 255 and 260.
241. Frend, Martyrdom 268.
242. Athenag., Legatio 1.
243. Grégoire, Persécutions 159.
244. Eus., HE 4.26.5.
245. Eus., HE 4.26.6.
246. Quoted Frühe Christ. 46-49.
247. Quoted Frühe Christ. 48/49.
248. Dio 71.35.
249. Vita Marci 3.3.
250. Hippol., Philos. 9.11.
251. Tert., Ad Scap. 3.
252. Marta Sordi, Crist. 212, calls their religious policy 'sincretismo severiano' with its inbuilt indifference to the official pagan cult.
253. For this subject I refer the reader to Ch. III.2c of this volume.
254. Spartianus, Vita Severi 17.1.
255. Eus., HE 6.1.
256. Frend, Martyrdom 321.
257. Molthagen, Röm.Staat 45.
258. Frend, Martyrdom 321.
259. Molthagen, Röm.Staat 40-43.
260. Sordi, Crist. 218.
261. Molthagen, Röm.Staat 43.
262. Clem.Al., Strom. 2.120 and 125.

263. Eus., HE 6.1.
264. Eus., HE 6.12.
265. Passio Perpetuae 2.
266. Passio Perpetuae 15. Her child was somewhat prematurely born in prison and adopted by a Christian woman in town.
267. Passio Perpetuae 6.
268. Passio Perpetuae 18-21.
269. Tert, Ad nationes 1.14.
270. Tert., Apol. 37.4.
271. Molthagen, Röm.Staat 47/48.
272. Sordi, Crist. 233-237.
273. Molthagen, Röm.Staat 52.
274. Grégoire, Persécutions 37.
275. Sordi, Crist. 238.
276. Lampridius, Vita Elagabali 3.4.
277. Herodianus, Hist.imp. 5.5.7.
278. Lampridius, Vita Elagabali 3.4.5.
279. Sordi, Crist. 238.
280. Sordi, Crist. 239, sees a resemblance between these priests and the Emperor, whose body was also dragged through the streets, were done away with, and ascribes this to the fact that Elagabalus had favoured the Christians.
281. Herodianus, Hist.Imp. 7.1.2.
282. Herodianus, Hist.Imp. 7.1.4.
283. Eus., HE 6.28.
284. Eus., HE 6.28.
285. Catalogus Liberianus, quoted Frühe Christ. 119.
286. Eus., HE 6.29.1.
287. Frend, Martyrdom 391.
288. Letter of Firmilianus, a Cappadocian bishop, quoted Cyprianus, Ep. 75.10.
289. Eus., HE 6.29.1.
290. Cyprianus, Ep. 55.9. After an interval of a year there was another bishop of Rome indeed, Cornelius (251-253).

291. Eus., HE 6.40.10-12.
292. Acta Pionii, quoted by Frend, Martyrdom 410.
293. Cypr., Ep. 59.10.
294. Acta Tryphonis, quoted by Frend, Martyrdom 411.
295. Frend, Martyrdom 413.
296. Eus., HE 7.10.3.
297. Victor, Hist.abbr. 32.4.
298. Karlhorst, Von Nero 139.
299. Frend, Martyrdom 422.
300. From their Passio, quoted by Allard, Dern.Pers.
301. Eus., HE 7.10.4.
302. Its text has not been preserved but can mainly be reconstituted from Christian testimonies.
303. Eus., HE 7.11.7.
304. Allard, Dern.Pers. 54.
305. From the Acta proconsularia S. Cypriani, quoted by Frend, Martyrdom 423/424.
306. Allard, Dern.Pers. 84, note 1 : 'a kind of intermediary class between senators and knights'.
307. Cypr., Ep. 80.1.
308. Allard, Dern.Pers. 88/89.
309. Allard, Dern.Pers. 84.
310. Allard, Dern.Pers. 89-92.
311. Ambrosius, De officiis 2.41.
312. In this context a story tells of a certain Tarsicius who brought the Eucharist, probably to Christians hiding in the catacombs. Stopped by a military patrol and refusing to deliver up his sacred charge, he was killed on the spot.The evidence for this is an epigram by Pope Damasus I (366-378) on the tomb of Pope Zephyrinus (198-217) where Tarcisius too was buried (text Allard, Dern.Pers. 76, note 1). As a boy I was told that Tarsicius too was a boy. I was so deeply impressed by his courage that, when I was to be confirmed by the bishop of Haarlem (NL) at the age of twelve, I chose him for my confirmation patron saint. Later I learned that Tarsicius in all probability had not been a boy but a deacon or an acolyte.
313. Acta Fructuosi 2, quoted by Frend, Martyrdom 428.

314. Acta proconsularia S. Cyprinai, in Frühe Christ. 155-159.
315. See Ch. III.6l.
316. Eus., HE 7.13.
317. Frend, Martyrdom 428.
318. Frend, Martyrdom 429.
319. Eus., HE 7.30.20-21; Lact., Mort.pers. 6.
320. See Ch. III.1c.
321. Frend, Martyrdom 480.
322. Acta Maximiliani 9, in Frühe Christ. 166-171.
323. Frend, Martyrdom 487.
324. Eus., HE 8.4.3.
325. Eus., Chron. ad annum 301.
326. Lact., Mort.pers. 10.1-11.7.
327. Eus., HE 8.2.4-5.
328. Lact., Mort.Pers. 14.1-15.7.
329. Eus., HE 8.6.7-8.5.
330. Eus., HE 8.8.6-9.3.
331. Eus., Mart.pal. 3.1.
332. Grégoire, Dern.Pers. 76.
333. Frend, Martyrdom 492.
334. Frend, Mart. 537.
335. See Ch. III.3b.
336. Eus., HE 9.7.3-14.
337. Frend, Martyrdom 493.
338. Eus., Mart.pal. 4.2.
339. Eus., HE 8.12.8-11.
340. Athanasius, Hist.Arian. 64.
341. Eus., HE 8.12.11.
342. Eus., HE 8.16.3-5; Lact., Mort.pers. 33.
343. Eus., HE 8.17.1; Lact., Mort.pers. 33.
344. Text in Eus., HE 8.17 and Lact., Mort.pers. 38.
345. Eus., Vita Const. 1.31.

346. Lact., Mort.pers. 44.
347. Eus., HE 10.7.1-2.
348. Eus., HE 10.6.1-5.
349. Frend, Martyrdom 534/535, note 282.
350. Eus., HE 10.5.1-17.
351. Lact., Div.inst. 5.13.
352. Lact., Div. inst. 5.22.
353. Tert., Apol. 50.13.
354. Julian, Misopogon 352C.
355. Greg.Naz., Or. 4.19.
356. Browning, Julian 36.
357. Amm.Marc. 22.9.4; Sozomenos, HE 5.2.10-14.
358. Sozomenos, HE 5.2.15.
359. Sozomenos, HE 5.2.9-10.
360. This does not mean that he intended to become a priest; the principal task of a lector is to read the lessons from the Old and New Testament during the service.
361. Sozomenos, HE 5.2.16. The life of this curious personage is described by Eunapius, Lives of the philosophers 473 sqq.
362. Julian, Or. 4.2 (Hertlein).
363. Julian, Ep. ad Themistium 259B (Hertlein).
364. Most historians assume this but Allard, Julien I, 330. doubts it since Eunapius 475-476 does not state this in as many words. On the other hand, there must have been a reason why Eunapius wrote that Julian "heard that there was a higher wisdom in Greece", and that he "hastened to the hierophant of the goddesses (Demeter and Persephone)".
365. Amm.Marc. 15.8.
366. Amm.Marc. 20.4.
367. Amm.Macr. 22.2.1.
368. Amm.Marc. 22.2.4.
369. Bouffartique, Julien 25.
370. Libanius, Or. 18.178.
371. Libanius, Or. 18.179.

372. Julian never spoke of 'Christians'; it was invariably the 'Galileans'.
373. Contra Galilaeos 43 A.
374. Contra Gal. 39A-B.
375. See for this section Braun, Julien et le Christianisme, passim.
376. Jul., Contra Gal. 43a.
377. Jul., Contra Gal. 39a-b.
378. Jul., Contra Gal. 243b.
379. Jul., Contra Gal. 218b-233d.
380. Jul., Contra Gal. 115d-e.
381. Jul., Contra Gal. 143a-b.
382. Jul., Contra Gal. 100c.
383. Allard, Julien II,225.
384. Allard, Julien II,222/223.
385. Libanius, Or. 18.125.
386. Goethe, Erlkönig.
387. Julian, Or. 7.237C-D (Hertlein).
388. Codex Theod. 13.3.51.
389. Julian, Ep. 422-424 (Hertlein).
390. Sozomenos, HE 5.18.3.
391. Amm.Marc. 22.10.7.
392. Bidez, Julien 264.
393. Browning, Julian 185.
394. Socrates 13.3.1.
395. See the relevant texts in Iul.Imp.ep.et leg., no. 50.
396. Julian, Ep.376C (Hertlein).
397. Julian, Ep.378B.
398. Greg.Naz. Or. 5.9.25; Theodor. 3.16; Joh.Chryst., In sanctum Babylum 22.
399. Caesarea Panias is now the small village of Bâniâs, in a nook of Mount Hermon, at an altitude of 329 m.
400. Rufinus, HE 7.14; Sozomenos, HE 5.21.
401. See Ch. III.6q.

402. Theodoretus 3.20 : "Νενίκηκας, Γαλιλαιε!"
403. Libanius, Or.17.7.

CHAPTER II

JUDAISM AND CHRISTIANITY :
A DUALISTIC RELATIONSHIP?

PART I PRELIMINARIES

1. My credentials

Where angels fear to tread, where demons feel at home, thus we may characterize the relationship of the Christian Church and the Jews in the first centuries A.D. (to say nothing as yet of later centuries) to which we now turn. When I wrote about the Gnosis, I deemed it necessary to present my credentials. I feel this is all the more needed now that I am going to speak of Jews and Christians. Let me repeat almost verbally what I wrote in a former volume [1]. I am a Roman-Catholic, a 'cradle Catholic', as the English use to say, a regular church-goer still, an assiduous, even daily Bible reader, accepting as true what the Church teaches as true - no more, as my father used to say, but certainly no less. If one were to object that, in consequence, my approach can never be objective, my retort is that it will probably different from that of a Jew - although I wonder whether this will be true in all respects (as a believer I am much closer to orthodox Jews than to liberal or agnostic Jews).

When declaring myself an orthodox Roman-Catholic and intending to speak of Jews and Judaism, I realize that I am making myself highly suspect. For are not all Christians, especially all Roman-Catholics, supposed to be viscerally and innately anti-Semitic? Has not the Church throughout all ages harassed, vilified, and persecuted the Jews? Didn't this depreciation already begin in the Gospels, to continue its fatal course until the present day? The theme of Christian anti-Semitism is omnipresent. One can hardly open a book on the question of anti-Semitism in general, whether written by a Jew, a Christian, or a non-believer, but soon enough one hits on accusations such as I mentioned. In a popularized, often more hateful form we meet this in the media, in dailies and periodicals, on radio and tv. I am writing this only a few weeks after the fiftieth anniversary of the liberation of the annihilation camp at Auschwitz which was solemnly commemorated on the spot. This proved a good occasion for repeating the age-old accusations world-wide, now including Pope Pius XII who is reproached for having been utterly silent with regard to the Holocaust [2]. The Church and the Christians, it is often suggested, although not directly responsible for the destruction of the Jews, are nevertheless guilty for having prepared the road to it [3].

As an editorial in a Roman-Catholic weekly put it : "Inevitably, the Church has been drawing much public attention to its own share of culpability in preparing the soil of European culture for the devilish seeds of Nazism". In the same article the Pope and those in authority in the Church at that time are accused of having "manifestly failed in their mission" [4]. In a letter to the Editor a subscriber commented that "the Catholic Church should be ashamed" [5].

Once again, I resist the temptation to present my own comment. After all, I am not writing about anti-Semitism in whatever form. But in view of the weight of the accusations and of the importance of the subject, I deem it necessary to say something about my own attitude. To be quite honest, I am mightily irritated that I, in one way or other, should be associated with the horror of Auschwitz. I was raised in a pious and practising Roman-Catholic family; until I went to the (neutral) University of Amsterdam, I attended Roman-Catholic schools, primary and secondary. At the age of eleven I joined a Roman-Catholic scout group of which I remained a member for many years. In all those years I never heard one anti-Semitic word, with one exception.

My father had Jewish friends and colleagues; when I was ten, he took me to visit a synagogue so that already then I became somewhat acquainted with the Jewish way of life. My mother always highly praised Jewish traders, more honest than the others, she used to say. From the pulpit I never heard a word uttered against Jews or Judaism; if there was polemizing (not much, not often, not vehement), it was against Protestantism. With monotonous regularity I hear it repeated that the priests constantly accuse the Jews of all centuries of having murdered Jesus. I cannot remember anybody expressing himself in this way. In the so-called 'lenten meditations' in the weeks preceding Easter the theme always was that it was the sinner (the Christian sinner, that is) who is the cause of Jesus' death. "It was not the Jews who killed you, but me, me!", wrote the seventeenth-century Dutch (protestant) poet Jacob Revius; this was also the leitmotiv in the sermons I heard.

In grammar-school our excellent teacher of RE did all he could to make us acquainted with the Old Testament; he invariably spoke of Jews with great respect. None of my other teachers ever said something against Jews or the Jewish religion. But as there is no rule without an exception, my first teacher of German was a convinced anti-Semite who often railed against Jews; it had perhaps something to do with the fact that he had lived for some time in Berlin. I don't think this made a great impression on us, at least not on me; we found him an ineffectual babble-box and used his lessons to do our homework for other teachers.

With all this in mind the reader will not be surprised to hear that my atttitude towards Jews and Judaism has always been and still is quite positive. During the occupation period I could do only very little, but I consider myself happy that I was able to help at least one Jew - a fellow-student - to escape to Switzerland, with considerable risk to my own safety, if I may say so. I hope the reader will now believe me if I categorically state that in this chapter I am not out to denigrate either Jews or Christians - which should not be taken to signify that I am neutral. I am not!

2. Clarification of terms

Speaking of the relationship of Jews and Christians (restricting ourselves to the first centuries of the present era), we should first of all clarify our terms [6]. Often enough the term 'anti-Semitism' is used in this context, rather glibly, I find. For 'anti-Semitism', like all other -isms, is a modern term [7], never used by ancient authors. Strictly speaking, when applied to Jews, as it invariably is, it is a highly inappropriate term, since all Arabs are Semites too. What is more, the term has decidely racist overtones; it stamps Jews as inferior and burdened with all kinds of unpleasant properties, even vices. Such racist anti-Semitism was completely foreign to all Antiquity and also to the Middle Ages. It originated together with the rise of nationalism and chauvinism in the nineteenth century.

It is also very disturbing that this term - and how could it be otherwise - is associated with the Holocaust. We have the habit of involuntarily reading history backwards from the horrible events which mostly are given the name of 'Auschwitz' and connect every anti-Jewish utterance in all ages with it, as though they were as many stepping-stones on the road to Hitler's destructive policy. But ancient authors, whether pagan or Christian, when agitating against Jews and Judaism, did not think of their wholesale physical annihilation. So I believe that, in studying these early centuries, we should studiously avoid the term 'anti-Semitism'.

3. The Jewish heritage of the Church

Our choice of terms, however, is not wide. If we do not want to speak of 'anti-Semitism', we are thrown on 'anti-Judaism'. But this term has its drawbacks too. Christian authors could scarcely set their faces against all that is Jewish. The founder of the Church, Jesus of Nazareth, was a Jew, circumcized according to the Law. His mother was a Jewess. All his apostles were Jews; even the great missionary of the heathen, Paul, was a Jew, and proud of so being. All the authors of the New Testament, with exception of Luke, were

Jewish. The first adherents were all Jewish. So the Christian Church is built on a Jewish foudation of which it was and is well aware.

The Roman-Catholic Church accepts, from the first letter to the last, all the books of the Old Testament; even to this day, in every Mass there is at least one reading from it. Its prayers, its liturgy, are replete with Old Testament texts; the Eucharist, the heart of the Catholic creed and its central mystery, is directly derived from the Jewish Passover meal. Even the sacerdotal hierarchy of Judaism has been duplicated by that of the Roman-Catholic Church, with the High Priest (the bishop), the priests (presbyters) and the Levites (the deacons). We find this literally expressed in the First Letter of Clement (written around A.D/ 100) [8].

All this means that the Church cannot be anti-Judaistic without belying her origin, her sacred books, and her ritual. 'Spiritually we are all Semites", it was Pope Pius XI (1922-1939) who said this. This phrase represents the deepest conviction of the Church. It is also my deepest conviction. I found this very pregnantly exemplified in one of the most profound movies I ever saw, 'Monsieur Klein' by the British film-director Joseph Losey [9]. Robert Klein is a young French art-dealer who, during the German occupation of Paris, buys for a mere trifle the art-treasures of Jews who will be transported eastward. He is a Roman-Catholic, albeit not exactly a fervent believer, and he is thoroughly anti-Semitic.

Much to his annoyance he appears to have a double, another Robert Klein. This second Klein, a member of the French resistance, constantly sends him notes and makes telephone calls to him; however, the two Kleins never meet face to face. Then the police begins to suspect that the art-dealer is identical with the resistance man; he might even be a Jew. The first Klein gets into trouble, for when interrogated by the police, he is unable to prove that he is not Jewish. Suddenly he remembers that he is a baptized Catholic, but his certificate of baptism does not turn up in time. Finally he is arrested and deported in a transport of Jews.

Klein the anti-Semite is 'klein' = small, because all anti-Semitism is petty. His double is what he should be but is not : a French patriot, a courageous resistance man. Obviously this second Klein is a Jew who prefers to go down fighting. What he does - and we may see in him the art-dealer's conscience - is to remind his double of his duty to act as a patriot, and of his existential background, that of Judaism. The message of the film is that Klein is incapable of escaping this; his fate is inexorably bound up with that of the Jews. Whether they like it or not, whether they are anti-Semitic or not, Christians are 'Jews'. There is, as Paul said, 'no distinction between Jew and Gentile'. Gentile Christians are 'grafted' onto the tree of Judaism [10]. That the Roman-Catholic but anti-Semitic Monsieur Klein has to share the fate of the Jews shows in a pregnant way that "spiritually we are all Semites".

4. What exactly is Judaism?

But what exactly do we mean when we speak of Judaism? The question seems as superfluous as the answer seems obvious : what else than the Jewish faith and the Jewish way of life? In fact there were several 'Judaisms' in Jesus' days, not rarely conflicting with each other. In his 'Antiquities' Josephus mentions three 'haireseis' in Judaism, three schools of thought, the Pharisees, the Sadducees, and the Essenes. To these we may add a fourth sect, that of the Zealots. So much for sects. Socially there were several groups distinct from each other. There was the priestly aristocracy, the top layer of Jewish society, then the scribes, and, at the bottom, the common people. All these seven sects and groups had their own idea of Jewish faith and practice, of 'Judaism'.

The priestly aristocracy had its base in the Temple of Jerusalem; its head was the High Priest. No High Priest could be appointed without the consent of the Roman governor. "The high-priestly officials ... were responsible to the Romans for the collection of the tribute and the maintenance of order in Judaea ... The political-economic interests and functions of the priestly aristocracy ... were inseparable from their religious role" [11]. They were not very popular with the common people : too wealthy, too haughty, too much hand in glove with the Romans.

Apart from the priestly class, we find the 'scribes'; they are often mentioned in the Gospels, not rarely in one breath with the Pharisees. We hear of them since the time of the Babylonian Captivity. They were the scholars, the professional experts of Mosaic Law; because of this generally acknowledged expertise their influence was great. Their exegesis of the Law tended to legalism, even to casuistry. Scribes - they were laymen - acted as teachers, lawyers, and administrators. Their form of address was 'rabbi' which is still in use in Jewish circles [12].

Both the Sadducees and the Pharisees may be characterized as religious parties. The Sadducees were an aristocratic group to which many priests belonged. Privileged and wealthy as they were, they looked down in contempt on the common people with the result that their influence was not great. Sadducees did not believe in an hereafter, in a personal immortality, in the resurrection of the body, and in the last judgment. Modern opinion would classify them as 'progressive', but in the Judaistic context they were the conservatives since they did not acknowledge the developments that had occurred in Judaism since the Babylonian Captivity.

The Pharisees [13] believed in the tenets mentioned in the former paragraph which had found a place in the Jewish creed in the centuries before Christ; today they would be dubbed 'conservatives', but then they were the progressives. They had their adherents among all classes of the population but not in the priestly class, only among the poorer priests. The scribes were mainly Pharisees. "Pharisees are simply identical with the early rabbinic Judaism", is the categorical statement of David Flusser [14]. They insisted upon a loyal and strict observation of the Law. They despised the high-priestly class whose members they saw as collaborators with the Romans; they themselves believed in the coming of the Messiah which, however, must not be taken to mean that they looked forward to an armed rising against the Roman power.

Whereas the Sadducees had the reputation of being harsh, even cruel "when they sit in judgment" [15], the Pharisees were "naturally lenient in the matter of punishment" [16]. To make things still more complicated, there were differences of opinion among the Pharisees themselves, the school of Shammai being more rigid than that of Hillel [17]. "Three hundred and sixteen controversies between the two schools were recorded, with the Shammaites 'on the strict side' in all but fifty-five of them" [18].

A very special group in the Jewish population were the Essenes. I write extensively about them in my Volume VII [19]. Essenes practised several forms of 'apartheid', the most conspicuous of these being that they did not take part in the Temple service in Jerusalem. A basically puritanical sect, they kept themselves apart from Jewish society. Their main settlement, in fact a monastery, was far from the centre of Jewish life, at Qumran near the shores of the Dead Sea. Theirs was an unusual brand of Judaism. But no more need be said of them in this chapter since they do not appear in the New Testament. And the Church Fathers too knew little or nothing of them.

Jacob Neusner describes the social following of the Sadducees, the Pharisees, and the Essenes in these words : "The Sadducees were most influential among landholders and merchants, the Pharisees among the middle and lower urban classes, the Essenes among the disenchanted of both classes" [20].

Yet another Jewish group, with specific ideas about the future of Israel, were the fanatically anti-Roman and anti-pagan Zealots [21]. They sought to effect the liberation of Israel by means of violence; they were also called 'sicarii', because they carried a 'sica', a curved dagger under their clothing. They too are not mentioned in the New Testament. There is, however, a reference to the 'Herodians'. Since no specification is given it is difficult to say who or what they were; they were probably courtiers of King Herodes Antipas I.

The last and largest group in the Israel of those days is the people. This was an undifferentiated mass comprising anybody from the inhabitants of the larger towns to small farmers in far away corners of the country, to say nothing of the despised shepherds. Since the Samaritans were not considered Jewish, I shall say nothing of them [22]. Then there was the distinction between Judaea and Galilee; sophisticated Judaeans saw Galileans as half-pagan. "The entire Galilee had been converted to Judaism only one hundred and twenty years before the common era" [23].

What the people from high to low had in common was their antipathy to (pagan) Hellenism and the (equally pagan) Roman domination. But of course some people were influenced by Hellenistic culture, while it was not always easy and sometimes simply impossible to shun all contact with Romans. Even for the most pious and zealous it was hard to observe all the innumerable prescripts of the Law. It is well-known how Paul campaigned against the Law, especially against those who would bind converted Gentiles to it [24]. But Peter too spoke of it as "a yoke that neither our fathers nor ourselves have been able to bear" [25].

Learned rabbi's and Pharisees had no high idea of 'that crowd who does not know the Law' [26], the 'am-haaretz". We may also suspect that the common people were not as strict in paying the religious imposts and the tithes for the Temple service as the Pharisees. This "was one of the main distinctions between the Pharisaic masters and disciples on the one hand, and the common people on the other. The former were meticulous in paying the priestly and Levitical dues, and the latter were not" [27].

The upshot of this section is that we should be careful when speaking of 'Judaism' and guard our words when referring to 'the Jews'. In particular we must ask the Church Fathers what or whom they mean when using the term 'the Jews'. We are obliged to conclude with Jacob Neusner that in the period under consideration "no such thing as 'normative Judaism' existed" [28].

5. Where did Jesus himself belong?

In this context an important question is where Jesus himself belonged. It is evident that he was not a member of the priestly aristocracy. Nor was he a priest of a lower rank. He was neither a rabbi nor a scribe; people stood astonished that he was so learned, although he had not attended a rabbinic school. His notions of the afterlife, the immortality of the soul, and the resurrection of the body put him at a very great distance from the Sadducees. A first reading of the Gospels already shows us that Jesus and the Pharisees did not see eye to eye. But this relationship is not so simple. "With important

Pharisean tenets Jesus had no quarrel at all", I wrote in Vol. VII [29]. Jesus fully acknowledged their authority, and he had a high opinion of the Mosaic Law. In some respects he was even more strict than the Pharisees; when he rejected, foir instance, the so-called 'writ of separation', a legal device which permitted a husband to divorce his wife. And not all Pharisees were opponents of Jesus.

Socially speaking, Jesus was a man of the people; his family was that of a simple carpenter in a forgotten nest in the mountains of Galilee. But already the fact that he was a descendant of King David in both lines and that the people knew this shows that he was more than a common artisan. He never denied his origin. The leaders of his people constantly accused him of siding with the common man and woman, of 'eating with publicans and sinners' (forgetting that he also dined with Pharisees). But does this make him a populist? I don't think so. Had he been a bona fide populist, he would have tuned in to the wishes of the people, in particular their hope that he should restore the Kingdom of Israel and become its king himself. This he steadfastly refused. From time to time he rebuked the people just as severely as he did the Pharisees. He reproached them for their materialism and sensationalism, because they wanted to see 'signs and miracles'.

6. Why Jesus had to be done away with and who were responsible

It is evident that Jesus of Nazareth represented a very specific brand of Judaism which made him stand apart from all its other tendencies; his stance drew the fire of other groups upon him. We know that, from a human point of view, he ended miserably, since he was condemned and executed, dying 'the death of a slave'. Every group had its own special reason to get rid of this firebrand. The priestly aristocracy had mainly political reasons. They feared that Jesus would bring them into difficulties with the Romans. Many of the people believed that the Messiah had appeared in him; the leaders found it entirely possible that Jesus could become the leader of an anti-Roman insurrection which would only end in bloodshed. They were well aware that there had been many false Messiahs. In the Sanhedrin the fear was expressed that "Jesus will find credit everywhere. Then the Romans will come, and make an end of our city and our race". The High Priest Caiphas advised his colleagues that "it is best for us if one man is put to death for the sake of the people, to save the whole nation from destruction" [30].

It is notable that in the Passion stories the Pharisees hardly play a role; Matthew does not mention them at all, and the scribes only twice, once as members of the Sanhedrin [31] and again when they derided Jesus on the cross [32]. The action against Jesus is led by the high priests and 'the elders' (the Sanhedrin). Mark mentions the scribes, and not the Pharisees; here too the high priests have the lead. It is the same in Luke. John says that Pharisees were present when the Sanhedrin resolved to execute Jesus [33], but when it comes to the execution of this plan, he speaks of High Priest Caiphas and his father-in-law Annas [34]. I guess that some Pharisees were involved in the initial plot but that the priestly class was not interested in their motives; they had their own score to settle with Jesus. In his public speeches in Jerusalem Peter never accused the Pharisees of having been instrumental in the death of Jesus.

Pontius Pilate, the procurator (governor) of Judaea, had to play the decisive role since the Sanhedrin did not possess the right of life and death; this was a prerogative of the Roman authorities [35]. He only comes late into the picture. It is sometimes contended by modern exegetes that the Gospels try to exculpate Pilate as much as possible in order to charge 'the Jews' with 'the murder of God'. If we take the Gospel stories at their face-value - which I believe is always the most sensible approach -, Pilate was far from happy with this case. In his eyes Jesus was a simpleton; he saw no proof that he really was a rebel. But put under pressure from Jewish elements, he proclaimed the death-sentence. Therefore, in his first public speech, Peter said that the Jews had delivered Jesus to the Romans but that it was 'the godless' (the heathen) who had nailed him to the cross and killed him [36]. He exonerated his co-religionists by stating that they had acted out of ignorance; even their authorities had been blind [37].

7. Jesus' conflict with the Pharisees

Since Jesus himself put Sadducees and Pharisees in the same boat, warning people against their 'leaven' (= their doctrine) [38], we had better concentrate on his difference of opinion with the Pharisees; these are often mentioned in the Gospels, the Sadducees only occasionally. Jesus did not attack their sticking to Mosaic Law. On the contrary! What he condemned in them was that they also bound the people to the 'oral law', the extensive system of rules, 613 in number (the rules are all to be found in the Torah, but the number itself is not found there). According to him, with this additional law they laid a far too heavy burden on the shoulders of the people so that they might even become indifferent to religion [39]. Jesus felt that the oral law should be abolished [40]. We may, however, well ask whether this dispute was a sufficient reason for the Pharisees to send Jesus to his death.

It must have angered the Pharisees in the extreme that this unschooled upstart, this self-made rabbi [41], made authoritative statements on the Law. There were two points in particular which, when taken together, made the Pharisees decide to have sentence passed on him. The first was the fear they shared with the priestly class that Jesus would set up himself as the Messiah and cause a rebellion. The second was that he began to suggest evermore plainly that he was of divine origin, that he was the equal of God, that he was the 'son of God'. This was the ultimate blasphemy which made him deserve death. It was in fact on the strength of this accusation that the Sanhedrin pronounced the death-sentence against him [42]. However, the Jewish leaders knew they could not sell this to Pilate (when the procurator heard of this sonship, it made him rather nervous [43]). Therefore before Pilate the indictment was changed into : "This man says he is the king of the Jews" [44]. So the priestly aristocracy, the Pharisees, and the procurator all had their own reasons to do away with Jesus.

8. A drastic change after A.D. 70

The varied picture of differently thinking groups that Jewish society offered in the days of Jesus changed radically after the failure of the rebellion in A.D. 70. Almost all groups disappeared then, never to return. In A.D. 68 Roman troops occupied the Essenian monastry in Qumran which went up in flames; nothing is heard of the Essenes after this. The Zealots, who had been instrumental in the outbreak of the revolt, perished with the Temple. With the destruction of the central sanctuary the Jewish sacrificial cult, with all its ritual, came to an end. Vague hopes that the cult would be resumed, just as had been the case after the Babylonian Captivity, were frustrated by the failure of Bar Kokhba's revolt in 135, when all Jerusalem went the way of the Temple, that of total destruction [45].

As a result, all those groups that had their headquarters in Jerusalem, as connected with the Temple service, and living from it, disppeared for good. No longer was there a High Priest, no longer was there a priestly aristocracy. Since most of the members of this class had been Sadducees, these are mentioned no more. With the disappearance of the cult centre and the end of the age-old ritual with all its sacrifices and ceremonies, the priests who had, with the Levites, always conducted the ritual, lost the most important part of their function. Thus the Jewish community became, to a large extent, a non-clerical one, a lay community, although there continued to exist - and still exists - a Jewish priesthood [46]. This is an essential difference with the Roman-Catholic Church which is a clerical and hierarchic community.

The one and only faction that more or less survived the catastrophe was that of the Pharisees. Not that after A.D. 70 they are mentioned as a coherent group; soon enough the word 'Pharisee' disappeared as a label. But it is perfectly possible that the Rabbis, who now assumed the leadership of Israel, were the spiritual descendants of the Pharisees (and the scribes) [47]. "While the historical connection between the Pharisees and the later Rabbis is not entirely clear, the Rabbis did eventually claim the Pharisees as their immediate forbears" [48]. The scribes had their successors in the so-called 'Tannaim' or 'teachers' (also addressed as 'Rabbi'), a loose group of about two hundred and twenty-five scholars belonging to several, often contending schools or academies in Palestine [49].

9. The miracle of the survival of the Jewish nation

With the annihilation of the Temple and all that it stood for, followed by the destruction of Jerusalem in 135, a horrible catastrophe had come over the Jewish nation. Palestine could no longer be seen as the Jewish homeland, with the great majority of the Jews now living in the Diaspora, in pagan countries. The promised country, the sacred soil, was now lost and defiled by the heathen. Jewish life had always been centred on the Temple and its cult; if possible, pious Jews 'went up' to Jerusalem to celebrate the great religious festivals. And now the Temple lay in ruins, never to be rebuilt, while Jews were forbidden to enter the holy city. "Sovereignty over the land of Israel and the continued operation of the priestly cult provided the Jews with a concrete symbol of their relationship to God and to the fulfillment of the Bible's covenantal promise ... The destruction of the Temple and the failed Bar Kokhba revolt accordingly meant for all Jews the end of Israelite history as it previously had been conceived at its own temple in its own land" [50]. Had Jahve forsaken his people, was the name of Israel destined to be eradicated?

That the Jewish nation survived as a distinct ethnic group and that there still is a Jewish religion as a separate creed, is the accomplishment of the Rabbis, the Tannaim. The vacuum that had been created by the disappearance of the authority of the leading groups in Jerusalem was filled by the 'Mishnah' [51]. This word means 'study' which implies that the idea was not to present something entirely new but to go on building on and explaining what already existed, mainly the Pharasaic interpretation of the Torah. The Mishnah, the fixation of the 'Oral law', is the final result of Tanaitic studies and discussions; in its definitive form it was published in about 200-220. It is three things at the same time : a legal source-book, a law code, and 'in general, a utopian vision of a world other than its authors' own' [52]. In its turn the Mishnah was interpreted and explained, and this finally led to the creation of the Talmud [53].

What is of the highest importance, in particular with regard to the differences between Judaism and Christianity, is the utopian character of the Mishnah. "The Rabbis present a cogent theory of the relationship between Israel and God. The result is an eloquent image of Israelite life in the aftermath of the destruction of the Temple" [54]. The overarching idea is that the religious life of all Jews had to be modelled on the Temple, as though the Temple still existed. Israelites had to "perfect and sanctify the life of their village on the model of perfection that existed in the Temple". The continued sanctification of the world is the response to "the notion that God originally created a perfect world" [55]. But if the Temple service were to be continued, the consequence, in view of the fact the heart had been cut out of the ritual and that there was no longer a High Priest, was that the priestly functions devolved on all Israelites, and especially on the family fathers. The authority over ritual and cultic matters that had been exercized by the priestly class now fell to the Rabbis.

Let Alan Avery-Peck, on whose essay I have been relying in this section, draw the conclusion. "Pharisaic and then rabbinic views created a Judaism that could survive the destruction of the Temple and the demise of the priestly cult. Placing priestly matters into the hands of individual Israelites allowed Judaism to maintain its vibrancy and power quite apart from the actual conduct of the cult, the existence of the Temple, and even Israelite political control of the land of Israel. In Pharasaic and later rabbinic Judaism, these things became secondary to common Israelites' conduct in their homes. The most important and crucial was what took place in the economy of Israelite life, in the individual family and village, not what took place on the stage of world history" [56]. It was in the shape of this new Judaism that the Jews would be confronted with emergent Christianity.

10. Who are 'the Jews' of the New Testament?

Yet another preliminary remark has to be made. Since modern anti-Semitism is always speaking of 'the Jews', and since the Fathers of the Church in their polemics also refer to 'the Jews', the question is who was the first to speak of 'the Jews'. A second question is what is meant by this term. Let us browse through the books of the New Testament.

a. Books without any Jews

To begin with the last book in the canon, the Revelation of John, the enemy there is the Roman Empire; Jews and Judaism simply are not mentioned at all. Not a single Jew figures in the so-called 'Catholic Letters', those of Peter, James, John, and Jude; the same applies to the (anonymous) Letter to the Hebrews (which, by the way, is a thoroughly 'Jewish' piece of writing).

Coming now to the letters of Paul, whether actually written by him or ascribed to him, we can immediately drop those to Philemon, to Titus, and the two to Timothy : no Jews in them. We find Jews neither in 1 and 2 Thessalonians nor in Colossians nor in Philippians and Ephesians. In Phil. 3:5-6 the author mentions not without pride that he is a circumcized Jew of the tribe of Benjamin, and even a Pharisee [57]. There is no talk of Jews in Galatians where Paul is polemizing against Peter and Judaizing Christians [58]. Nor are Jews to be found in Ephesians and in 1 and 2 Corinthians.

b. Paul's Letter to the Romans

This leaves us with Paul's Letter to the Romans where the apostle speaks extensively of his relation to Israel. I wrote about this relation in Volume VII [59] and can only repeat what I said there. Paul admonishes the Christians that they, in the history of salvation, are only second choice. Israel - he does not speak of 'the Jews' but of Israel - is and will remain the chosen people that was never rejected by God. Christians have been 'grafted onto the tree (of Israel)' because part of Israel has not recognized the Messiah; Paul criticizes them for their blindness, but the really hard things he has to say concern the heathen, not the Jews.

c. 'The Jews' in the Gospels

Leaving aside the Acts of the Apostles for a moment, we must now inspect the Gospels. In the three synoptic Gospels a collectivity called 'the Jews' does not appear. But this expression regularly occurs in John, forty-five times. Of these forty-five times fifteen are absolutely non-polemical; they refer to the Jews as a collectivity. So for instance in 2:6 where 'the custom of the ceremonial washing of the Jews' is mentioned, in 3:11 where Nicodemus is called 'one of the chiefs of the Jews', or in 4:9 where it is stated that "the Jews have no dealings with the Samaritans". Twice the generic term is applied to 'the Jews who believed in him', in 8:11 and 11:45; in these cases the term is even used in a friendly way. The most positive of these non-polemical references is in 4:22 where Jesus says that "salvation is to come from the Jews". This is a fundamental and categorical statement that is essential for John's opinion of 'the Jews'.

The thirty or so references to 'the Jews' which have a polemical or antagonistic tinge never concern the collectivity. This appears already from their very first mention in 11:19 where it is said that 'the Jews' sent priests and Levites to John the Baptist to ask him : "Who are you?". These Jews can be none other than the highest leadership around the High Priest. These authorities are also meant in the section about the man who was cured by Jesus on the Sabbath; here they are mentioned four times (Jo. 5:10-15); in the same pericope it is also stated that they planned to kill him (also in 7:11). When he was teaching in the Temple, 'the Jews' found that he was not authorized to do this since he had not attended a rabbinic school; these 'Jews' refer to the official, authorized teachers are meant, the rabbis (Jo. 7:14).

Jo. 7:32-36 makes it very clear who are meant by 'the Jews'. The High Priest and the Pharisees order their servants to arrest Jesus. He tells them : "Where I am you cannot find me". And then 'the Jews' ask themselves what this might mean. That not all Pharisees were inimical to Jesus is proved by the story of the man who had been blind from his birth. When cured, he was brought to the Pharisees who could not arrive at a common opinion, for there were some who said that it would not be possible for a sinful man to perform such miracles. Then the term 'Pharisees; is dropped and the rest of the text speaks of 'the Jews'. These Jews are the Pharisees who are enemies of Jesus (Jo. 9).

That with 'the Jews' only a small part of the nation is meant is made evident by Jo. 10:22-24 where it is related how Jesus stood in Solomo's porch in the Temple, and how 'the Jews' gathered around him. Since we are in the Temple, a group of priests must be meant. When 'the Jews; say to Pilate : "we have no power to put any man to death" [60], this too can only refer to authorities. Similarly in 19:7 where 'the Jews' tell the procurator that, according to the Law, Jesus has to die since he is calling himself the Son of God. In 19:21 we find the High Priests mentioned specifically when they ask Pilate not to write : "He is the King of the Jews".

The conclusion can be no other than when John is speaking of 'the Jews' in a negative sense [61], he is always referring to the top layer of the people, to the leading authorities, and not even to all of them, since John also mentions well-intentioned members of this group, such as Nicodemus, a Pharisee, and Joseph of Arimathea, a member of the Sanhedrin. 'The Jews', therefore, are that party among the authorities that was inimical to Jesus. John is not very specific about these; they seem to be members of the priestly aristocracy and/or Pharisees, most of the time Pharisees, I think.

Now the great question is why John, although aiming at a relatively small group of the Jewish people, none the less uses a generalizing term. And a generalization like this one may easily give rise to anti-Semitism; all Jews become enemies of Jesus in this way. Of course, this was not the intention of John who was a Jew himself. But if he did not intend to accuse the collectivity of the nation, why then did he use this word so often in a pejorative sense?

d. 'The Jews' in Acts

In order to understand why John adopted a so much sharper tone than the other Gospel authors, it is necessary to realize that his Gospel is the latest work in the New Testament; it must have been written at the end of the first century A.D., perhaps about the year 100, in all probability in Ephesus. This means that it is some decades later than the synoptic Gospels and the authentic Pauline Letters. In the meantime Jewish-Christian relations had taken a turn for the worse. We find an account of what happened in Acts; this book preceded John's Gospel by about a decade. The hardening of the respective standpoints is clearly discernible in it. Luke, its author, relates how in the first years of the Church the Jewish authorities tried to prevent the apostles from preaching 'the name of Jesus'. They did not obey, and there was a growing number of converts, even among the Jewish priesthood [62].

Then the first victim fell. Stephen, a deacon, was brought before the Sanhedrin, condemned to death, and stoned [63]. It was the first time that the Jewish-Christian conflict had led to bloodshed [64]. Later King Herod Agrippa I, since A.D. 41 the ruler of Judaea and Samaria, began to persecute the Christians. James, the brother of John, was killed by the sword, while Peter miraculously escaped from prison [65]. Herod did this, says Luke, because "he saw that the Jews approved of this". This is the first time that Luke uses this generic term (which he did not use in his Gospel); it suggests that the Jewish nation as a whole was inimical to the Christians. However, he cannot have meant this since the Christian victims too were Jews. Almost in the same breath Luke relates that thousands of Jerusalem Jews, even priests, had become Christians. So once again we should think of authorities.

When, from Chapter 13 onward, Luke describes the missionary journeys of Paul through Asia Minor, Macedonia, and Greece, he not rarely uses the term 'the Jews'. In many towns of Asia Minor Paul began by being successful, but then 'the Jews' reacted, and the apostle and his company were expelled, sometimes under threat to their lives. In Corinth, where Paul stayed for one and a half year (A.D. 51/52), he was even brought before the Roman proconsul who, however, washed his hands of such theological disputes [66].

In A.D. 56, when Paul had come to Jerusalem, 'the Jews' from Asia, viz. from towns where he had founded Christian communities, who saw him in the Temple, started an uproar against him; he had to be saved by a Roman patrol. Since a Jewish plot to kill him was discovered, he was transported to Caesarea; when he appealed to the Emperor, he was sent to Rome. There he lived in some sort of gilded custody where he had the opportunity to discuss with Jewish leaders. He had no success with them. Paul gave up the Jews as hopeless and turned to the Gentiles [67].

The conversion of Jews to Christianity had begun very hopefully, but at the end of the century the stream had slowed down to a mere trickle. Perhaps in the period after the destruction of the Temple Jews felt it to be treason to their afflicted nation if they went over to another religion. Who was Jewish then remained Jewish. The disappointment about this shines through the pages of Acts and John. If, after the first promising blosoming, Luke starts to speak of 'the Jews', he is, so to speak, already pre-empting the final verdict that their conversion had become a hopeless matter.

e. The Jewish anti-Christianism of the first century A.D.

With regard to the difficult and often painful relationship of Jews and Christians, I want to be as irenic and objective as possible. This objectivity implies that what is a fact must be stated as a fact. The decades following the death of Jesus were characterized not by Christian anti-Judaism, still less by anti-Semitism, but by the anti-Christian attitude, verging on dualism, of leading Jewish circles. Their ferocious stance becomes somewhat more understandable if we realize, not only that, in the first place, many Jews defected to the new sect, but, even more, that the Jewish leaders felt the whole venerable Jewish heritage threatened and jeopardized by men like Paul [68]. It is possible to go somewhat deeper into this subject.

One of the most important Jewish prayers is the 'Shemoneh esreh' or the 'Amidah', a prayer that had to be recited daily in a standing position and facing Jerusalem; it consists of nineteen (originally eighteen) 'benedictions' [69]. Now the twelfth of these benedictions is the so-called 'Birkat ha-Minim' - more a curse than a benediction since it is spoken against the 'heretics' (minim). After the fall of Jerusalem in A.D. 70 the centre of Judaism was moved to Jamnia, the present-day Yavne, some thirteen miles south of Tel Aviv. There the Sanhedrin, the Beth Din, which was the Court of Justice, and a great rabbinic school were established. In the decade between A.D. 80 and 90 the Beth Din approved a revision of the Benedictions in which the twelfth benediction acquired a special emphasis. It now ran as follows. "For the apostates let there be no hope and let the arrogant government be speedily uprooted in our days. Let the Nazarenes (the Christians) and the minim (the heretics) be destroyed in a moment and let them be blotted out from the Book of Life and not be inscribed together with the righteous (the Jews). Blessed are thou, o Lord, who humblest the proud" [70].

This is something of momentous importance. As Kikuo Matsunaga writes : "prior to this decision, there seems to have been some uncertainty among both Jews and Christian Jews as whether the Jesus-is-the-Messiah movement should be regarded as one of the Jewish sects" [71]. It will be evident that, for Jewish Christians, it was now no longer possible to take part in a cult which condemned them openly as 'heretics' and worse. From this moment Judaism and Christianity considered themselves as different from each other [72].

f. John again

To return to the Gospel of John. First of all, we should realize that the book was written after the decision of the Beth Din. Jewry had formally and officially distanced itself from Christianity, and had even shown itself inimical to it. John reacted to this attitude by speaking of 'the Jews'. According to J. Louis Martyn [73], in three places in John there is probably an allusion to the 'Birkat ha-Minim'. 1. "They will ban you from the synagogue" (16:2); this is what happened in fact. 2. "Even among those in authority many believed in him, but would not acknowledge him on account of the Pharisees, for fear of being banned from the synagogue" (12:42). 3. "The Jewish authorities had already argued that anyone who acknowledged Jesus as the Messiah should be banned from the synagogue" (9:22). It is indeed, as Matsunaga says, hard to accept that during the lifetime of Jesus himself those who believed him to be the Messiah were actually banned from the synagogue; we know that Jesus for a long time was extremely reticent in calling himself so.

What John states in these three passages reflects the situation of about A.D. 100, when the Jewish Christians were banned indeed from the synagogues. They can also shed some light on what John had in mind when he spoke of 'the Jews'. This term too may mirror the situation of the turn of the century. Taking account of the fact that 9:22 speaks of 'Jewish authorities', we are allowed to guess that John will have thought first and foremost of the leading Jewish circles who were inimical to Jesus and his followers. "'The Jews', just as 'the Pharisees', are for John no longer an empirical group that one could relate quantatively to each other, but stylized types : the Pharisees are the official, the Jews the ideal representants of a Judaism that, basing itself on the Law, rejects Jesus" [74]. With the virtual disappearance of all other groups and tendencies, only the Pharisees remain as discussion partners of Jesus, and they are identical with 'the Jews' [75].

11. Where Jews and Christians disagreed

A final preliminary remark must be made. What exactly made Judaism and Christianity differ from each other [76]? For some time the first Christians kept moving in the ambiance of Judaism. They visited the Temple and the synagogue, they observed the Law and celebrated the Jewish feasts. Many of them must have thought that they formed a branch of Judaism; the Romans too had their problems in distinguishing Jews from Christians in the first decades. Even after the separation had become a fact, a form of Christianity, called 'Jewish Christianity', subsisted for several centuries.

Those who felt this way were the victims of an optical illusion. From the beginning both religions were different. Some Jewish authorities were less dupes of this than others. It was already in the first days and weeks after Pentecost that Peter and John got into trouble with the authorities. Cited before the Sanhedrin, they were forbidden to teach or to do anything in the name of Jesus [77]. A short time later this prohibition was repeated. But, it is stated, "they went on proclaiming that Jesus is the Messiah" [78]. Evidently the stone of stumbling was that the apostles preached Jesus as the Messiah.

a. Jesus as the Messiah

Jews and Christians disagree about the person of Jesus of Nazareth. In Christian opinion he is the promised Messiah; for Jews, however much many of them may respect him, he is not. They feel that the coming of the Messiah - which is still to be expected - will bring about the fulfilment of the promises of the prophets : peace and harmony will then reign on earth. They object that the appearance of Jesus of Nazareth did not make much difference in the general condition of mankind. And he had been crucified. This fact proved definitely that he could not possibly be the Messiah. "You (the Christians) put all your hope in one who was crucified", said Tryphon, a Jew, to Justin the Martyr, "but Scripture obliges you to expect him who is great and glorious and who, as the Son of Man, receives the eternal kingdom out of the hands of the Ancient of days (God)" [79].

According to Marcel Simon, the Christian contention that Jesus is the Messiah, was "one of the essential causes of the Jewish refusal" [80]. But although we have to do with a real and telling difference, I don't believe that this can have led to such animosity. After all, the Jews were quite used to the appearance of false Messiahs; they might have tolerated Christianity as a Messianic branch of Judaism. This was the consequence of what Rabbi Gamaliel I advised his colleagues in the Sanhedrin : "Let them! If this plan or work comes from man, it will fail. But if it comes from God, you will be unable to stop it". And he pointed to the example of two false Messiahs in the past who both were killed. His colleagues agreed with him [81]. And indeed, the historical person of Jesus does not have pride of place in Jewish anti-Christian polemics [82].

b. Jesus' divinity

What was far more important was that, according to early Christian theology, Jesus was divine, was the Son of God, was God, in theological terms, the second person of Holy Trinity. The Jews believed that a Messiah would come, but it was viscerally impossible for them to accept the idea that a human person - and the Messiah would be human - could be God. We saw that for the Sanhedrin this was a sufficient reason for condemning Jesus to death; in their eyes it was sheer blasphemy. A century later Tryphon, this intelligent defender of the Jewish viewpoint, is alleged to have said : "All of us (Jews) expect a Messiah who will be man among man ... That you Christians say that this Messiah is God, that he has pre-existed before all ages, next that he has consented to become man and be born, and that he is not man among man, seems to me not only paradoxical but plainly absurd" [83]. Marcel Simon states the essence of the controversy very precisely. "The opposition between Christianity and Judaism has as its essential cause that the Jews ... have always refused to connect and confound the two entities, the human Messiah and divine Wisdom which, in different degrees, were both familiar to them" [84].

c. Ideas of the redemption

Gershom Scholem calls our attention to another point of difference, in connection with the Messianic idea. Both in Judaism and in Christianity the Messiah is the Redeemer, but the idea of redemption is understood quite differently by Jews and Christians. It is not only that, according to Christian doctrine, the Redemption has been brought about by Jesus Messiah, whereas for Jews the Messiah, and therefore also the redemption, is still to come. No, the nature of the redemption is different in both religions. "Christianity conceives of redemption as an event in the spiritual and unseen realm, an event which is reflected in the soul, in the private world of each individual, and which effects an inner transformation which need not correspond to anything outside ... Judaism, in all its forms and manifestations, has always maintained a concept of redemption as an event which is to take place publicly, on the stage of history and within the community. It is an occurrence which takes place in the visible world and which cannot be conceived apart from such a visible appearance" [85].

d. The Christian rejection of Mosaic Law

What definitely separated Christians from Jews was that the first mentioned no longer observed Mosaic Law. At first, the converts from Judaism doubtless did so. But a problem arose when Gentiles presented themselves, a problem that assumed ever vaster dimensions in proportion to the growing numbers of pagans that entered the Church. Peter was the first to be confronted by it, when the Roman centurion Cornelius desired to be baptized. This officer was not expressly told that he need not observe the Law, but Peter realized at this occasion that the strict food taboos had lost their validity. A divine vision, however, was needed to get this pious and law-observing Jew thus far [86].

The problem got really pressing when Paul made many pagan converts in the Hellenistic cities of Asia Minor, Macedonia, and Greece. A new category of Christians came into being, the pagan Christians who, in the course of time, began to outnumber the Jewish Christians ever more. Could new Christians be forced to observe a Law with which they were totally unacquainted? The faithful observance of all those innumerable commandments and prohibitions would have turned their daily existence upside down. It would have been particularly abhorrent to the men to have themselves circumcized (circumcision was not a Greek or Hellenistic habit). Paul soon realized that this was impossible; asking this of pagans would have seriously impeded his missionary work.

There were, as will be understood, Jewish Christians, mainly converted Pharisees, who opposed this. They found it necessary that pagan Christians be circumcized and observe Mosaic Law. The apostles, however, appealing to the Holy Spirit, decided otherwise, for they absolved Gentile Christians from the observance of the Law [87]. Jewish Christians remained true to the old precepts, but since after A.D. 100 their numbers began to dwindle ever more, observance of the Law ceased among the Christians, at least among the great majority.

e. Paul the great enemy

Reading Acts proves how furious the synagogal authorities were with Paul, the traitor, the ex-Pharisee; obviously he was the Satan, the opponent of all that was Jewish. This was to be heard in Jerusalem, when the culprit paid a visit there for ritual reasons. "Israelites, come to the rescue! Here is the man who goes about everywhere, teaching everybody to despise our people and our Law, and this place (the Temple). He has brought Gentiles into the Temple, too, profaning these sacred precincts" [88]. Whereas the Talmud hardly ever mentions Jesus, it is Paul who is there the great enemy [89]. The unforgivable crime of the apostle was, of course, to have abolished the Law, to have declared it no longer valid.

12. The Jewish predicament

To understand why the Jews were so furious about this, we must comprehend their awkward situation. Everything was lost : the cult centre, the sacrifices, the High Priest, the pilgrimages to the Holy City; after A.D. 135 there was not even a Holy City or a Holy Land. Judaism had become a decapitated religion. In modern terms we could say that the whole superstructure had disappeared. Roman-Catholics should try to imagine what it would mean if Saint Peter and the Vatican were burnt down and Rome was no longer the centre of their religious community, if were there no longer a Pope and bishops, and if even the celebration of the Mass had been suspended. This is no pure phantasy : this is what would have happened - and mutatis mutandis to the Churches of the Reformation too - in case Hitler had won the war.

What remained was the infrastructure. Although sacrifices were no longer performed, the village communities and the families would go on to observe the Jewish feast days and to celebrate the special occasions : the weekly Sabbath, the annual Passover, Yom Kippur, the Feast of the Tabernacles, and so on (in my youth there were still tabernacles on the balconies in the Jewish quarter of Amsterdam). The rules for ritual purity and food cleanliness would be strictly observed. Judaism became a religion of households where the housefathers took the place of the priests. Male children were circumcized; the boys did their Bar Mitzva at the age of thirteen by which they became full members of the Jewish community. And of course, there was the weekly gathering in the synagogues.

What remained was above all Mosaic Law which now acquired a paramount importance. In this lay religion the Law is the binding and inspiring element. The miracle of the subsistence of Judaism, throughout the ages and in spite of all, is due to the strict observance of the Law, as explained by the Rabbis with the Mishnah in their hands. The Law was more than a collection of prescriptions and prohibitions. This it was too, but it was also, and most of all, a link between heaven and earth, between mankind and its Creator, between man and his fellow-men; it was what made the nation into a truly religious community [90]. One who realizes this does not find it hard to observe the innumerable stipulations of the law, for instance that no fire should be made on the Sabbath, so that strict families need a non-Jew, a 'shebbes-goy', to switch on the lamps for them (some of my friends were 'shebbes-goys').

The most powerful expression of this significance of the Law we find in Psalm 119 that sings the blessings of the Law. It is an alphabetical psalm and not without reason, with its hundred and seventy-nine verses, by far the longest in the Psalterium. "Blessed are they, who cherish his (God's) decrees, make him the whole quest of their hearts. Buried deep in my heart your warnings will keep me clear of sin. I claim no other heritage, o Lord, but to obey your word; life-giving are your commands, never by me forgotten. More wisdom I have than all my teachers, so well have I pondered your decrees. There is no lamp like your word to guide my feet; other defence, other shield I shall have none. In your law I trust; revelation and light your words disclose to the simple. Unnumbered, Lord, are your blessings. Under all the assaults of my oppressors I keep true to your charge. Very great peace is theirs who love your law; their feet never stumble. Vigilantly I observe your precept and bidding, living always a sin your sight." Only a few quotations out of the many, chosen at random, but they demonstrate what I mean, or rather what the Jews found in the Law. It is now not hard to understand how strange and wrong they found it of Christians to set the Law aside.

13. An ethnic nation

There is yet another distinction between Jews and Christians, and again one that did not make cohabitation easier. Christians belong to all possible nations and languages; the term 'people of God' can only be used in the spiritual sense of the word. But the Jews were members of an 'ethnos', even in the Diaspora; they differed from others by their ethnic specificity. The Romans treated Jewry as an ethnos with special privileges, whereas the Christians were not a specific nation in their eyes. This has always conferred on Jews a strong sense of belonging together; this even pertains to the many secularized Jews of our own days who do not observe the Law and who are no longer believers. But the Nazis were not interested in the question whether or not a Jew practised his or her faith or was a believer; to them they were all in the same boat.

How even a non-believing, non-observing Jew can experience his fundamental ethnic identity was expressed by the Polish author Adam Michnik. In April 1991 he addressed an audience at the Central Synagogue in New York, on the occasion of his receiving the so-called Shofar Award. He expressed some surprise at this because of his unbelief and non-observance; he does not, he said, feel part of the Jewish religious community. First and foremost, he considers himself a Pole. He does not deny his Jewishness but there is a negative ring to it. "As a Pole, so far as anti-Semites were concerned, I always wanted to be a Jew." But further on he repeated : "I am a Pole".

This reiterated statement forced him 'to explain why he accepted an award created for Jews'. For he is not a member of a synagogue nor does he think of himself as a member of the Jewish nation (his grandparents did but he did not). "I am not speaking of solidarity with Jewish religion, with Jewish history, or with Jewish traditions or customs, or with the Jewish nation, or with the state of Israel. With what then?" Yes, with what then? For Michnik cancelled out every connection with Jewishness that is real and organic, from his grandparents to the state of Israel, thus making things extremely difficult for himself.

But he finds a way out of this quandary by declaring his solidarity with the Jewish fate. "The Jewish fate is the fate of a threatened people." This fate is not identical with Jewish history, because the speaker denies having a connection with it. "The Jewish fate is a certain condition", he stated. "If that condition (viz. the Jewish fate) is not understood, contemporary civilization, contemporary spiritual life, contemporary ethics would be the poorer in something essential" [91]. Dispiritingly vague as this is, it makes clear that a Jew like Michnik in one way or other wishes to remain Jewish. Can one imagine an ex-Roman-Catholic speaking of the 'Catholic fate' or the 'Catholic condition' which, whatever this might mean, would remain his home?

Far more profound than this hesitating statement and deeply moving is what the German author Lion Feuchtwanger, who is Jewish, wrote in his novel 'Jud Süss' (1925). The main character of this book is a Jew, Süss Oppenheimer, who had a great career in the service of the Duchy of Württemberg; although he has no official function, he controls all the financial and political affairs of the country. At the same time he becomes immensely rich. But although he is Jewish and although he knows this and does not hide it, he is neither a believer nor an observer of the Law; in no way he lives up to Psalm 119. Quite the contrary! His morals are loose.

Süss the Jew is an historical person [92]; the framework of the novel is authentic. But at a certain point the author inserts a fictitious, non-historical element. Süss discovers that he is the illegitimate son of his mother and a 'goy', who is nobody less than the German field-marshal Heydersdorf. This goes a long way to explain his aristocratic bearing and his taste for luxury. However, he keeps this secret to himself. Is this because he is ashamed of being illegitimate? Not at all! It is because he wants to remain united with the Jewish nation. This becomes apparent when his protector, Duke Karl Alexander (an anti-Semite!) suddenly dies. Then the enemies of Süss contrive to bring him down. He is arrested and condemned to death on the charges of treason, embezzlement of state funds, mismanagement, and what not.

He might, however, have had a far lighter judgment, or perhaps, like his accomplices, have been acquitted, if he had not been a Jew. But even in this predicament he does not make use of his secret; he does not disclose to his judges that he has a Christian father. Even in this moment of great danger to his life, he, the non-believer, remains one with his nation. He is executed by strangling on the main square of Stuttgart, the capital of the Duchy. A large crowd is present, vilifying the Jew. But there are also ten Jews, representing, by the number ten, the totality of the nation. They pray, loudly, the prayers for the dying. "One and eternal is He who is, the more than real, the God of Israel ... Shema, Yisrael, hear, o Israel, one and eternal is Jahve Adonai." And just before his throat is squeezed, the son of the Christian field-marshal tunes in, crying loudly as a Jew : "One and eternal is Jahve Adonai".

14. A sore spot : the question of proselytism

A sore spot in the question of Jewish-Christian relations is often said to be that, in the first centuries of our era, Jews and Christians were after the same prospective converts, the Jews by proselytizing, the Christians by missionary work. This is thought to have caused much asperity between the two religions. The question is whether or not the Christians were not only poaching in the missionary fields of the Jews, but, in the last resort, poaching with more success.

a. What is a proselyte?

The word 'proselyte' comes from the Greek 'prosêlutos' which, in its turn, is derived from the verb 'proserchomai' = to come over. It is the rendering used in the Septuagint for the Hebrew 'ger' = somebody who changes his religion for another one. In Jewish parlance it has come to mean a pagan who converted to Judaism. Male proselytes were circumcized and thus "entered into the assembly of Jacob" [93]. Although having a heathen background, they were considered in every respect Jewish. They adopted the Jewish customs, kept the Sabbath, celebrated the Jewish feasts, and, above all, observed the Law. Proselytes were subjected to certain restrictions : they could not be appointed as public officials or be judges in criminal courts, while female proselytes were not allowed to marry a priest.

b. The 'God-fearers'

Speaking of proselytes, we should not forget the so-called 'God-fearers'. Not a few people in the ancient world felt attracted to Judaism without, however, wishing to become full Jews as proselytes. Being disgusted with the large pagan pantheon, they adhered to the Jewish dogma of the one and only God. They attended the services in the synagogue and kept the Sabbath. But males did not have themselves cricumcized since this would mean that they and their families would be obliged to observe the Law in every detail. This they found too hard, especially with regard to the laws of purity and the food taboos [94].

c. Modern views of Jewish proselytism

The tone of modern scholarship was set by Harnack in 1902 in his book on the mission and expansion of Christianity. In his opinion Christianity was the superior religion, with a natural right to supersede and replace all other religions [95]. Harnack's idea was that, whereas Christianity was youthful and energetic, Judaism, on the contrary, had lost its vitality and did not make many converts; it had to leave the field to the Christians. "Since the fall of Jerusalem there was ... hardly any Jewish counter-mission; the Christians ensconced themselves in the strongholds of Jewish propaganda and of the Jewish proselytes : Japhet moved into the huts of Sem and Sem had to cede place" [96]. Harnack's view would imply that there was no Jewish-Christian conflict over converts, for after the first decades Judaism had obviously ceased to be of consequence for the Christian Church. This concept of the great German historian of religions was dictated, not by historical objectivity but by a theological parti pris, that of the natural superiority of Christianity. It was the Jewish historian Marcel Simon who developed the 'conflict theory' as a correction to Harnack's way of seeing things [97]. According to him, Judaism displayed a remarkable vitality during the first centuries of our era, when many converts were made. This, writes Miriam Taylor, "afforded him a ready-made explanation for the Church's expressed opposition to the Jews during the course of the early Christian mission to the gentile world". The 'conflict theory' - of two opposed religions competing for the same missionary fields - could also account "for the vehemence and the persistence of anti-Jewish arguments in the writings of the church fathers ... The conflict-theorists aim to present us with a well-rounded, global explanation for early Christian anti-Judaism" [98].

The idea of strong Jewish vitality, resulting in successful proselytizing, has come to stay [99]. "Proselytism ... must have been a tremendous force in Jewish life ... Uninterrupted religious propaganda seems to have gone on throughout the dispersion (the Diaspora)" [100]. The most recent description of Jewish successes is an essay by Louis Feldman of 1992 [101]. Such theories about a supposed religious rivalry between the Church and the Synagogue are dubbed by Miriam Taylor 'competitive anti-Judaism' [102].

d. Proselytes and proselytism

I think that we should first of all carefully distinguish between proselytes and proselytism, that is, between the existence of converts to Judaism and an active drive by Jews in order to win such converts. There can be no doubt that there were proselytes. At the first Pentecost after Jesus' death there were many of them in Jerusalem coming from all possible countries [103]. Pagans of all classes felt attracted to Judaism, more women than men, among them persons of high social rank, even royalty. Even the Herodians may be seen as proselytes, since as Edomites (Idumaeans) they were not of ethnic Jewish stock. A nephew of Vespasian, Flavius Clemens, embraced the Jewish religion [104].

When it comes to active proselytizing, there is first of all the fact that some Rabbis were opposed to it. "Rabbi Eliezer is credited with the opinion that the nature of proselytes is corrupt and that hence they are apt to become backsliders" [105]. He was not the only one to distrust the newcomers. There were bitter experiences behind this distrust. In difficult days proselytes frequently became backsliders. They "and their offspring became renegades, often slandering their new religion and denouncing their new religion and its leaders to foreign rulers" [106]. Simon admits that the Talmud does not offer 'any uniformity of attitude toward proselytism, or any consistent teaching concerning it' [107]; he even goes so far as to state that we cannot conclude from the rabbinic writings that "real missionary activity did go on" [108]. This does not assert, of course, that there was no such activity at all, but only that proselytism obviously was not a rabbinic priority [109].

e. The lack of evidence

It is extremely difficult to find evidence corroborating the view that Jewish missionaries were active in the Empire. Much is made of a saying of Jesus that the Pharisees "compass sea and land to make one proselyte" [110]. This should be seen in its context which forms part of the fierce polemic against the Pharisees; as such it is a rhetorical exaggeration. We possess not the slightest evidence that Pharisees really travelled around in order to make converts. Simon, the main spokesman for the conflict theory, admits that pagan and Christian sources have very little to tell about Jewish proselytizing. He tries to explain this by stating that ancient authors were so deeply impressed by the efficacious and highly successful missionary activities of the Christians that they simply overlooked what the Jews were doing [111].

The fact that there were indeed converts has led Simon and others to the conclusion that they had been converted by missionaries. But no ancient author says as much. Gentiles will have felt attracted to Judaism because they knew Jews and came to admire their way of life and the seriousness of their religious convictions. "It is the failure of scholars to make this distinction between positive acceptance and active pursuit that is, in part, responsible for all the confusion in this field of study" [112]. The conclusion must be that, if there was friction between Judaism and the Church, it was not caused by competing for the same people.

f. Was the great number of Diaspora Jews the result of proselytism?

People felt attracted to Judaism because it "became one of the substitutes adopted in place of the empty state cult which failed to fill spiritual and emotional needs, and some encouragement may be taken for granted" [113] ... But in all probability "comparatively few of those who turned to Judaism became full proselytes, accepting circumcision or in the case of women a ritual bath, and the full rigour of the Law. The majority became what may be called ... 'Judaizers' (or 'God-fearers - F.); these were loose adherents of Judaism, ... shrinking from the decisive commitment of stamping themselves as Jews" [114]. "The national (that is 'ethnic' - F.) basis of Judaism precluded large-scale missionary activity" [115].

This may leave us with the question where, if there was no active proselytism to speak of, did the great number of Diaspora Jews come from. Jewish communities in the Diaspora grew because Jews love to have large families; they saw children as a visible sign of Gods's blessing - this in sharp contrast to the pagan population where couples were not very eager to have a quiver full of children. Emigration from Judaea was a source on which Diaspora Jewry drew. This was already the case long before the Romans became the masters of Palestine. We know that after the Exile, which was a form of compulsory emigration, a great many Jews stayed in Mesopotamia. In the same period Jewish emigration to Egypt and Cyrenaica began.

This sort of emigration had a political background, as when in later centuries Jews began to emigrate because they were displeased with Ptolemaic and Seleucid rule. Economic reasons too played their role : Smallwood suggests over-population, land shortage, and promising commercial prospects in other regions [116]. In the wake of the two Jewish revolts many others left the Holy Land.

g. The question of Jewish vitality

The hub of the discussion on Jewish proselytism in the first centuries of the present era has been the question whether or not Judaism had lost its vitality after the catastrophes that hit it. This is what Harnack implied when he wrote that not many converts were made after these events. The reaction was predictable. Under the vigorous leadership of Marcel Simon a plethora of scholars, Jewish and non-Jewish, argued that Judaism had retained all its vitality, and the evidence of this was the great inflow of proselytes. Some of the few dissenting voices are those of Miriam Taylor and Mary Smallwood, whom I have quoted. Having pondered on the question as a historian, I think both are right. There is almost no support in the sources for the thesis that there was active proselytizing.

In my opinion one is on the wrong tack when the question of Jewish vitality is put at the centre of the debate or, in other words, if the question whether or not Judaism remained vital, is to be decided on the ground of the number of converts. "The strength and 'vitality' the conflict theorists attribute to Judaism, and this is so central to their main assumption about the conflict between the two groups", writes Taylor, "ultimately proves to be a pseudo-vitality which ... contains within it the seeds of Jewish defeat and hidden presumptions about Jewish inferiority vis-à-vis the Church" [117]. For even on this theory Judaism lost out to the Church, when converts were no longer made. The only difference with Harnack is that in the conflict theory the loss of vitality occurs later.

However, when we look at the question from a different angle, we come to a different conclusion. To go on quoting Taylor, "Judaism was no less vital for its lack of an organized missionary drive ... If the Jews had different goals and aspirations from the Christians, then it can be no longer assumed that they were the Church's main competitor for converts" [118]. Such different goals and aspirations Judaism doubtless had. I must refer the reader to what I wrote earlier in this chapter. After the catastrophes Judaism showed a remarkable, even miraculous resilience, a new 'vitality', if one wants to employ this word. It reorganized itself on a new spiritual basis by becoming a lay religion, bound together by and receiving its vital strength from the observance of the Law. This enabled Judaism to survive throughout the ages.

15. Christian anti-Judaism compared with that of pagans and Gnostics

Studying the utterances of the Christian authors of these centuries, mainly the Fathers of the Church, we shall be confronted with a sizeable quantity of unfriendly, disagreeable, and even nasty remarks about Judaism. This may lead to the conclusion that the early Church was basically anti-Judaistic - not rarely the term 'anti-Semitic' is used in this context. I am not going to excuse what was said, but we should see it in perspective.

a. Pagan anti-Judaism

There was quite a lot of anti-Judaism, or anti-Semitism, in the pagan world. The evidence presented in Chapter V of Volume X gives ample proof of this. Many ancient authors, Greeks as well as Romans, saw fit to express themselves in denigrating and insulting terms on the Jews and their religion. And when we speak of Christian assaults on synagogues in the fourth century and later, shouldn't we also think of the wilful destruction of the great Jewish cult centre in Jerusalem by Titus?

b. Gnostic anti-Jewish polemics

Since the Gnosis hits on the blind spot of almost all scholars, of whatever discipline, it is overlooked how ferociously, how rabidly anti-Judaistic the Gnostics were. What they had to say of the Jewish religion was far, far worse than whatever emanated from one or another Church Father. Rosemary Ruether is almost the only one to pay attention to this. She spoke of 'the diabolizing of the Jewish God in Jewish Gnosticism' [119]. There is, of course, no parallel section on 'the diabolizing of the Jewish God' in the Fathers : for them there was no specific Jewish God; the God of the Jews was their own divinity. As I wrote in Volume VII, "from the onset, the Gnosis was diametrically opposed to both Judaism and Christianity" [120].

Simon the Magician, who is often seen as the first Gnostic, was sharply opposed to Judaism. He accused Moses of 'agnoia', of ignorance, since he did not know the creator of this world - by which Simon meant that, in his eyes, Jahve was responsible for the deplorable state of cosmos and mankind [121]. In the ideology of his second successor Saturnilos Jahve is one of the bad angels, an evil godhead, whereas the 'heavenly Father' (quite different from Jahve) is a benevolent one. "There is a strong vein of anti-Judaism in this system" [122].

There is equally "a distinctly anti-Jewish bias in the Pseudo-Clementina. Judaism must be swept aside to make place for a new and superior religion (= the Gnosis)". Mosaic Law is full of lies inserted as it was into the Old Testament by the Evil One (= the devil) [123]. A still more fierce attack on Judaism and the Bible was made in the Sethian ideology [124]. The patriarchs are 'counterfeit fathers', the prophets are only sham prophets, great biblical figures like David and Solomon are mere 'laughing-stocks'. By way of contrast the Sodomites are glorified.

For the Archontics there are two godheads, the Supreme Father and 'Sabaoth', the god of the Jews and the law-giver; his son is the Devil [125]. About the Ophites I wrote that, if "Ophitism had a strong Jewish background, then its adherents took care to distance themselves as far as possible from their origin" [126]. According to them, the Jewish God is to be identified with 'Jaldabaoth', an inferior divinity, the creator of an evil world. In the Barbelo-Gnosis the Demiurge is called 'Jaltabaoth', the origin of all that is wrong in the world; he too is the Jewish God [127].

The picture does not differ in the important Gnostic sects of the Basilidians and the Valentinians. In Basilidian ideology we find one of the oldest accusations against the Jews : their God (who is an evil and ambitious being) strives to subject all other nations to the Jews. We "detect here, for the first time in history, the idea of a Jewish conspiracy to rule the world" [128].

The apex of anti-Judaism is reached in the doctrine of Marcion. His attitude towards the Jewish people was entirely negative; "he could not imagine a worse lot. For it was they who had acknowledged and proclaimed the Demiurge (= the Jewish God) ... His rejection of the Jewish religion was total and dualistic in nature" [129]. He not only repudiated the whole of the Old Testament, but he also wanted a New Testament that was entirely free of Jewish influence. In the Marcionite Church all links with the Old Testament and Judaism were severed [130]. At the end of Volume VIII I concluded that the real hotbed of anti-Semitism and anti-Judaism in the first centuries was not Christianity but the Gnosis [131].

PART II CHRISTIAN AUTHORS ON JEWS AND JUDAISM

1. The Christian authors of the first hundred years

a. The Letters of Clement

Let us now turn to the earliest Christian authors. Probably the oldest non-biblical text we have is the First Letter to the Corinthians by a certain Clement; we need not go into the question who this Clemens Romanus was, a bishop of Rome or somebody else. The Letter can be dated in the period between A.D. 75 and 110 [132]; it is the Church of Rome here that addresses the Church of Corinth. In it the Jews are non-existent, that is to say, as an target for polemics. But in other respects no writing could be more Jewish; the text is almost entirely based on the Old Testament which is used in the most positive way.

It is exactly the same in the Second Letter of Clement to the Corinthians. Not a word about Jews. The date and the author are matters of conjecture; it may have been written about 150.

b. Ignatius of Antioch

We are better informed about another early Christian author, Ignatius, who was bishop of Antioch in Syria around A.D. 100. He ended his long life as a martyr in a Roman arena, in A.D. 108 according to Eusebius [133]. There exist six letters under his name addressed to as many Christian communities in Asia Minor, and one to Polycarp, the bishop of Smyrna. In two of these letters, those to the Christians of Magnesia and Philadelphia, Judaism is mentioned [134].

In the Church of Magnesia there was obviously discord; Ignatius exhorts the faithful to be obedient to Damas, their bishop [135]. There were dissenters in this Church, people who held their bishop in disregard and who did not come to the communal services but were holding meetings of their own [136]; they even seemed to have their own Eucharist [137]. To express this in formal terms : they were schismatics. Ignatius warns the Magnesian Christians not to fall 'into the snare of false doctrine'. He goes on to explain what this false doctrine is : not be convinced of 'the birth and passion and resurrection of Jesus Christ which took place in the time of the procuratorship of Pontius Pilate' [138]. These words make it clear that Ignatius is speaking here of Docetists, people who held that Jesus was a divine person but had only had a human body in appearance, not a real, a physical one.

It is possible, and even probable, that Ignatius feared that a body of Magnesian Christians was reverting to Judaism, or were taking an intermediary position between this and Christianity [139]. A few chapters further on he warns the Magnesians that "if we are living now according to Judaism, we confess that we have not received grace" [140]. "It is wholly wrong", he writes, using the word 'atopos' = out of place, misplaced, "to talk of Jesus Christ and to practice Judaism" [141], for instance, by preferring the Sabbath to the Lord's Day [142]. Judaism he calls 'the old leaven which has grown old and sour' [143].

In his anxiety that he will lose his newly won believers to Judaism, he uses a curious argument that is at variance with Paul's opinion that Christians are grafted onto the tree of Judaism [144]. "Christianity", says Ignatius, "did not base its faith on Judaism, but Judaism on Christianity" [145]. He explains this by stating that "the divine (Jewish) prophets lived according to Jesus Christ", for, inspired by God's grace, they were convinced that "there is one God who manifested himself through Jesus Christ his son, who is his word" [146]. Tortuous as this argument is, it proves that to this early Father of the Church the lure of Judaism seemed a real threat.

We detect the same fear in his Letter to the Christians of Philadelphia, also a town in Asia Minor. Here he does not attack Judaism as such but, instead, its propagandists, whom he calls 'tombstones and sepulchres of the dead". The curious thing, however, is that these judaizing persons are not Jews but Christians, who obviously were presenting their own version of Christianity. Ignatius, combating them, even adds that "it is better to hear Christianity from the circumcized" by whom he means converted Jews [147]. In this context he expresses his respect for the Jewish religion; he says that its priests are noble. But the High Priest, by whom he means Jesus Christ, is greater, because "only to him the secret things of God are entrusted". He mentions the patriarchs, the prophets, the apostles, and the Church in one breath [148]. I feel that Ignatius is not so much polemizing against the Jewish religion proper, which he holds in honour, but against judaizing tendencies among Christians.

It seems that this danger of judaizing did not exist among the communities of Ephesus, Tralles, and Smyrna, and also not in Rome, for writing to these Christians, Ignatius nowhere mentions Judaism or Judaizers; instead, he warns against heretics, especially against Docetists. It is the same in his Letter to Polycarp, the bishop of Smyrna.

c. The Didache

In the second half of the nineteenth century a remarkable document was discovered, called the 'Didache, or the Teaching of the Twelve Apostles'. Its author is unknown; probably it is a compilation of catechetical texts of the first and second centuries. Kirsopp Lake dubs it 'a manual of Church instruction' [149]. Must we not expect in such a manual a stern warning against Judaism and Judaizers? But these are nowhere mentioned in the text.

d. The Epistle of Barnabas

In the earliest discussions between Judaism and Christianity the Epistle of Barnabas occupies a place of its own. Barnabas is known as a companion of Paul, but it is not very probable that he would be the author; the real author remains anonymous and its date uncertain, perhaps the end of the first or the beginning of the second century. As Kirsopp Lake writes, "its main object is to warn Christians against a Judaistic conception of the Old Testament" (which Christian community it has in mind is unknown) [150].

What the author is explaining at some length - it is a treatise rather than a letter - is that the Jewish and Christian religions, although having much in common, are not the same; Christianity is not a variant of Judaism. In doing so, he is doubtless polemizing but succeeds in avoiding hard terms. Simon sees in this letter the beginning of anti-Jewish polemics. Recruitment from Judaism had almost stopped by then; converts were coming nearly exclusively from paganism. On the personal level the Church was already 'pagan'. Now "the scission between the two religions was becoming a fact on the doctrinal plane" too. Faced with the ancient and venerable Jewish religion, the still tender Christian one felt the urgent necessity to delineate with great precision where the dividing line ran, the more so because Christianity had so much in common with Judaism [151].

Quoting the Jewish prophets who spoke out against sacrifices, 'Barnabas' states that they have been abolished now "in order that the new law of our Lord Jesus Christ ... might have its oblation not made by man" [152]. The Covenant which once was Jewish has now become Christian; they (the Jews) lost it because they turned to idols [153]. Thus the Christians have succeeded to the Jews as the covenantal people. But when Barnabas comes to speak of the reason for the death of Jesus on the cross, he imputes this not only to the sins of the Jews but equally to those of the Christians [154]. He nowhere says that the Jews were exclusively guilty of Jesus' crucifixion.

Certainly the Letter does not reject the Old Testament out of hand, as Marcion did, but explains it in a spiritual way; the Jews err when they take its pronouncements literally. Circumcision, for instance, had not apply to the flesh but should be of the heart (the prophets are quoted to this effect) [155]. And of the food laws "Moses spoke in the spirit" [156].

At the end the author states that "there are two ways of teaching and power, one of Light and one of Darkness. And there is a great difference between the two ways". The first is the way of God, the second that of Satan [157]. There is, however, not the slightest suggestion that the way of the 'Black One' was that of the Jewish religion. It is the way of the vices that are common to mankind : pride, lust, magic, speaking evil, and what not [158].

Throughout this long treatise its author is revindicating the Old Testament for the Church. We should not only see an anti-Jewish move in this, perhaps not even in the first place. The early Church was not only stating its fundamental position vis-à-vis Judaism, it did the same regarding the Gnosis. As we saw, Marcion rejected the Old Testament in its entirety; the Church, on the contrary, salvaged it for Christian orthodoxy. "Opposite the heretics who dissociated and opposed, as two irreducible values, biblical revelation and the message of Christ, the Church affirms their continuity and their fundamental identity. At the moment that, in practice, the events are achieving to turn the two religions against each other, the Church, with ever greater precision, recognizes itself as being tributary to the Synagogue" [159]. It is for this reason that the Letter of Barnabas reads as an exegesis of the Old Testament rather than as an exposition of Christian doctrine. According to A.L. Williams, its object was not so much to combat Judaism but rather 'to rebut the objections brought by Jews against Christianity' [160].

e. The Pastor of Hermas and the Martyrdom of Polycarp

There exists a long treatise known as the 'Pastor', or 'Poimên' (it is in Greek), the Shepherd. It is ascribed to a certain Hermas and probably dates from the first half of the second century A.D. For our purpose we may pass it over in silence; the author is obviously not interested in Jews and Judaism and nowhere mentions them. The same applies to the story of 'The Martyrdom of Polycarp' the most probable date of whose death is February 23, 155.

f. The Letter to Diognetus

The last work to be studied in this section is the anonymous 'Letter to Diognetus', an apologetic treatise of uncertain date. It is not improbable that it should be dated later than the middle of the second century. With regard to Judaism it assumes a tone that differs from that of the previous treatises. This Diognetus is obviously a convert who is being instructed in the Christian creed. The author acknowledges that the Jews venerate the one true God, but for the rest there is not much good in their religion. Their customs - Sabbath, circumcision, food laws - do not show reverence for God but foolishness. He sums it up by stating that it is all 'silliness and deceit and fussiness and pride' [161].

g. Conclusion

Regarding the Jewish-Christian relationship, the harvest of texts in the first century of the Church is rather meagre. We have now perused fifteen treatises of which only four occupy themselves with Judaism. With the exception of the Letter to Diognetus (that probably belongs to a later period), the tone is not harsh. The aim of Ignatius and Barnabas is clearly to prevent Christians from judaizing or even from reverting to Judaism. It is remarkable that an important catechetical work like the Didache does not have a word to spend on this subject. We may safely conclude that for the early Fathers the relation of Church and Synagogue did not present a great problem.

2. Christian authors of the late second century

a. Justin the Martyr

Justin the Martyr was born in a pagan family at Flavia Neapolis (the present-day Nablus) in Samaria. He was educated as a philosopher but remained dissatisfied with the several philosophical schools. For a time he adhered to Plato's doctrine, in all probability in the form of Middle Platonism. In his autobiography he relates how he encountered an old man - a Jew? a Christian? - who directed him to the Jewish prophets. He then became a Christian. Wandering about as a peripatetic teacher, he everywhere propagated the faith. Later he went to Rome where he founded a philosophical school. He met his end as a Christian, for he was condemned by the city prefect Rusticus and executed in A.D. 165, which earned him the nickname of 'the Martyr'.

Justin the Martyr wrote two Apologies for the Christian faith [162]. In the second half of the First Apology he speaks of the Jewish prophets; we should not forget that it was through them that he became a convert to Christianity. What he wants to show is that their prophecies refer to Jesus Christ. He reproaches the Jews of his day that they do not understand this sense. They view the Christians as their enemies; during the Bar Kokhba revolt they have persecuted them [163] - an accusation that is not without foundation. They hate the Christians because these hold that the Messiah has already appeared [164]. The catastrophes which have hit the Jewish people were also foretold by the prophets [165].

The short Second Apology does not mention Judaism at all. Taken together, both works are polemizing against pagans rather than against Jews. However, Justin took his chance to discuss Judaism in his Dialogue with Trypho, a far longer work [166]. It is by no means improbable that a discussion of this kind really took place, although the author will have given his own version. Trypho is presented to the reader as a circumcized Jew who has fled his country because of the Bar Kokhba revolt. According to Eusebius, he was one of the most respected Jews of his time [167]. Perhaps he is modelled on the historical Rabbi Tarphon whom we know from the Mishnah and who was a famous teacher of the Law. The dispute took place in Ephesus, spread over two days.

After an exchange of courtesies and a short discussion on the significance of philosophy, Trypho begins by stating that he has read the Gospels and finds them sublime; he is not ready to believe the usual anti-Christian slander. But what he does not understand is that the Christians do not live up to Mosaic Law - no Sabbath, no circumcision -, and, instead, put their hope in an crucified man. "You claim to be pious and believe yourselves to be different from others but do not segregate yourselves from them nor do you observe a manner of life different from the Gentiles" [168].

Justin retorts, drawing on the Old Testament. He accuses the Jews of having executed Jesus and of their failure to show any signs of repentance; "after the crucifixion they sent out from Jerusalem emissaries through all the land (Palestine must be meant - F.) to tell everybody that Christianity is a godless heresy" [169]. In almost the same breath he accuses the Jews of having attacked the Christians, in the first decades, as often as they could. This, however, is no longer the case in Justin's days, "thanks to the power of those who rule us". He also refers here to the Birkat ha-Minim [170].

This is an important passage, since it proves that, contrary to common opinion, the real issue was not only that second-century Christians were hostile to the Jews but also that the memory of the Jewish aggression in the first century still lingered on so that the Christians thought that the Jews were inimical to them. In this context it is appropriate to quote a famous quip by Tertullian who around A.D. 200 wrote that "the synagogues of the Jews were the springs of the persecution" [171]. He was referring to the early days of the Church when, as he added, the apostles had been scourged by the Jews, but by the same token his words make it clear that fear of the Jews had not wholly disappeared yet [172].

The line persistently taken by Justin is not that the Jewish religion is wholly wrong. By no means! He accuses the Jews of not having observed their own Law and quotes the Old Testament prophets to this effect [173]. The Jewish and Christian creeds have the same origin : belief in the God who led the Jewish people out of Egypt [174]. He counters the Jewish tenet that Mosaic Law had lost nothing of its validity by averring that it had been transitory, its aim having been to make the Jews conscious of God. The Jews could have known from their own prophets that what they foretold referred to Jesus Christ, "but you, when you read them, do not understand their sense" [175]. Hence the Old Covenant has been superseded by a new Covenant, better than all others. The old Law was given for one people only, but the new one is destined for all mankind; all those who aspire to the heritage of God must stick to it [176].

It is in this context - and as far as I know this is the first time - that Justin employs the term 'the true Israel', 'verus Israel'. "The true, spiritual Israel and the descendants of Judah, Jacob, Israel, and Abraham - Abraham who, although he was not circumcized, became the father of many nations -, those descendants are we" [177]. It is perfectly understandable that making the Christian Church the 'true Israel' irritates the Jews, but it should not be lost sight of that Justin establishes an intimate, an organic connection between the people and the faith of the Old Testament and the Christian Church.

Perhaps the modern reader will feel that Justin expressed himself in a way hostile to Judaism so that he and his Jewish interlocutor must necessarily have fallen out with another. However, at the end of their talks the two men part in the most friendly manner. Trypho states that the conversation had pleased him immensely, and that he had profited by it. And Justin declared that he would love having such a discussion every day [178]. Williams delivered the following judgment on this conversation. "The discussion was conducted in a seemly way ... Justin, no doubt, was the most learned of the two in Jewish matters, but Trypho was perhaps the more polished man of the world. Both were earnest and sincere, and neither shows any sign of desiring a merely verbal victory" [179]. And in fact, why should they have been angry with each other? They expressed their opinions civilly and never insulted one another or vilified their reciprocal tenets. Both must have felt an intellectual satisfaction in having an intelligent, well-informed, and courteous discussion partner.

This dialogue may well picture the situation of the middle of the second century. The Christians were no longer harassed by the Jews but had not yet wholly overcome their visceral fear of Jewish agitation. Some sort of peaceful cohabitation proved possible, at least on the theological and intellectual level. We also see that the parties did not fully understand each other. For both, it boiled down to the same thing : how is it possible to misinterpret the Old Testament in this way? What is evident is that their mutual positions were frozen. It is as though the two gentlemen concluded a kind of armistice on the basis of the status quo. But would this armistice hold firm?

b. Melito's paschal homily

We hear a different, a harsher tone in a sermon delivered by bishop Melito of Sardes between 160 and 170. This sermon is a paschal homily, the very first we possess [180]. It makes displeasing reading, for this homily "contains the most prolonged, vitriolic, even violent, attack on Israel known in pre-Constantine writings" [181]. Its successor would be the anti-Judaistic sermons by John Chrysostomus in the fourth century. The leading theme of the sermon is that Jesus Christ is prefigured throughout the whole of the Old Testament. Melito's typological interpretation leads him to the view that Jesus was "murdered in Abel, bound in Isaac, banished in Jacob, sold in Joseph, exposed in Moses, slaughtered in the (paschal) lamb, persecuted in David, despised in the prophets" [182]. Jesus is, so to speak, personally and persistently present everywhere in the Old Testament. This is, of course, no rejection of the Old Testament; it is, on the contrary, of the highest importance for Melito. It is even so that he derives the word 'pascha' from 'paschein' = to suffer [183].

The attack on the Jews occupies the last quarter of the text. It is not an incrimination of the religion of Israel but of the alleged sins of this nation. If the preacher had the Jews of his own day in mind, he does not say so. He reproaches Israel for the 'strange crime' it had committed, this crime being the repudiation and crucifixion of Jesus Christ. "You denied him that acknowledged you; you disclaimed him that proclaimed you; you killed him that made you live [184] ... O criminal Israel, why did you commit that unheard of injustice of plunging our Lord into unnamable sufferings [185] ... O ungrateful Israel, come, be judged before me for your ingratitude" [186]. And much more in this vein.

Even the heathen have treated Jesus better, for "the Gentiles prostrate themselves before him, and the uncircumcized admire him, and those of another nation glorify him" [187]. At this point disappointment over the obstinacy of the Jews is evident enough. "You have destroyed your Lord, but then you were thrown down yourself. You are lying dead but he rose from the dead" [188].

The question now is what made Melito so vehement. One supposition is that the eloquent bishop was a so-called 'Quartodeciman', one who celebrated the Passover on 14 Nisan, the classical date in the Jewish calendar, a day that not necessarily was a Sunday. The Church, wanting to celebrate Easter always on the Lord's Day, was opposed to this custom. It is possible that Melito feared that he was laying himself open to the reproach that he was too close to Judaism, and for this reason emphasized that he had no sympathy for Judaism at all.

It has also been suggested that the bishop felt his flock threatened by the large Jewish community in Sardes. But we actually do not know whether this community was really so wealthy and powerful as is sometimes supposed. There is in any case not the slightest suggestion of an anxious animosity towards Sardesian Jewry in Melito's text. "Our understanding of Melito's psycho-social response to his Jewish neighbours must remain in the realm of speculation" [189]. Carefully perusing the text will be helpful. There is no indication that the bishop was speaking of his Jewish co-citizens or of contemporary Jews in general. His Jews are Jesus' contemporaries, for Melito already historical Jews. It is possible, of course, that his vehement diatribe might influence his hearers, but he nowhere incites them to vilify or to assault the Jews of his town. In fact, he clearly states that they have already received their punishment.

In other words, we are in the presence of a theological treatise. This treatise is characterized by Melito's peculiar theology which was 'Christological' to a degree. This signifies that he makes no distinction at all between God and Jesus of Nazareth. Not only is Christ permanently almost physically present in the Old Testament, so that the great men of Israel seem to be 'modes' of him (for which reason some scholars speak of Melito's 'modalism'). Furthermore, in his view all that is said of the Messiah is equally applicable to God himself. The unavoidable consequence is that the execution of Jesus was 'deicide'. This was, perhaps to the preacher's own surprise, the outcome of his theological quest, but it was not his starting-point. It was not his intention to nail down the Jews as 'God-murderers' and he takes no pleasure in it. "Who is the murderer? I am ashamed and I am obliged to tell" [190]. The tragic thing is that it was the chosen people who committed the deed. If only it had been the pagans ... "He had to suffer, but not by you; ... he had to be judged, but not by you ... Let him suffer by foreigners ...; let him be judged by the uncircumcized man" [191].

I am not attempting to explain away the unpleasant sensation caused by the bishop's harsh words. After all, he was the first to formulate the accusation of deicide, an accusation that would have catastrophic consequences. Of course, Melito could not foresee this nor did he intend it. But we may reproach him for speaking of Israel as a thing of the past. It is true that he was not stirring up his faithful against the Jews, but he was forgetful of the fact that Christians and Jews had to live together as citizens of Sardes and of the Empire; this fact should have made him more careful in his choice of words [192].

c. Irenaeus of Lyons

Saint Irenaeus became bishop of Lyons in 177; probably he died a martyr's death around 200. His main work (in Greek), 'Adversus haereses', against the heresies, dates from about 180, but was certainly not written in one go. It is also called 'Exposure and refutation of the so-called Gnosis' [193]. This makes it clear that the heresies in question are Gnostic doctrines.

Considering the main theme, we should not expect special sections on Jews and Judaism. However, throughout the whole work Jewish religion, or rather the Old Testament, has pride of place; it is the great source on which Irenaeus is drawing. To him the Old and the New Testaments form a unity [194]; in his view Abraham is 'the patriarch and the prophet of our (the Christian) faith' [195]; the prophets were speaking in the name of the true God [196].

The visceral fear Christians of the second century still had of Jewish enmity is exemplified by Irenaeus in the story of Esau and Jacob - a story that keeps recurring in patristic writings. Just as Jacob took away the blessing of his father Isaac and on account of this had to suffer the persecution of his brother, "the later people (the Christians) snatched away the blessings of the former (the Jews) from the Father (God)"; therefore the Church suffers persecution from the Jews, as Jacob did from Esau [197]. But, says Taylor, "there is no reason to believe that the fathers (in casu Irenaeus) are referring to actual accidents in their own day" [198].

There is a short reference to the guilt of the Jews in the crucifixion of Jesus, but although Irenaeus in the same breath asserts that Jesus is the Son of God, he does not speak of deicide. Another slightly polemical passage is that on the fall of Jerusalem. He does not say that it was destroyed because of the sins of Israel but rather that it had lost its significance once it had brought forth Jesus and the apostles. Jerusalem was a temporal thing, with a beginning and an end in time [199]. Rather more polemical is the statement that Mosaic Law was given to Israel because of the hardness of their hearts.

d. The first 'Adversus Judaeos'

There exists a treatise against the Jews which is probably the first instalment of the 'Adversus Judaeos' genre [200]. We know nothing of its author except that it was certainly not Saint Cyprian of Carthage to whom it has been ascribed; we speak of the author as 'Pseudo-Cyprianus' [201]. We are equally uncertain of its date of origin, probably the end of the second century. It is also probable that the author lived in Rome.

The tone of this short essay is decidedly unpalatable to the modern ear. However, the addressees are not the Jews but the Christians : "You, the heirs of Christ, listen to this testament" [202]. The Jews have killed their own prophets and later they have killed Jesus too (although the term 'deicide' is not used). For this reason Israel rightly suffers by wandering around on earth [203]. The anonymous author describes the Jewish attitude in particularly spiteful and unjust terms. "The apostles grieved and the (Jewish) people glorified. The earth trembled and the people rejoiced. The Lord was condemned and Israel was exultant. The Lord suffered and the impious shouted for joy. The Lord was crucified and the people were glad. The Lord was buried and the people sat down to dine; with this scandalous solemnity (what can the author mean if not the Passover meal? - F.) it set the seal on its iniquitous counsels with their crimes and cruelty" [204]. As a consequence the Jews have lost their kingdom; this is now 'among us' [205].

This is a massive attack on Jews and Judaism. In any case the author implies the people of Israel in its entirety, not only historical Jewry but his contemporaries as well. There might, however, be another reason why the author is speaking of the Jews without any nuances. This becomes apparent from a passage in which the word 'hic' = here, is repeated no less than thirteen times; by this 'here' the Church is meant. "Here is the castle, here is the army, here is the commander, here is the king, here is the Christ ...", etcetera, etcetera. It is conceivable that the real addressees are neither 'the Christians' nor 'the Jews' but Christian Jews and Judaizing Christians. Perhaps it had to be made clear to them that they should no longer hark back to the past that had lost its meaning and validity. "Here is he who broke the Old Covenant and wrote a new ... Israel is deprived of its heritage" [206].

The Dutch professor Klijn remarks that from the beginning the Church of Rome had its problems with the cohabitation of Jewish and pagan Christians; Paul had to write to this Church about this. Klijn supposes that this homily was an ultimate attempt to stop the Jewish Christians and Judaizers appealing to their particular heritage [207]. That the author was not exactly fastidious or sensitive in his choice of words might have been caused by his exasperation over what he considered 'Jewish pretensions'.

e. What Theophilus had to say to Autolycus

There were in this period more apologists. Of some of them (Aristo of Pella, Miltiades, Apollinaris, Hermias) we only know the names. Others, like Tatianus, did not polemize against the Jews; to him Hellenism was the enemy, not Judaism. But another treatise, that by Theophilus, has been preserved.

What he had to say stands in sharp contrast to the tone and the substance of the homilies of Melito and the anonymous author of 'Adversus Judaeos'. What he does not say of them is, paradoxically, highly revealing too. Theophilus was a bishop, maybe of Antiochia, in the years 169-177 [208], or perhaps till a still later date. He wrote extensively, but most of these writings are lost. His main target were not the Jews but the Gnostics, Marcion for instance. Jews figure in an apologetic work in three books called 'Ad Autolycum' [209], this Autolycus being a pagan with whom Theophilus had a discussion.

The bishop's words show great respect for Judaism. "Moses, who was God's servant, was the minister of the divine law (= the Ten Commandments) to all the world, in particular to the Hebrews, who are also called Jews, whom an Egyptian king in ancient times had enslaved, and who were the righteous seed of godly and holy men, Abraham, Isaac and Jacob. Mindful of these men, God, by means of miracles and stupendous signs wrought by Moses, liberated them and led them out of Egypt, and after having conducted them through the region called 'desert' established them in the country of Canaan, later called Judaea. He gave them a law (= the Mosaic Law) and taught them these things" [210]. A direct line runs from Judaism to Christianity. The Jews are 'our ancestors' [211]; Abraham is 'our patriarch' [212], Moses 'our prophet' [213], David 'our father' [214]. The 'Hebrews' too are 'our ancestors' who "transmitted to us the sacred books" [215]. The sacred texts are older and more true than the books of the Greeks and the Egyptians [216].

Miriam Taylor is of the opinion that Theophilus simply annexes Judaism and "freely appropriates the Jewish past" [217]. But I don't see that he relegates them to limbo; the texts I quoted prove the contrary. To him Judaism and Christianity are bloodbrothers. I think he needed this close alliance to make a common front against paganism and the Gnosis.

f. Minucius Felix and his 'Octavius'

The next author to claim our attention is Minucius Felix who wrote a little book called 'Octavius'. Its date is uncertain; probably it was written around the turn of the century. The author is said to have been born in North Africa and was a convert. The excellent literary style shows that he was an accomplished rhetor. His books played an important role in the Christian polemics against paganism, although their theological value is minimal. The namegiver, one Octavius, in all probability a fictitious character, is shown discussing with a pagan, Caecilius, whose objections against Christianity he refutes. So the main subject of the treatise is paganism, not Judaism. The Jews are mentioned only once by Octavius, in Ch. 33.

There he states that "it did not help the Jews at all that they have venerated one God only with altars and temples in a great superstition" (that the Jewish religion is a superstition was a standard reproach of pagans which, rather suprisingly, we find here in the mouth of a Christian). Octavius has obviously only the present predicament of Jewry in mind. For as long as the Jews adored their God - who is also the Christian God - in purity and innocence and obeyed his commandments, they grew from few to many, from poor they became rich, from servants rulers. In that time they had God and the elements on their side during their wars. But later they grew unfaithful to God; what happened to them - the fall of Jerusalem and the Temple - is the result of this disloyalty. They abandoned God before God abandoned them [218]. That the catastrophes that had befallen the Jewish nation were caused by its disobedience is an idea that was also current in Jewish circles. Hence it cannot be said that this text is inimical to Judaism.

3. Fathers of the third century

a. Clement of Alexandria

Clement of Alexandria was a vintage Greek coming as he did from Athens, where he was born into a pagan family, probably around 140-150. Later he became a Christian; one of those who instructed him in the faith was a converted Jew [219]. He was thoroughly educated in classical and philosophical scholarship. After having travelled for a time, he established himself in Alexandria where he attended the diocesan catechetical school; it is not certain whether he became its principal. Anyhow, he wrote and taught a lot. Around 202 he migrated to Jerusalem and died at some time during the years 215-221 [220].

Alexandria, where there existed a very large Jewish community, was a hot spot for the Jews; major clashes between Greek (hellenized) Egyptians and Jews had taken place there, with many victims on both sides [221]. Resident as he was for so long in this town, Clement was fully aware of the anti-Jewish mood of the pagan population. Apion, he says, wrote so venomously against the Jews, because he was an Egyptian [222]. Clement himself, however, did not internalize such anti-Jewish feelings; he was a mild man, who was not out to browbeat either Jews or pagans. What he hoped for was the conversion of both nations so that they can become one people. "The middle wall which separated the Greek from the Jew has been taken away, in order that there might be a peculiar people. And so both meet in one unity of faith, and the selection out of both is one" (by 'Greek' the author means the Gentiles) [223].

This opinion implies that the Greeks owe to the Jews the best they have. The Greeks have plagiarized the Law and the prophets [224]. Clement was deeply convinced that all that is good and true in Greek philosophy had been derived from Judaism to which thinkers like Socrates and Plato were deeply indebted [225]. When the author enumerates all that Greek wisdom borrowed from the Jews [226], the modern reader is in for a surprise; Clement even claims that the Greeks knew that the seventh day is holy [227]. In his Hellenic way of thought it is only natural that Abraham is the father not only of the Jews but also of the Greeks [228]. The Jews are led to salvation through the Law, the Gentiles through philosophy. "Philosophy clears the road preparing the way that will be completed by Christ" [229]. Therefore, there is no difference between the really just, "whether they come from the world of the Law or are Greeks. For God is the Lord not only of the Jews, but of all mankind, especially of those who recognize him" [230]. The main thrust of Clement's missionary activity was directed towards the Greeks, the Gentiles, the heathen; he was not greatly concerned with Judaism, and he does not not polemize against it.

God is the same in both the Old and New Testaments. "The providential order in which the Old and New Testaments form only one single diathêkê, one single salvific order, is one of the fundamental concepts of Clement" [231]. Both are given by the same Logos (a concept dear to a man steeped in Greek philosophy) who acted through Moses in the old dispensation and directly by Christ, the incarnate Logos, in the New Covenant [232]. But in the last resort the Jews have become enslaved to the letter and ignore true justice; in consequence, they have forfeited their place as the chosen people, and now the Gentiles have been called [233]. This does not mean that he thought badly of Jews or spoke ill of them. Not at all [234]! Jews and Christians alike are told that they must live lives holier than those of the heathen [235]. When Christ said : "Your faith has saved you", he said this to those Jews who lived blamelessly according to the Law; what failed them was faith in the Messiah [236]. Moses, the truly holy, the all-wise [237], receives high praise from Clement.

But this Father of the Church can be critical of the Jews too. He rebukes them for having stuck to their own traditions and misunderstood the Law [238]; he singled out the Pharisees who strayed from the Law and introduced human opinions [239]. And then there is the standard accusation that the Jews rejected the Messiah and nailed him to the cross [240]. His conclusion, at the end of his 'Stromata', is that "the great mass of the Jews have the words of God on their lips, but do not have the faith and the manner of walking that leads through the Son to the Father and is based on truth" [241].

b. Tertullian

The writings of Tertullian straddle the turn of the century. He was born into a pagan family in Carthage around 160. Probably he became a lawyer in Rome; when he was thirty-five years old, he was converted to Christianity. Whether he also became a priest is an open question. In any case he was a lone wolf, ill at ease in the communities he successively joined. Around 203 he left the Catholic Church and joined the Montanists with whom he later broke too. He died some time after 220.

Tertullian was a prolific writer, and a great one at that. Many of his theological and exegetical works remained very influential. His polemical works are directed against several Gnostic sects and 'adversus Judaeos' [242]. Far more than the Jews the Gnostics were his enemies, for there are four books against them, to one against the Jews [243]. Miriam Taylor enumerates twenty places in his writings where he reproaches the Jews with having rejected Jesus and crucified him [244]. To quote only one of them : "The whole synagogue of the children of Israel killed him" [245].

The last chapter of 'On the spectacles', a book in which Tertullian fulminates against (pagan) spectacles of all kinds, speaks of the spectacle of all spectacles, the ultimate Day of the Last Judgment. Then the Jews will stand before the 'carpenter's son' whom they have despised and insulted and rejected and maltreated. But although he says that the (pagan) authorities who persecuted the Christians, will perish in the flames, together with the philosophers who argued against God, he does not say that the Jews will be punished in the same way. He obviously hopes and expects that at last they will recognize the Messiah [246].

Tertullian did not deny that the Old and the New Testaments belonged to the same dispensation; he spoke of "that same God to whom belong the old and the new ... I do not deny a record of things spoken, in precepts of good behaviour and in rules of law, provided that all those differences have reference to one and the same God, that God by whom it is acknowledged that they were ordained and foretold" [247]. These phrases are directed against Marcion [248] to whom the Old and New Testaments were entirely different and squarely opposed texts [249], but they are also highly important for our theme. If in Marcion's view the distinction between both parts of the Bible is radically dualistic, this is not so in Tertullian's opinion, not even relatively dualistic. Although the two parts are different indeed, what is essential is their agreement, depending as they do on the revelation of one and the same God. The fundamental difference between the Jewish and Christian faiths, according to Tertullian, was that the Jewish religion did not know the Trinity

: the Jews believed in one God without referring to the Son. "What other difference would there be between us and them except that disagreement? What need is there of the Gospel (i.e. if the Son is denied - F.)?" [250].

One of the main objections made by pagan authors against Christianity was that it was so new. Newness was no recommendation in those days. Tertullian was conscious of this. "We fully admit that it dates from a comparatively recent period, not further back than the time of Tiberius", which, as he said, might raise doubts about its standing. He refuted this objection by asserting "that our religion is supported by the writings of the Jews, the oldest which exist" [251]. The Jewish reproach that the Church had abolished the Law he countered in the following way. "We declare that the Law is abrogated in the sense that the burdens which it imposed no longer rest upon us ... However, those of its precepts which have to do with righteousness not only continue in force but have been extended" [252]. And elsewhere : "The yoke of the works has been cast off, not the yoke of moral precepts" [253].

Reading what Tertullian has to say of Judaism and Jews, it is a striking thing that he hardly ever mentions the Jews of around 200; it is always biblical Judaism he is envisioning. Claude Aziza sums up Tertullian's opinion of Judaism as follows. "The Hebrew nation has passed, on account of its impiety, from its situation as chosen people to the state of a people condemned by God, this well before the coming of Christ. This nation, later called the Jewish people, has from being blind become criminal, because it killed Christ after having misjudged him. For this reason it has been punished temporarily with the destruction of the Temple and the capture of Jerusalem. The consequence is that this people cannot be the true Israel which is now found in the Church. The Chistian religion, since long announced symbolically, is now substituted for the Jewish religion, because it is ameliorated and enriched" [254].

One might conclude from this stern judgment that Tertullian was creating an immeasurable distance between Christianity and Judaism, something utterly dualistic. But this is certainly not true. He declares emphatically that "the Christians are close to the Jewish religion" [255]. Where he faces the pagans or Marcion, he becomes, paradoxically perhaps, a defender of Judaism. He is quite ready to refute the anti-Jewish calumnies of Tacitus [256]. Regarding Marcion, he expresses the opinion that Mosaic Law had not been abolished in its entirety : the spiritual commands, the moral law, are as valid as ever [257].

c. Origen

Origen was in all probability an Egyptian, born in Alexandria around 185 into a Christian family; his father even died a martyr's death. He seems to have had a radical temperament which, in an excess of chastity, caused him to castrate himself - a deed he later came to deplore. He became a priest only when he was forty-five years old, but his own bishop banned him from his Church on the ground that an eunuch could not be a priest. However, his opinions may perhaps have given umbrage too. He was a thoroughly educated man, well-versed in many fields of scholarship, and a prolific author; his output in writing is enormous. He loved to argue with heretics, Gnostics, Jews, and pagans. He also found the time to travel widely through the whole eastern half of the Empire and to Rome and to teach and preach in many places. During the persecution of Decius in 249/250 he was arrested and tortured for days on end, but kept firm. Finally he was set free and died in 254, probably at Tyre.

Before we are going to examine what Origen had to say of Judaism, it must be remarked that many of these early Fathers were not only genuinely concerned with it but often showed considerable knowledge of this subject. How did they pick up this knowledge? None of them had a Jewish background. That these theologians were well at home in the Old Testament will not surprise us. But they were also acquainted with non-biblical material, Jewish legends for instance. There is no other solution - and there is evidence to sustain it - than the supposition that these Christian scholars sat at the feet of Jewish teachers.

First of all, since many discussions turned on the exact meaning of a biblical text, the Fathers had to consult the original Hebrew. Having not much

Hebrew themselves, or none at all, they had to seek the help of Jewish scholars - and expensive they were, sighed Jerome. Eusebius said these teachers were "people gifted with an uncommon strength of intellect, and whose faculties have been trained to penetrate the very heart of Scripture" [258]. The apologists needed this assistance in interpreting the Old Testament. "There is much evidence", writes Parkes [259], "in fathers such as Justin, Clement of Alexandria, Origen, Aphraates, Ephraim the Syrian, and above all Jerome, of knowledge which must have been the result of hours of patient discussion. It is impossible to believe that these were never carried on in the tranquil spirit of the student." Enough to show that we should not think of Jewish-Christian relationship as one of permanent acrimonious sparring.

All this applies to Origen too. Already in his home town Alexandria he had learned to read Hebrew in order to be able to consult the Old Testament in the vernacular; his teachers were Jews. Whether he really had much Hebrew is another question; Robert Wilde believes that his knowledge of this language was 'very limited'; he had to consult people (i.e. rabbis) who knew Hebrew much better than he did [260]. After many peregrinations, Origen established himself in 201 or 202 for many years to come in Caesarea in Palestine. This town, writes Trigg, "may also have appealed to Origen because it, unlike Jerusalem, was a major centre of Jewish learning" [261].

There he founded an important school of theology that attracted many outstanding students [262]. In many passages of his works he mentions Jewish scholars from whom he had specific explanations of scriptural texts [263]. One of the Jews he met in Caesarea was Rabbi Hillel, the son of Rabbi Jehuda, the great Mishnah editor. Often Origen refers to 'a Hebrew' or 'the Hebrews' or, in the singular, 'the Hebrew'; with this term he seems to be speaking of an individual Jew, a rabbi to all intents and purposes. But it is not certain whether he always refers to the same rabbi with it, Hillel, for instance [264]. Not rarely we see the author quoting from rabbinic literature.

We find in Origen the usual judgment that the Jews had been punished for their sins since they were a most wicked nation but above all for the crimes that were committed against Jesus. He punctuated this by remarking that he knows of no other nation that has been deprived of its fatherland and its sanctuary [265]. It deserves attention that the Church Father is writing in the past tense, that is, of historical, biblical Jews, not his contemporaries. But in another passage he asserts that the Jews of his own day justify the crime of their fathers against Jesus [266]. Through this crime the Jews lost the privilege they had as the chosen people. Taylor makes the point that Origen applies a double standard to the sufferings of the Jews and the Christians (he was not the only one to do so). The sufferings of the Jews were a fitting punishment for having rejected the Messiah; were the Christians persecuted, then it was a token of divine favour [267].

In the opinion of Origen the Jews had been unbelieving right from the start. Already in the desert they put no trust in the divine revelations; it is, therefore, no wonder that they did not believe the Messiah when he came [268]. As a result they have lost their entire inheritance. "After Jesus' advent the Jews have been entirely forsaken and possess nothing of those things from Antiquity they have regarded as sacred, and have not even any vestige of divine power among them. They no longer have any prophets or wonders, though traces of these are found to a considerable extent among Christians" [269].

That the Mosaic Law had lost its validity is a standard argument in Origen too. Christ had instituted better and more divine laws than ever existed, and these supplant all posssible other customs, whether pagan or Jewish, however ancient [270]. Opinions like these arose from the Church's claim to universalism. Against Celsus's remark that every nation lives according to its own particular laws and customs, Origen argues, so it seems, that natural law is valid for all mankind; this law he equates with the divine law [271].

When it comes to the question of how the enemies of the Church are to be classified, Origen does not sharply distinguish between pagans, Jews and heretics. In one passage he states that the heretics persecute the Church together with pagans and Jews [272]; in another he speaks of heterodox people who do not build the house of the Lord [273]. Was the Church Father really thinking here of his Jewish contemporaries? The Jews of his days, the first decades of the third century, did not harass the Church at all. His passages to this effect have a strongly historizing flavour referring back as they do to biblical instances of heathen peoples threatening Israel.

I feel that Origen, like so many other Fathers, is showing the mentality of the beleaguered fortress : they see opposition all around; all opponents are alike. We should not forget that in his days the Church felt herself to be living alone in an inimical world, criticized, vilified, combated from all sides, and not rarely subjected to bloody persecutions. The Christians still formed a tiny minority in the Empire. And could a man like Origen ever forget that his own father had been executed on account of his faith? The prevailing circumstances were not conducive to subtle reasoning. A nice example of this lack of subtlety is where the author contends that the Jews are "moved in insatiable hatred against the Christians, who have abandoned idols and turned to God" [274]. Why should strictly monotheistic Jews grow angry when they saw pagans abandoning their idols and turning to the true God?

All this may suggest that, if the Jews hated the Church, Origen paid them back in kind. This would not be correct. He was really concerned with the problem of Jewish enmity; he broke his head over it. Like other Fathers, he thought the Jews were jealous of the Christians. Their envy was supposed to result from the fact that Israel had been supplanted by the Church. Origen quotes a Deuteronomy text to this effect : "I will stir them to jealousy with those who are not a people" [275]. He interprets this prophecy as referring to the Christians : "We are this non-people" [276].

Commenting on Paul's saying in Romans that the Jews were still beloved by God because of their election, but the enemies of the Christians because of the Gospel (i.e. of the Messiah) [277], he says that the Jews envy the salvation of the Christians [278]. He can find no other explanation for the Jewish attitude, and in assuming this he is remaining strictly in the theological (Christological) line. But whatever Origen might say in places against Judaism, he knew from his reading of Paul that Israel's rejection was not definitive. With the apostle he believed that in time "the whole of Israel would be saved" [279].

To him the Old and the New Testament are parts of the same divine dispensation, because God is one. Taking a position against Marcion, he "refutes those who think that the Father of our Lord Jesus Christ is a different God from him who gave Moses the sayings of the Law and sent the prophets, and who is the God of the Fathers Abraham, Isaac, and Jacob" [280]. Because of the divine revelation the Jews, free from all superstition (i.e. idolatry), are possessed of a higher wisdom, higher not only than that of the common vulgus but also of those who are supposed to be philosophers. What a pity they have sinned, or else we would have had that celestial city of which Plato dreamed [281]. The Jews were ready to suffer countless tribulations for their religion [282]. And if he somewhere called them 'wicked', he has also much praise for their probity and high moral precepts. In fact, Origen had so much good to say of Judaism that Bietenhard could speak of an 'apology' [283].

In his book against Celsus Origen figures as a staunch defender of the Jews and their religion. His replies to Celsus's objections are 'cool and well-reasoned' [284]. Christians and Jews are united in their strict adherence to monotheism [285] and their aversion and avoidance of idolatry; they will not be seen in pagan temples, around pagan altars, and before pagan images. De Lange remarks that Origen's reasoning on this point is very close to that used by rabbinic authors [286]; "he sees the Church and the Synagogue standing side by side to face the pagan attack" [287].

Bernhard Kötting characterizes Origen's attitude towards the Jews in the following terms. "In accordance with his nature (he) does not choose insulting terminology; (he shows) respect for the Jewish past, but the unbelief of the contemporaries of Jesus is found also in the later Jews. For this bad sin God deals out the same punishment as in the Old Testament for idolatry and contempt of the admonitions of the prophets. That the Jews suffer is rightly so. Their fate is the punishment for their unbelief" [288]. This scholar adds that Origen was not thinking of Christians as instruments in the punishing hand of God, but the inbuilt risk was, although the Church Father could not foresee this, that politicians would take over the birch from God.

Yet another facet of Origen's stance regarding Judaism has to be mentioned. He knew that there were Christians in his flock who were judaizing, for instance by visiting the synagogue on the Sabbath and a church on the Lord's Day. They tended to take the ritual injunctions of Mosaic Law literally. As De Lange says, "there was sufficient religious promiscuity to cause alarm" [289]. By pointing out that the Law should not be interpreted to the letter he steered the middle course between the Scylla of its total rejection - after all it was in the Bible - and the Charybdis of a virtual return to Judaism.

d. Successors of Origen

As a biblical scholar Origen had some successors. One of these was Sextus Julius Africanus, probably a Libyan writing in Greek, of whose life little is known. His dates are ca. 160-240. After having served as an officer and taken part in a campaign, he began to devote himself to biblical studies. Of his writings not much has been preserved [290]. His main work was the Chronographia. This chronicle was centered on the people of Israel, in his view the pivot on which world history turned, at least until the coming of Christ. It amazed him that the Jews had not believed in him [291].

Still less is known of Methodius who, late in the third century, was bishop of Olympus in Lycia [292]. He too wrote in Greek. Only one of his works, the 'Convivium decem virginum', had come down to us in its entirety. His main aim was to combat Origen where he deviated from orthodoxy. His attitude towards the Jews was, as Wilde expresses it, 'regulated by the minimal demands of orthodox theology' [293]. It was Israel's task to announce the Church ('that which is ours', says Methodius) typologically [294]. But the Jews did not understand their own prophets; they failed to see that the prophets predicted the future [295] and understood the prophetic oracles only in a corporeal, i.e. literal sense. As a consequence of this blindness, Israel has become a non-spiritual and worldly nation, aspiring more to the things of this earth than to the treasures of heaven [296].

e. Hippolytus

Hippolytus was a Roman presbyter who lived in the decades before and after 200, but whose main works were written well after the turn of the century. He fell out with Pope Calixtus I and founded a schismatic community of his own, more orthodox than the orthodox one. It came to a reconciliation when the Emperor Maximinus Thrax in 235 banished both Pope Pontianus (230-235) and Hippolytus to Sardinia where they both died in the first year of their exile [297]. Hippolytus was a prolific writer, but a great part of his works have not come down to us. It deserves attention that his main target was heretics, mainly Gnostics. A work called 'Adversus omnes (= 32) haereses' or 'Syntagma' is lost. Later, in the twenties of the third century, he took up this theme again and wrote the voluminous 'Refutatio omnium haeresium', also entitled the 'Philosophoumena', in ten books, which has been preserved. It is doubtful whether he was also the author of a short treatise with the title 'Adversus Judaeos'.

He himself stated that he was able to read Hebrew texts but in all probability his knowledge of the language was meagre [298]. His etymologies often are rather queer [299]. God, he thought, gave the Israelites the Law because they were a wicked people who feared neither God nor man; for this reason the Law had to be very severe [300]. They must not think they would be saved because of their circumcision; they have been rejected [301]. The reason that they are so badly off now is that they killed Christ [302].

But, as in other Fathers, reproaches and praise alternate. Israel is God's holy race, favoured by him above all other nations; the instrument of holiness is Mosaic Law that is a guide to salvation and an initiation to celestial life. The Logos was present in Israel from the beginning, illumining the children of the circumcision. This nation has not been rejected for good; if it comes to conversion, it will be saved. Once converted, the Jew will occupy a special position because he knows both the Old and New Testaments. He even warns the Christians against arrogance with regard to Jews [303]. We discover in Hippolytus, as Robert Wilde writes, a mixture of two traditions : "that of the rigoristic, sometimes heretical, Christians who were unsoundly literal in their scriptural exegesis, and that of the sane and hopeful exegesis of Justin, and of the factual presentation of Irenaeus" [304].

f. The Didascalia

Of an uncertain date, but certainly belonging to the third century are the so-called 'Didascalia apostolorum' = the teaching of the apostles. This work pretends that it had been written by the apostles themselves [305]. In our days this would be considered a literary hoax, but in the third century this kind of fiction was not seen as a problem since the contents were perfectly 'apostolic'. The real author was, perhaps, a Jew, a converted one, and this would explain that, as Parkes writes, it is "a work remarkable throughout for the lack of hostility which it shows to the Jews" [306]. Whoever he may have been, he was a bishop writing as a pastor with the care of souls, not as a theologian [307].

The anonymous author is at pains to show that Mosaic Law (by which he understands first and foremost the Ten Commandments) and the Law of Christ agree with each other : "For those men who obey God there is only one law" [308]. The faithful are admonished not to hang around in the streets but to do their work and read the Old and New Testament at home, instead of the books of the heathen. But he utters a warning against the 'second legislation' : one may read it, but should read it 'simply'. He is referring here to the vast body of commands and prohibitions; the faithful should not bind themselves 'with the bonds of heavy burdens' but, instead, rejoice that God "has redeemed us from all these bonds" [309]. This is clearly directed against judaizing Christians. Or still more directly, "beloved brothers, you who have come from the people (of Israel) to believe in God, our Saviour Jesus Christ, do not persevere in your former customs, those meaningless obligations like purifications, aspersions and washings and the distinction in kinds of food" [310].

Positive though the author is, he is nevertheless critical of the Jewish attitude. "When our Lord came to the Jewish people, they did not believe him ... They did not understand him, not from the writings of the prophets nor from his deeds and healings ... (Therefore,) by reason of the blindness a great darkness has surrounded them." The priests and elders are guilty of Jesus' death, but it seems as though the author seeks to excuse the common people of Israel. The authorities chose exactly the Passover festival for the execution of their plans because then "the people of Jerusalem were occupied with the sacrifice and the eating of the Passover" [311]. This notwithstanding, he asserts bluntly that "God has abandoned the people of the Jews and the Temple and has come to the Church of the Gentiles ... Indeed, he took away the Holy Spirit (from the Jews), and the power of the ward, and the entire ministry from that people, and restored it in his Church". But then he says something curious, namely that "Satan, the tempter, removed (himself) from that people and came against the Church" [312].

Perhaps, we may see this document as a semi-official, quasi-authoritative statement of the atttitude of the Church regarding Judaism. The author expresses no hostility, indeed [313], but is partly favourable, partly critical in his judgment [314]. Here too the Judaizers can be discerned in the wings. According to Schreckenberg, combating judaizing is even the central theme of the Didascalia [315].

g. Cyprian

If a Christian might think that he or she would automatically be saved by adhering to the Church, there was Cyprian, the bishop of Carthage, to warn such a person against this fatal misunderstanding. "A Christian should persevere in prayer and supplication so that we do not fall away from the heavenly kingdom, just as the Jews, to whom this promise had first been given, fell away" [316]. Cyprian, a North African, born in the early years of the third century into a pagan family, was a well-educated man who excelled as a (Latin) rhetor. Around 240 he became a Christian and later a priest. In 249 or 250 he succeeded to the episcopal see of Carthage. Two years later, during the persecution of Decius, he had to flee his town for some time; his possessions were confiscated by the state [317]. During the persecution of Valerianus in 257 Cyprian was banished to a provincial town, but returned in the following year. A month later, in September 258, he suffered a martyr's death [318].

Cyprian is categorical about the rejection of the Jews. "We Christians, when we pray, say Our Father, because he has begun to be ours, and has ceased to be the Father of the Jews" [319]. The reason for this rejection is that "they put to death the prophets and all the righteous men, and plunged even into the crime of the crucifixion and the shedding of the blood of the Lord ... The heretics in the Church act against the peace and love of the Lord in which they resemble the Jews" [320].

This bishop of Carthage was one of those who wrote a treatise against the Jews, the 'Testimonia adversus Judaeos', in three books [321]; it is, however, not voluminous, taking also into account that the third and longest book is not about Judaism at all. The argument is that the Jews have forfeited their heritage by being unfaithful and by not comprehending their own Scripture. Therefore, the Old Covenant has come to an end and has been replaced by a new one. However, the Jews will be forgiven if only they will wash off the blood of Christ and enter the Church. The text is coolly theological and does not use invectives.

4. Fathers, synods and councils of the fourth century

a. The canons of the Elvira synod

When we now cross the treshold of the fourth century, we first of all encounter the Council of Elvira, held around 306, an ecclesiastical meeting of the bishops of the whole Spanish Church. It issued eighty-one canons, four of which refer to Jews. As far as my knowledge goes, these are the very first canonical stipulations with regard to them; they had, however, no general validity, since the Elvira synod was a provincial one.

Canon 16 says that a Catholic girl may not marry a Jew (or an heretic) "since a believer cannot have communion with an unbeliever". The prohibition of intermarriage was reciprocal; the Rabbis too opposed it. Canon 49 admonishes landlords not to have their fields blessed by a rabbi "so that our blessings do not become unworkable and powerless". A curious text that deserves attention! It must obviously have occurred that farmers invited a rabbi to bless their fields, doubtless in the belief that an incantation by a representative of such an old religion would have more potency than that by a priest of a new religion. The Spanish bishops evidently saw this as an (unfair) competition with their own benedictions. Even those prelates feared that they would be worsted by the rabbis. In the background the fear of the judaizing tendency is lurking.

Canon 50 forbids clerics and faithful from having meals with Jews; in all probability joining in ritual meals like the Passover one is referred to. Once again we may suppose that some Christians accepted Jewish invitations on this occasion [322].

b. Eusebius

The first great author, writing in Greek, after Christianity had become a 'religio licita', is Eusebius of Caesarea. He was a Palestinian, born about 264, who spent nearly all his life in Caesarea, of which town he became the bishop in 313. He was personally acquainted with Origen. He used the years of the last persecution, 303-313, for writing. His inclination towards Arianism brought him into trouble, but he succeeded in defending himself successfully. He died around 340.

Eusebius was the first ecclesiastical prelate in whom the collusion between ecclesiastical power and the state becomes visible; Ambrose was to be the second. Eusebius is sometimes even referred to as the 'state bishop' or the 'court bishop of the Emperor', this Emperor being Constantine the Great whom he venerated, as his 'Vita Constantini' [323] may prove. Schreckenberg presents the intriguing supposition that his idea of the monarchy had something to do with his theology. For him God the Father was the supreme world monarch, just as Constantine was the universal ruler on earth; the Son was in his view subordinated to the Father but not fully identical in being with him, a tenet that brought him near to Arianism [324].

The leading idea of his Chronicle [325], composed about 303, is that Judaism is much older and in consequence more venerable than all pagan traditions. Together with his History of the Church [326], this Chronicle deeply influenced medieval historiography. The History intends to prove that Christ was typologically present in the Old Testament, but that the Jews failed to recognize him; therefore, they were rejected and punished by God. The Christians have now taken their place [327].

Later, when the Church had become free [328], Eusebius, a very learned man, wrote two voluminous books, the 'Praeparatio evangelica' [329] and the 'Demonstratio evangelica' [330] (half of which is lost). Parkes characterizes these works as "the most complete example of the instruction given at this critical epoch in Church history to the pagan world. In the first book Eusebius proves the superiority and greater antiquity of Christianity in comparison with all other religions; in the second he proves the superiority of Christianity over Judaism and the uniqueness of the person of Christ" [331].

Eusebius makes a curious distinction between 'Hebrews' and 'Jews'. The 'Hebrews' are the descendants of Eber, an ancestor of Abraham [332]. According to him, they were a much older tribe than the Jews; in fact, they were the most ancient people in the world, and neither Jews nor Gentiles. Greek philosophy was derived from their peculiar religion [333]. The inevitable conclusion is that they were 'Christians'; Abraham and all the Patriarchs led Christian lives, eminently virtuous as they were [334]. For "without doing violence to truth, one may call Christian all those whose justice is attested since Abraham, even going back to the first man; they were, in fact, Christians without having the name" [335]. The divine revelation was given to these Hebrews and not to the Jews [336].

The idea behind this strange theory seems to be to make the Christians the spiritual descendants of those hypothetical Hebrews. "The Christian religion renovatingly ties up with one that is more ancient and venerable than the Mosaic, to a religion according to which Abraham, agreeable to God, and his ancestors have lived" [337]. The idyl of a Christian life long before Christ was disturbed by Moses who gave the 'Jews', the descendants of Judah, the oldest son of Abraham, a law of their own. It is through this Mosaic Law that the Sabbath, the feasts, the food taboos, and the rules of purity were instituted. The only addressees of this Law were the Jews, but neither the Gentiles nor the 'Hebrews', and by implication not the Christians [338]. This device clearly tries to establish that the Church had no obligations with regard to the Law. I feel that we should see this as an oblique reference to Judaizers.

The religion of the Hebrews had been a 'free religion' in which God was the deity of all nations and not of the Jews alone; it was a religion without legislation, based on natural law. These people had an innate instinct for divine truths [339]. The link between the Hebrews and the Christians is formed by the prophets who were not Jews but Hebrews [340]. The prophetic utterances were the only part of the Old Testament that was really valuable in Eusebius's eyes [341].

It is true, as Parkes says, that Eusebius made 'a complete caricature of the history of the Jews' [342]; his construction is wholly artificial, indeed. He will have had two reasons for this weird strategy. The first was to make Christianity as little indebted to Judaism as possible; he tried, in particular, to cut the links with Mosaic Law. The real intention was to invalidate the position of the Judaizers. Secondly, his attempt to disqualify Judaism can also be explained by pointing to a tendency that is prevalent in many of the Fathers who saw in Greek philosophy, especially in Platonism, something Christian or pre-Christian. This presuppposes a belief in a universal natural religion of which Christianity is the highest and fullest expression; the wish to provide it with an older origin than it historically had may also have played a role.

c. Lactantius

Lactantius was a North African, born a pagan in the second half of the third century. He became a rhetor and an author renowned for his beautiful Latin. He got an imperial nomination as professor of rhetorics at Nicomedia in Bithynia. The last rounds of persecution just after 300 had the effect of making him a Christian; he resigned his professorship and devoted henceforward his considerable gifts to the service of his new creed. Later he became, in Treves, the teacher of the Emperor Constantine's son Crispus. He died in or around 325.

It seems that he planned to write an anti-Judaistic apology which is lost or was perhaps never written. What he really wrote and what has been preserved was a catechetical handbook, mainly destined for educated pagans and called 'Divinae institutiones', in seven books. He comes to speak of Judaism in his fourth book.

His tone is rather unfriendly, but there is no absolute opposition of Judaism and Christianity. "The Jews make use of the Old Testament, we of the New; but yet they are not discordant, for the New is the fulfilling of the Old, and in both there is the same testator, even Christ, who, having suffered death for us, made us heirs of his everlasting kingdom, the people of the Jews being reproved and disinherited" [343]. Here too we find the usual accusation of the Jews being the murderers of Jesus - a deed in which, as Schreckenberg remarks, the Romans did not take part in Lactantius's version [344]. We do not find the Pauline prophecy that in the end the Jews will be saved. Quite the contrary! Lactantius has in mind a final punishment for the crucifixion which was, indeed, already anticipated by the destruction of Jerusalem [345].

Even in the Last Judgment there will be no hope for the Jews, "unless they come to conversion, are repentant and purify themselves from the blood with which they have soiled themselves". The further we get in time from the New Testament, the less interested Christian authors show themselves in the conversion of the Jews [346]. This is understandable in as much as in the three preceding centuries there had been no signs of a Jewish mass conversion.

d. The Council of Nicaea

The first general council ever was that of Nicaea in 325 where three hundred bishops were present; it took place under the aegis of the Emperor Constantine the Great rather than that of the Pope of the day, Silvester I (314-335). It was convened mainly to discuss the question of Arianism. With regard to Judaism, the Emperor had a special wish, namely that the date of Easter would be fixed. From the beginning of Christianity the faithful had celebrated the first day of the week, the Sunday, as the Lord's Day, but many had also stuck to observing the Sabbath on the Saturday. In the course of time the Sunday supplanted the Sabbath, and the Saturday lost all its liturgical significance. There remained, however, (judaizing) Christians who, in some way or other, continued to celebrate the Sabbath; 'sabbatizing' was almost a synonym of 'ioudaizein' [347]. The shift to the Sunday was not specifically anti-Jewish, although it was a means of distinguishing the two religions : on the Sabbath the liberation of Israel from Egyptian bondage was commemorated, on the Sunday the resurrection of Jesus.

In the fourth century, and long after, there were many Christian communities who celebrated the feast of Easter on Nisan 14, the traditional Jewish date; these were the so-called 'quartodecimani', the 'fourteeners'. Others, however, felt the need of distinction from Judaism on this point too. In a letter to the council fathers Constantine the Great expressed the wish that another date than Nisan 14 would be chosen. His terminology was decidedly unfriendly. "It seems unworthy to celebrate this sacrosanct feast according to the custom of the Jews who have soiled their hands with a heinous crime and for this reason have been smitten with blindness ... We should, therefore, have no communion at all with this thoroughly hated people" [348]. This is one of the ominous signs that the political sphere was now ready to occupy itself with the Jewish question, and this in a none too subtle way.

The Council fulfilled the imperial wish by fixing the Easter date on the first Sunday after the first full moon after the vernal equinox; fixing is perhaps too strong a word since Easter may fall on any Sunday between March 25 and April 25. It lasted centuries before all the ecclesiastical provinces had accepted the Nicaean rule. As Simon writes, this "reveals the persisting prestige of synagogal practices and norms in the eyes of certain faithful" [349].

There is only one other canon, no. 25, that refers to Jews. "No priest ... should have communion or a fraternal relation with Jews nor consume food and drink in their company", this on the penalty of excommunication [350]. The canon speaks of priests, not of laymen; in combination with the prohibition of having meals together, this suggests that what was forbidden was not so much social intercourse (having a glass together) but rather 'communio in sacris', the taking part of Christian priests in Jewish rituals. The heavy penalty suggests first that this occurred not rarely and secondly that distinguishing the two religions was still a matter of prime importance.

e. Silvester I

The name of Silvester I (314-335) is attached to two texts, the first being an 'Adversus Judaeos' of which only a few fragments have been preserved [351], and the second the 'Acta Silvestri', the so-called 'Silvester-legend'. This is a totally unhistorical Vita of this Pope. It was originally in Greek, dating from about 500 in Syria, and was later translated into Latin. The theme is a disputation in the presence of Constantine the Great between one hundred and twenty Jews, of whom twelve actually take the floor, and seventy-two bishops with Silvester as their spokesman, and two pagans who are acting as referees. Seldom will the three religions of Late Antiquity have been so fraternally united. All the usual arguments - the reader has met them already often - pass in review. At the end all the Jews present become Christians; their example is followed by three thousand more, and also by the Empress Helena, by the whole court, and the two referees.

Schreckenberg states that this legend (which is free of verbal aggression) originated in a time when the Church was certain of her triumph over Judaism and expressed her joy in legends like this one. I feel that there is something more to it. More than once I have mentioned the great disappointment the Christians felt at what they called the obstinacy of the Jews, a disappointment that often was the cause of harsh words. The other side of the coin is that there persisted a secret hope or pious wish that in spite of all the Jews would come in. Of this wish the Silvester-legend is a colourful example. It remained popular; Schreckenberg mentions a carnival play of the fifteenth century entitled : 'The combat of the Jews and Christians before the Emperor Constantine' [352].

f. Aphrahat

The first Christian author we meet after the Council of Nicaea is a Syrian, Aphrahat (or Aphraat), who lived from ca. 290 to ca. 350 and who was a bishop and the abbot of a monastery on the Persian side of the Tigris [353]. What we have of him are twenty-three homilies which together form an exposition of the Christian faith. He too warns his hearers not to observe the Sabbaths, the new moons, and the annual festivals of the Jews [354]. Homily XI deals at length with circumcision [355]; faith is more important than this. He calls baptism the second circumcision; one should be circumcized in the heart, not in the flesh. Those who are blessed in this way and live righteously will rightfully be called children of Abraham, the father of all nations (i.e. not only of Jewry). Of course, he also takes up the subjects of the Law having become invalid (in Homily XIV), of the vocation of the Gentiles (in Homily XVI), and of the Messiah (in Homily XVII) [356] in which he directly addresses the Jews [357].

The conclusion of Williams is that the abbot "knew a good deal about Jews, doubtless from coming into close contact with them". There is 'little direct reference to the Judaism of his time', but "he seems to have felt very strongly that some of his people were exposed to the danger of being led astray by Jewish practices and even Jewish arguments. This fear indeed seems always to have been at the back of his Homilies" [358]. This notwithstanding, there is no trace of asperity against Jews and Judaism in them [359]. Jacon Neusner even finds "Aphrahat the worthiest participant in the Jewish-Christian dialogue put forward in antiquity by either side ... (He) is most impressive for his reasonable arguments, his careful attention to materials actually held in common by both sides, and the articulated and wholly lucid, worldy character of his argumentation" [360].

g. Hilary of Poitiers

An evident personification of anti-Judaistic tendencies was Hilary of Poitiers, a Latin author who was bishop of this town where he died in 371; he was an erudite and influential man whose influence reached into the Middle Ages. As a staunch opponent of Arianism he earned the nickname of 'the Athanasius of the West'. He was so painfully orthodox that he shunned all contacts with heretics. It was perhaps not from personal enmity but in order to preserve his Christian purity that he did not even greet Jews when he passed them in the streets [361].

'Wicked' is a word that often crops up in Hilary when he speaks of the Jews. They even 'gloried in wickedness' and were 'mighty in wickedness' [362]. No wonder, for they were the prey of the devil. "Before the Law was given, the Jews were possessed of an unclean devil which the Law for a time drove out, but which returned immediately after their rejection of Christ" [363]. He equates the Jewish people with Cain and the Christian with Abel. The jealous Cain persecuted his brother in whom the 'just' (the Christians) are prefigured [364]. "The offering of the younger one (Abel) is welcome; the Jew feels malevolence towards Christ. The prophets showed (Christ) to him (the Jew) long before, but he (the Jew) let himself be carried along far enough to murder him (Christ). He does not want to be forgiven, not even by confessing himself repentant, but sticks brutally in the face of God to his crime. Without hope of the glory of the resurrection and subjected to (new) potentates after the conquest of Jerusalem, he is preserved, anxious and in fear, for the judgment of retribution" [365]. Here are, in a totally unwarranted sweep and hopelessly confused, mixed up past, present and future, Cain and the Jews, Abel and Christ and the Church.

h. John Chrysostom

We now get to the hardest nut to crack, the eight anti-Jewish homilies of John Chrysostom. Johannes Chrysostomus was a Syrian, an Antiochene born around 350 into a wealthy Christian family. His pious mother provided him with an excellent education in which two important elements were combined, the best of pagan culture - rhetoric and (Stoic) philosophy - and Christian doctrine. He had himself only baptized, however, when he was twenty-two. He had a strong tendency towards asceticism, stayed for four years in a monastery, and then became a hermit. His fierce temperament made him castigate himself so much that his health became impaired; after two years, in 381, he left his cell. His bishop ordained him a deacon and charged him with the care of widows and virgins. In these five years his first writings saw the light.

When he was ordained a priest, in 386, he began to combat the opponents of the Church and her orthodoxy with all the force of his powerful rhetorical gifts. "I have to do battle", he said, "not only with Jews, but also with Gentiles and many heretics" [366]. He polemized against the Arians (eleven homilies), against the pagans, particularly against Julian the Apostate, against the rich and powerful, and then, in the context of this chapter, against the Jews, or rather against judaizing Christians (eight homilies). We would, however, do him an injustic, if we saw him only as a disputant hitting left and right at everybody who did not agree with him. By far the greater part of his speeches, dozens of them, concern Christian life, the liturgical year, and biblical exegesis, destined for the ordinary church-goer.

Antioch was an unruly city where imperial troops had to beat down a revolt; fearing stern measures against the citizenship, bishop Flavius went to Constantinople in order to plead for leniency. He charged John with the task of calming down the populace, which he did in twenty-one homilies preached in 387. In 398 he became Patriarch of Constantinople. He was extremely popular with his flock, but hated by the court and the powerful whose luxurious way of life he constantly criticized, not sparing the Emperor himself, Arcadius, and his wife, Empress Eudoxia. In 403 he was banished, soon to be recalled, because the Empress had had a miscarriage, a misfortune which she saw as a divine punishment for the way the Patriarch was treated. But in 404 he was banished again, and this time for good, to the small town of Kukusos in Armenia. Since this did not spell the end of his polemical activities, he was to be deported to Pityus, north of the Caucasus range. His guards forced him to march bareheaded in sun and rain across mountains and streams. He did not reach his new place of exile. On September 21, 407, the exhausted man died in Comana in Pontus.

In the early Church and much later, until not so long ago, John Chrysostom was celebrated and commemorated as the pastor, the teacher, the prophet, as a great theologian and an outstanding Father of the Church. Even in my youth I heard of him as 'the one with the golden mouth', the chrysostomos. But today, after the Holocaust, he is mainly remembered as the father of anti-Semitism [367]. He is sometimes spoken of as though he was a direct precursor of Adolf Hitler [368]. Now I am not prepared to explain away the nasty things Chrysostom said against Jews and Judaism, but since the modern attitude towards him is highly reductive, a somewhat broader perspective can do no wrong.

For a start, it should be realized that his anti-Jewish sermons form only a small part of his total literary and rhetorical output. Next, it must be understood that rhetorical customs in ancient times were different from ours. Inhabitants of northern countries, Scandinavia, Germany, the Netherlands, the Anglosaxon ones, are somewhat distrustful of rhetoric, especially when a speaker works himself up into a flourish. I suppose an ancient expert would have considered that we have no art of rhetoric at all. Rhetors in Antiquity knew all the tricks in the game, for they were trained in it, and the public knew them too. They admired them for being great orators.

"Of all the devices at the rhetor's disposal, the one that stands out is hyperbole, exaggeration", writes Wilken [369]. He presents a telling example of rhetoric hyperbole. After stating that not even the testimonies of the prophets and the apostles were sufficient proof for him, "I (John) went up to heaven itself and displayed to you the chorus of angels" [370]. "The rhetors overstate, they magnify, they use poetical and grandiloquent words for the simplest actions; everything is writ larger than life" [371].

Speaking of a person or a group, the speaker might exuberantly praise them, that is, use the rhetoric device of 'encomium', or just as exuberantly vilify them, in which case he turned to 'psogos' = rhetoric abuse. How to be effective in psogos was taught in the schools of rhetoric. It was normal usage to compare one's opponents to wolves or to accuse them of inebriety. Terms like 'wretched, wicked, rabble, foolish, dogs' were freely bandied about. Christian rhetors make no exception to this; "the Christian vocabulary had become as stereotyped as that of the rhetorical schools" [372]. However, elements not to be found in pagan rhetoric but stemming from Christian theology can also be detected; for instance, when Chrysostom dubs the Jews 'Christ-killers' which he does more than once [373].

But because the public knew the genre so well, it did not take everything a speaker said at its face-value. By no means! The nearest approach to this nowadays is what the public thinks of a candidate for a political office during an election campaign; every sensible person knows that one should not believe all that he promises. If he says that he is going to lower the taxes, one may be glad if he, once in office, does not raise them. So the Antiochene public will have taken John's sermons for what they (partly) were : rhetorical tours de force. Add to this that it will have known that he was a vehement man who was often carried away by his own words, especially when he was getting up steam.

Having stated this, I have no problem, although not without some reservations, with the verdict of Parkes who writes that Chrysostom "has left us the most complete monument of the public expression of the Christian attitude to the Jews in the century of the victory of the Church (i.e. the fourth century A.D.)". All the same, I ask myself whether really all Christians thought and expressed themselves in this way. Chrysostom held no brief from Rome to agitate against the Jews; he had commissioned himself and was not the official spokesman of the Church. True enough, "in these discourses there is no sneer too mean, no gibe too bitter to fling at the Jewish people. No text is too remote to be twisted to their confusion, no argument too casuistical, no blasphemy too startling for him to employ" [374]. However, the possibility cannot be excluded that the text of the homilies, as we have them, does not exactly correspond to what the rhetor actually said. His sermons remained highly popular and knew a long tradition of transmittance; this means that there may be interpolations and adaptations from a later date in them [375].

Chrysostom throws invective after invective at the Jews, using curious arguments. As long as the Jews were subjected to the Law they did not observe it; now that it has been abolished they cling to it. "The sun of justice rose over them, but repelling its rays, they sit in darkness. Hard of head as they are, they are incapable of bearing the yoke of Christ, light though it is, so that they become brutish beasts" [376]. The cause of their bestiality is their debauchery and voracity; all their evils result from their drunkenness. Like cattle, they are unfit for serious work but only good for the butcher (sic!). Their festivals are shameful; barefooted they dance in the marketsquare, pretending to rejoice but in reality gorging themselves with drink. They assemble women of a bad reputation and bring the whole theatrical world and the actors to the synagogue, for there is no difference between this and the theatre [377].

What on earth, the reader would like to ask him, and probably his hearers too, put these ideas into your head? It is evident that Chrysostom never in his life visited a synagogue. Well, he will have retorted, they themselves, of course, we find it in their own prophets. Chrysostom never tires of quoting the prophets when they were admonishing and reprimanding the people of Israel. They are his warrant that what he is saying is perfectly true. It does not bother him that he is magnifying and distorting the prophetic utterances, that he is citing them out of context, that he should not apply what one specific prophet said at a given historical moment to the entire biblical nation, and above all that he should not take the metaphors literally. If Jeremiah says to Israel : "You have the shameless face of a prostitute" [378], then Chrysostom takes this to mean that synagogues are brothels, and not only brothels, but also robbers' dens and lairs for wild beasts [379].

God has forsaken the Jews, and now what hope remains for them? Without God their prayer-house is the dwelling-place of demons. If they don't know the Father and have crucified the Son and reject the help of the Holy Spirit, what else can a synagogue be but a place of idolatry? God is not adored there. Impossible! And he comes to the astonishing conclusion that no Jew adores God [380]. Thus he goes on ranting. The Jews have committed all kinds of crimes. The orator cites Ps. 106:37 to the effect that they have sacrificed their children to the demons. And he quotes Jeremiah to prove that everyone of them is neighing after the wife of his neighbour [381]. Worse than animals they are [382]. They are guilty of robberies, of avarice, of leaving the poor to their fate, of stealing, of bartering [383].

In the sixth homily he returns to the charge, no longer taking 'the Jews' as his target but, instead, Judaism, the religion. Or rather what the Jews, in his opinion, had made of it. Once the Jewish cult was really venerable, but now it is no more than a joke, a laughing-matter. True enough, they possess the sacred books, but this does not suffice to sanctify the synagogue. They have brought these books to their synagogues, not to honour them but to insult and dishonour them [384]. Since it is evident that God hates the Jews, the Christians are obliged to hate them too. Just as the beasts in the arena once having tasted blood cannot easily abstain from this kind of food, so the Christians should not give up the battle with the Jews [385]. A most imprudent and ominous comparison!

The six other homilies are more moderate in tone dealing mainly with the ordinary stuff of the theological discussion with the Jews; there is no need to tread this path again.

Since John Chrysostom was a passionate man, he made the most of the rhetorical devices at his disposition : exaggeration and abuse. His was a radical nature, temperamentally incapable of striking a means between conflicting opinions. Nuances formed no part of the rhetor's art, still less of that of John Chrysostom. Even more easily than others he was carried away by the flow and glow of his phrases, not rarely saying more than was wise or than he could answer for. One gets the impression that he sometimes sensed that he was going too far, when he saw his hearers - so to speak - shifting uneasily in their pews (in reality they were standing around the cathedra); he then became rather less strident [386].

But knowing so well the ins and outs of the art of rhetoric, he can hardly have believed all that he said of the Jews himself. Maybe he did when he had warmed up to his subject, but it is not probable that he remained just as excited in his more sober moments. And did he really think that his audience believed all he said? And did he imagine that his audience thought that the speaker believed that his hearers believed him? I don't think they were one another's dupes [387]. Those crowding around the cathedra - to say nothing of the man on it himself - knew Jews, without any doubt as neighbours, colleagues, shopkeepers, artisans, and what not. They must have been perfectly aware of the fact that the Antiochene Jews were, as a group, no worse than they were themselves, not robbers, thieves, crooks, adulterers. Some in the audience were Jewish Christians or Judaizers; they knew, from their own experience, that synagogues were no robbers' dens or brothels. Conversant as they were with rhetorical tricks, they knew what to subtract from the speaker's words.

I do not think that it was Chrysostom's intention to convince his flock that 'the Jews' were such a bad lot. Who were his 'Jews', anyhow? Certainly not his co-citizens, the Antiochene Jews of the later fourth century! It is utterly impossible to construe, on the basis of these sermons, a picture of how the Jewish community of his town lived and thought. Were his opponents the Old Testament Jews then? Hardly! For Scripture must have informed him about so many pious, holy, God-fearing Jews. His Jews were hypothetical beings, not existing in reality; they were, as Parkes says, a 'theological necessity' [388]. But whence this theological necessity?

To answer this question, we must turn, perhaps somewhat paradoxically, to an historical situation, namely that of the Jews in Antioch. The numerous Jewish community in this town was of old standing, its origin reaching back some six centuries. Most of its members were Greek speaking, some wealthy and well-educated, 'active participants in the Hellenistic culture of late Roman society' [389]. But they had remained Jews, which signified that they kept themselves apart from the rest of citizenschip. They had their synagogues and bath-houses, they celebrated the Jewish feasts, they observed the Sabbath, they practiced circumcision, and kept, at least partly, the food laws [390]. Thus facing the Christians, was an active, lively Jewish community which presented some fascinating aspects to Christians and raised some poignant questions. For instance, might Jewish (ritual) baths be more efficacious than Christian baptism [391]? Add to this that the Christian community itself was hopelessly divided, what with the Arian controversy. Chrysostom himself admitted that many of his flock had "a high regard for the Jews and think that their present way of life is holy" [392].

There is nothing to show that the relations between the Christian and Jewish communities of Antioch were anything else than peaceful. Neither do we hear of Christians swooping down on Jews as a result of Chrysostom's preaching. Nothing in his sermons suggests that this was his intention. What then caused him to denounce Jews and Judaism so vehemently?

It was what we found in other early Christian authors too : the fear of judaizing, the fear that Christians, many Christians perhaps, would backslide into Judaism. That this fear sometimes assumed obsessive proportions - as is especially evident in Chrysostom - can easily be explained, as I pointed out before, by the circumstance that the Church was still engaged in defining her identity. It did so with regard to paganism and to the Gnosis too, but the problem of Judaism was more pressing, since the two religions were twin sisters. For Chrysostom it was no abstract theological problem at all, since the Jews of his city were so much in evidence. The Christians could see them walking to their synagogues on Friday afternoons, saw with their own eyes how all Jewish business stopped on the Sabbath, witnessed how Jewish families made their short Sabbath walks, looked at the temporary Sukkoth during the Feast of the Tabernacles, and knew that the Jews joyously celebrated their festivals [393], even dancing in the squares - to the immense irritation of Chrysostom who was an inveterate enemy of all kinds of theatrical performances.

In all probability the Christians found the colourful and joyous Jewish celebrations attractive. I wonder whether a humourless and stern preacher like the puritanical Chrysostom was able to talk his faithful out of this. Isn't it possible that he, gauging their reluctance, put on more steam? He knew perfectly well that not a few of his flock convened with Jews on occasions like Passover and the Jewish New Year. "Many who belong to us and say that they believe in our teaching, attend their festivals and even share in their feasts" [394], he said mournfully. There were even members "who consider themselves yoked to us but participate in their religious rites" [395]. At moments even Chrysostom came near to understanding why Christians admired the Jewish way of life. "You Christians should be ashamed and embarassed at the Jews who observe the Sabbath with such devotion and abstain from all commerce beginning with the evening of Sabbath. When they see the sun hurrying to set in the west on Friday, they call a halt to their business affairs and interrupt their selling" [396].

Chrysostom accused the Judaizers of wanting to have the best of both worlds and ignore the difference between the two religions. They attend the services in the synagogues and then go to church to take part in the eucharistic meal. This is inadmissible, the speaker declares. If a catechumen does this, he should not be baptized, and a baptized Christian should be barred from the Eucharist [397]. The date of Easter constituted a special problem. Sixty years earlier the Fathers of Nicaea had ordained that Easter should not be celebrated on the fourteenth of Nisan, the date of the Jewish Passover. But in Antioch, Judaizers still stuck to the Jewish date. In their opinion Nisan 14 was the authentic date which should not be changed. What! thundered Chrysostom, "three hundred fathers, and even more, convened in Bithynia (Nicaea), and you heap abuse on them!" [398].

There are instances in abundance which prove that Chrysostom was not really attacking 'the Jews' but, instead, judaizing Christians; he accused them roundly of dividing the holy assembly [399]. He prods them to make a definite choice. "If you think Judaism is true, why do you bother the Church?" [400]. We should take into account that the eight 'adversus Judaeos'-homilies were delivered within a period of a few months; seven of them were preached in quick succession in the autumns of 386 (nos. 1 and 2) and 387 (nos. 4-8). In his very first sermon he said that in this season Jewish feasts were 'continuous and frequent' [401], revealing by these words his reason for assuming his self-appointed task : the fear that his faithful would join in the celebrations. The third sermon was delivered in the early months of 387, when Jewish Passover was approaching [402].

It is almost inevitable that the modern reader feels that the Antiochene Christians were thoroughly imbued by John Chrysostom with the anti-Semitic line. But much as they admired his rhetorical bravour, applauding after the sermons, they went their own way. In his last sermon he had despondently to admit that his diatribes even made people curious about the Jewish way of life [403].

The tactics followed by Chrysostom to turn away the faithful from judaizing were the usual means of the art of rhetoric : psogos, abuse. Judaism must be belittled as much as possible, downgraded, declared worthless, and void, a thing of the past. His very vehemence show how great he judged the danger. His anxiety for the spiritual safety of his flock prompted him to become unfair and unjust, totally ignoring what Paul had said of the relationship of Church and synagogue. To a modern reader the sermons make disagreeable reading. In later times John's homilies were readily used as ammunition in anti-Judaistic and anti-Semitic polemics. Times had changed then. The art of rhetoric had been lost, and people succumbed to a tendency to take what the orator had said at its face-value. But I feel we should not hold John responsible for the use made of his homilies in totally different circumstances centuries after he had left this world.

j. Synods of the second half of the fourth century

In, probably, 364 a provincial synod was held in Laodicea, a town in Phrygia; several canons of this assembly had judaizing Christians as their target. Canon 29 stated in as many words that "Christians should not judaize". If they did, they had to be excommunicated. They should not observe the Sabbath by not working on Saturdays. Canon 37 forbade the faithful to share in Jewish festivals, and canon 38 to accept unleavened bread from them [404].

In, probably, 398 the fourth provincial synod of Carthage was held; here too prohibitions against Judaizers were enacted, in particular against taking part in Jewish festivals (canon 89). On the other hand, canon 84 ordered that the bishops of North Africa should not prevent anyone - and here the Jews are mentioned too - from attending the so-called 'mass of the catechumens' (the first, non-sacramental part of the mass). Oviously all hope of making converts among the Jews was not yet given up [405].

5. Fathers of the late fourth and the fifth centuries

I don't think there is much sense in presenting the opinions of Christian authors of the late fourth and the fifth centuries. I am thinking here of Zeno of Verona, Athanasius of Alexandria, Ephraim the Syrian, Basilius the Great, Cyrillus of Jerusalem, Gregory of Nazianze and Gregory of Nyssa, to quote only the most renowned. Arguing against Judaism was not their main aim; Athanasius, the Patriarch of Alexandria, is mainly remembered for his long-drawn-out battle against Arianism. Not one of them wrote an 'Anti Judaeos' with the exception of bishop Diodorus of Tarsus, at the end of the fourth century, of whose work not a single letter remains, and that of Augustine, of whom more later on.

For almost all of them Judaism is simply a side-issue, references to which are found throughout their books. The Judaizers can often be detected in the background. The arguments are always the same; we have met them over and over again already. Some of these authors are vehement; others use a courteous tone; this obviously depends on their temperament.

a. Ambrose

I feel, however, that we should mention two Fathers, because they remained so influential, Ambrose and Augustine. Ambrose mixed in imperial politics; we shall have to come back to this later in this chapter. He was the son of a Roman official and had a political career as a provincial governor himself. But then he became a cleric and was in 374 chosen as bishop of Milan, in which see he remained until his death on April 4, 397. As bishop he was instrumental in the conversion of Augustine. He too did not write an 'Adversus Judaeos', but this does not mean that he was friendly disposed towards the Jewish people. What he had to say of them and of Judaism is mainly found in some of his letters; these offer the usual array of well-worn arguments which all these authors never tire of repeating. There is something obsessive in this.

Two things deserve attention. The first is that, although the bishop considers the Jews as rejected, he nevertheless hopes for their ultimate conversion and final salvation. The other is that he occasionally has something good to say of them. The Jews have a high morality, read the Scriptures assiduously, and are highly conscientious. With regard to Bible reading, the Christians remain far behind. "You, Christian, you are sleeping ..., (but) the elders of the Jews ... peruse day and night the sacred writings"; they are experts in the interpretation of the texts [406].

b. Augustine

Augustine needs no introduction. I quote him here because of his immense and enduring influence. He was certainly not primarily occupied with Judaism but, all the same, the Jewish-Christian relationship was important to him. He remains mainly in the theological sphere, since he does not seem, just like his mentor Ambrose, to have been personally acquainted with Jews [407]. He wrote an 'Adversus Judaeos' which actually was a sermon extended into a treatise; its date is after 425 [408].

His arguments are identical with those of other authors. It seems that he feared Judaism as a still potent presence which attracted Christians. In one of his letters he mentions Christians who gave themselves the name of 'Jews' and who combat the idea that the Church would be the 'verus Israel' [409]. In North Africa too the Judaizers were numerous; more than once Augustine uttered warnings against them [410].

In his polemizing against Judaism Augustine is occasionally vehement, not to say rude. He uses terms as 'shameless' and 'blind', 'sinners' and 'evil-doers', even 'murderers'. Jews are 'hard, unjust, worldly", etcetera [411]. We should, howver, not forget that he is not speaking of his contemporaries but of those biblical Jews who did not recognize the Messiah and crucified him. It deserves attention that Augustine takes only the contemporaries of Jesus under fire. Judaism of the ages preceding Christ was the ancestor of the Church; occasionally he defended it against pagans and Gnostics. His real

181

aim, as Blumenkranz states, was to keep the faithful from judaizing, even from converting to Judaism [412].

PART III STATE LEGISLATION REGARDING JEWRY

1. Judaism as a religio licita

We shall now have to turn to the official policy of the Empire regarding the Jews once Christianity had become a religio licita. Since Constantine the Great the Empire was governed by Christian Emperors, orthodox or Arian, with the exception of Julian the Apostate, while Constantine himself was a catechumen and not formally a Christian. Judaism had always been a religio licita and remained so after 313 [413]. The privileges of the Jews were preserved : exemption from military service and no obligation to take part in the imperial cult (which was not abolished).

2. Measures of Constantine the Great

In 315 Constantine forbade Christians to convert to Judaism (obviously a real possibility!) and Jews to make proselytes; Jews who wanted to become Christians should not be hindered in this (presumably by their co-religionists). In this rescript Judaism is called 'a pernicious and a nefarious sect' [414]. Another law forbade Jews to have their Christian slaves circumcized;, if this prescription was contravened, the slave had to be set free [415].

By these measures no new policy was inaugurated. Under the pagan Emperors circumcizing (pagan) slaves had been forbidden, while several of them put a ban on conversion (of pagans) to Judaism [416]. The public status of the Jews was improved because, since taking part in the imperial cult was no longer obligatory, they were now free to become officials and serve on town councils [417]. Constantine also allowed the Jews to enter the forbidden city of Jerusalem on the anniversary of the destruction of the Temple [418]. However, Schreckenberg is of the opinion that this imperial edict made things for the Jews wanting to visit the Holy City rather worse than better, since in the course of time Hadrian's decree had fallen into abeyance so that Jews had become more or less free to enter the town at will [419].

3. Sharpening of the legislation under the sons of Constantine

Under Constantine II (337-340) the legislation regarding Jews was sharpened. When a Jew bought a slave 'belonging to another sect or nation' (= mainly a Christian one), this slave would immediately be confiscated. Circumcision of such a slave was to be punished by death [420]. But here too the lawgiver is harking back to decrees of pagan times, even in respect of threatening execution. Constantius II (337-361) repeated the prohibition against Jews winning Christian converts; when a Christian changes sides, his fortune will be confiscated [421]. Since this did not apply to pagan proselytes, the intention of these decrees is evidently to prevent the leaking away of Christians to Judaism.

4. Benevolent measures of Valentinianus I

The Emperor Valentinianus I (364-375) was relatively well-disposed towards the Jews. There is, for instance, an edict of his forbidding the seizure of Jewish prayer-houses (by military quartermasters) in order to billet troops in them (this did not apply to the private houses of Jews) [422].

5. The policy of Theodosius I the Great

a. Legislation

Theodosius I the Great (379-395) repeated the interdiction on Jews against keeping Christian slaves and circumcizing them, but the death penalty was no longer mentioned [423]. Marriages between Jews and Christians were now forbidden; since this was equated with adultery, the death penalty was applicable to it [424]. Schreckenberg remarks that, although the rabbis too did not like mixed marriages, this decree was yet another element in the policy of isolating the Jews from the Christians; of course, 'Rassenschande', to employ the Nazi terminology, was not what the Emperors had in mind [425].

b. The Kallinikon incident

During the reign of Theodosius an incident took place which made Ambrose, the bishop of Milan, manifest himself as an enemy of the Jews. In 388 a Christian mob, led or incited by the local bishop, fell on the synagogue of Kallinikon, a village on the Euphrates in Mesopotamia, and burned it down. The Roman governor - the comes - punished these Christians and reported the affair to the Emperor. The ruler issued a rescript [426] by which the bishop was ordered to indemnify the Jewish community for the objects stolen form the building and to have it rebuilt at his own costs [427]. The culprits should be bastonnaded [428].

Ambrose, in Milan, got wind of the affair and wrote a letter to the Emperor [429]. He begins with stating that the information may be unfounded. But then he begins to employ excessive language, roundly threatening the ruler, and showing his most unsympathetic side. He is taking the guilt, by proxy, upon himself. "It was me who set this synagogue on fire ... so that there may be no place where Christ is denied." There is no sufficient reason for punishing people so severely because they have destroyed a place of unbelief, the house of impiety. "Will you grant the Jews this triumph over the Church ...? Is there any communication of the pious with the unbelievers?" If the Emperor will not retrace his steps, he must face the consequences [430].

At first, Theodosius did not waver but stuck to his guns. But then, on a Sunday, the bishop preached in the cathedral, while the Emperor stood near. Ambrose expatiated on the relation of the Church and the synagogue, how (spiritually) rich the one was and how poor the other, and more in this vein. The Emperor asked, for the sake of asking, whether the sermon was directed at him. Why, yes, retorted the bishop, I do it in order to save you. Theodosius said, meekly, that he had already modified his measures somewhat; perhaps he had been too severe. But no, this was not enough.

Ambrose declared that he was not ready to continue with the service and administer the sacraments to the Emperor, if he did not promise to totally stop the proceedings. "I am ready to do this", answered Theodosius. "Can I count on your promise?", asked the bishop. "You can", was the last word [431].

One thing should not be lost sight of : we see the whole affair from beginning to end solely through the eyes of Ambrose; he is our only reporter but at once the main actor who is assigning the great role to himself. He saw his chance, and he took it, to put an Emperor in his place, a few steps lower than an ecclesiastical dignitary. Was Theodosius really so complacent as the bishop claimed? Ambrose stated that legislation on synagogues was the task of the Church, but the rulers never honoured this claim. When Simon has it that Ambrose succeeded in modifying the law on the protection of the synagogues [432], he contradicts himself on the next page by writing that this legislation remained unchanged for the time being [433].

Of course, Ambrose's words to the Empeor were imprudent and his intervention was unasked for, but the one who really was at fault was Theodosius who gave in where he should not have given in. His weakness in this matter may have given Christian rowdies the impression that they could do what they liked against Jewish property. It proved very difficult to turn the wheel back again.

There is yet another intriguing point which, I believe, is rarely touched upon. What exactly made Ambrose intervene in this affair? He had nothing to do with it, being only the bishop of Milan in northern Italy, whereas the diocese in which Kallinikon lay was at the other end of the world. Perhaps we must take into account that he had been a provincial governor; he had evidently not yet lost the zest for handling political affairs. Maybe we see here the very first instance of the conflict of the Church and the state, of the secular and the spiritual power.

Respecting the Kallinikon affair, the Emperor and the bishop regarded it with different eyes. To the Emperor it was a political affair : disorderly behaviour should be punished; every citizen of the Empire had the same right to protection of his person and possessions. To the bishop the thing was first and foremost of a spiritual nature : Christians, who were the true believers, were not to be punished because of Jews, who were 'perfidi' = unbelievers. But it is also possible to suppose that Ambrose seized the opportunity for showing that the secular power was subordinate to the spiritual one. In this context it should be pointed out that this was a one-man-action. It deserves attention that the highest authority in the Church, the bishop of Rome, never turned against the Emperor nor made pronouncements against the Jews.

6. Legislation after Kallinikon

In 393 an imperial decree declared that Judaism was not interdicted by the law - on other words that it was and remained a religio licita; persons who in the name of the Christian religion arrogated to themselves the right to rob and destroy synagogues should be punished with all due severity [434]. A rescript of 397, for the Orient, repeated that the synagogues should be left in peace [435]. Then again in 412 [436] and 418 [437].

No attack was made by the state on the religious rights of the Jews. Infringements on the observance of the Sabbath were not permitted [438]. On the other hand their public position became curtailed. Slowly but certainly they were pushed out of all public functions [439]; they could no longer be court dignitaries or lawyers [440]. Gradually all public functions, even the lower ones, were closed to them. Only baptized Jews could become functionaries and state officials [441]. In this way the Jews were, for centuries to come, excluded from public life.

7. Attacks on synagogues

The repetition of warnings at frequent intervals against molesting synagogues may signify that incidents of the Kallinikon type occurred from time to time. Whether they were as numerous as Simon asserts [442] is another question. In a letter by Ambrose we are told that in 388 a synagogue in Rome was set on fire [443]. In 418, at Magona in the island of Minorca, a synagogue was pillaged and burned after the Jews had defended the building in vain; the local bishop and the clergy were not innocent of this act of vandalism [444].

In the Spanish town of Dertona the local bishop was the leader of a group of Christians who seized the synagogue and turned it into a Christian church [445].

In the East there were more incidents of this kind. In Palestine, in the beginning of the fifth century, a fanatical monk, called Barsauma (or Barsumas), wandered around for many years, accompanied by a number of monks who resembled robbers rather than clerics, attacking synagogues and Jewish property; sometimes Jews were killed in the course of such actions [446]. In Antioch the synagogue where the remains of the seven Maccabaean brothers were said to rest, was confiscated by the Christians in the second half of the fourth century [447]. Such deplorable things happened sometimes with the connivance of the local bishop or even with his active collaboration, while the protests of the authorities proved ineffective. When the Emperor Theodosius II ordered the Antiochene Christians to restitute the confiscated buildings to the Jews, the famous hermit Simeon the Stylites protested so loudly that the ruler countermanded his order [448].

We have seen earlier that in Alexandria the relations between Jews and pagans were strained. It seemed that in this difficult and often anarchical city the Jewish-Christian relationship was also bad. In 414 there were incidents between the two groups. Tumults occurred in the square where the Jews assembled to dance on Sabbath days, a spectacle that attracted many onlookers. The city prefect Orestes forbade these happenings but, according to our Christian source, the Jews did not obey. "And since the Jews are the spiritual enemies of the Christians, they showed themselves more inimical to them because of these pantomimes" [449].

When a town festival was to be celebrated in the theatre, under the auspices of Orestes, adherents of Cyrillus, the patriarch of Alexandria, went there too. A certain Hierax, a scholar, denounced the presence of so many Jews among the public. The Jews reacted vigorously, there were disturbances in the city, and according to the Christian historian Socrates, Jews attacked Christians in the night and made many victims. When daylight came, the Christians, fired on by their patriarch, invaded the synagogues and killed quite a number of Jews. As a result, the Jews were banished from the town [450].

All this is highly deplorable. no doubt, but some caution is necessary. Isaac writes that Cyrillus, the patriarch, organized a pogrom and he, rightly, blames him for this [451]. But what he does not mention is that the pogrom was preceded and probably caused by Jewish aggression, which, however, was preceded by Christian agitation. As I said, Alexandria was a city with an history of violent clashes between its population groups; the incidents of 414 fit neatly into this age-old tradition.

8. Legislation with regard to synagogues

The imperial authorities never condoned the Christian aggressions, but neither did they take a strong line against offenders. At the end of the fourth century the construction of new synagogues was only permitted with special authorization; in 415 the Jewish patriarch Gamaliel VI was robbed of his dignity as honorary prefect because he had contravened this rule [452]. The rule was then sharpened : even for the restoration of an existing synagogue a special authorization was needed [453].

In 423 Theodosius II decreed that synagogues and ritual objects that had been appropriated by Christians had to be restored to their original owners. However, if such buildings had already been consecrated for Christian use, indemnities should be paid [454]. In this way the illegal appropriation of Jewish ecclesiastical buildings was more or less condoned : the local bishop, after having consecrated them, needed only to pay (if he ever did). The Jews got permission to erect a new building on a site ceded to them by the local Church [455] (which was not always done) [456]. Juster concludes that the greatest risk a local Church might run by confiscating a synagogue was that it had to cede a few acres of land [457].

9. The general attitude of the imperial authorities

It must, however, not be thought that all imperial legislation was unfavourable to the Jews. The sons and successors of Theodosius I ruled in 397 that insulting the patriarch constituted a punishable offence [458]. More important was a rescript of July 1, 379, to the effect that the age-old privileges of the Jews would remain inviolated; these were, the decree continued, the same as the clerics of the Christian religion enjoyed [459]. This means that despite the fact that Christianity had now become the official religion, the ancient Jewish privileges, which dated from the days of Julius Caesar, had not been rescinded. A decree of 404 said that the privileges of the Jewish patriarch and those of the authorities nominated by him remained valid [460]. A curious regulation, one of the Emperor Theodosius II, stipulated that Jews who, for some practical reason, wanted to join the Church, should be prevented from doing this, if they were not sincere converts. 'Conversions' like these, the decree declared, were not in the interest of the faith [461].

Although the decrees mentioned were favourable to the Jews, two things must be remarked, however. The first is that these official documents referred to Judaism as a 'superstition'; the pagan Empire too had always considered it a 'superstition'. The second point is that Jews were often mentioned in one breath with Samaritans, heretics, Donatists, Manichaeans, etcetera, which, of course, was not meant in a friendly way.

10. The abolishment of the Jewish patriarchate

It was also disadvantageous to the Jewish position that the patriarchate of Tiberias was abolished in 425. Since the time of Caesar the Jews had had an eminent head, first the ethnarch, later the patriarch, the 'nassi' in Hebrew, nominated by the Emperor [462]. He possessed certain (non-sovereign) rights not only over the Palestinian Jews but also over those in the Diaspora. The Patriarchs were descendants of Hillel, a doctor of the Law, who was born in Babylonia but lived and worked in Jerusalem in the time of Herod I the Great. The famous Rabbi Gamaliel II was his great-grandson. In 425 the House of

Hillel became extinct. Theodosius then took the line that the function was a prerogative of the Hillelites but of nobody else, so that no new Patriarch was nominated.

11. An overall view

a. Why synagogues were attacked

Should we imagine that, after the last decades of the fourth century, the nightly sky was lit by the flames of burning synagogues all over the Empire? That there was a long-drawn-out 'Reichskristallnacht'? That would be a gross exaggeration. During this period over the whole extent of the Empire such incidents were really not the order of the day. All the same, we must ask why synagogues were attacked and/or confiscated. I feel that behind this indefensible behaviour of Christians lurked the fear of 'judaizing'. Synagogues were prayer-houses where not infrequently Christians went in order to join in the services. They were, therefore, even literally 'stones of offence'; they were seen as traps into which unsuspecting faithful might walk. It was for this reason that the Fathers fulminated against them; it was for the same reason that local bishops, uneasy about the loyalty of their flocks, sometimes instigated or even led the attackers. It was particularly the prayer-houses they aimed at; attacks on Jewish persons and private property remained extremely rare.

The Christians did not dispose as yet of the vast and grandiose churches of later ages. But Jewry, whose cult had always been licit, could show the most beautiful, large buildings, kept in repair and decorated by the cares of the whole community - buildings that, together with the venerable and colourful cult celebrated in them, exercized an almost irresistible attraction on non-Jews and, by the same token, evoked the jealousy, the irritation and the rage of another section of the Christians. Violent feelings that had their origin in fear and anxiety [463].

b. Jewish retaliations

Modern sensibility is inclined to consider the Jews as innocent victims of the Christians always and everywhere. But the Jews of Late Antiquity could be provocative and aggressive. Isaac admits as much, but, he continues, "could one be surprised about this since they had had to endure without reacting a regime of vexations, exclusions, humiliations ..." [464]. Without reacting? What about the revolt of 67-70 and the Bar Kokhba rising? The repeated rebellions in Palestine? The retaliations by the Jews against their pagan adversaries in Egypt, Cyrene, and Cyprus? And doesn't Isaac forget that for centuries on end anti-Jewish reactions came from the pagan Empire and its authorities? Doesn't he equally forget that for three centuries the Christians had been submitted, not so much to humiliations but to harassments of a serious kind, and even to bloody persecutions? In the first three centuries it was far more dangerous to be a Christian than to be a Jew.

Occasionally Christian churches were attacked by Jews [465]. In Egypt and Syria it also happened on more than one occasion that, during the Purim feast, when the 'gallows of Haman' were erected, a Christian cross was burned. Theodosius II instructed the provincial governors to prevent the Jews from doing this, on the penalty of losing all their privileges [466]. Another nasty incident is reported to have taken place in the Syrian city of Imnestar or Immestar; the Christian historian Socrates has it that drunken Jews seized a Christian child, bound it to a cross, and beat it to death. This heinous crime led to a formal battle between Jews and Christians, after which the perpetrators of the deed were duly punished [467].

c. Conclusion

Let us attempt to come to a conclusion. First of all, was there an inimical relationship between the two communities? I repeat that we have not one doctrinal statement on the subject of Judaism emanating from the highest authorities in the Church; no Pope condemned Jews 'ex cathedra' [468]. Whatever the Fathers of the Church might write or say, this body of opinion has no doctrinal or dogmatic value; their opinions do not form part of the 'depositum fidei'

It is not impossible, nor even improbable, that their anti-Judaistic stance exercized some influence on certain sections of the Christian population, so that, for instance, bishops felt entitled to seize Jewish synagogues. On the other hand, the constant harping by the Fathers on the theme of judaizing - that is showing sympathy with Jewish ritual and customs - proves that judaizing remained an attractive option for parts of their flocks. There are, however, no indications that Jews and Christians did not normally live peacefully together in the towns and villages all over the Empire. However, the seizure of synagogues, although by no means universal, must have caused bad blood with the Jews.

The Christian Emperors stuck throughout to their policy that Judaism was a religio licita. As well as they could they protected the religious rights of the Jewish community and tried in certain places to repair the damage done to them. However, the tone they assumed when speaking of Judaism was decidedly unsympathetic, although not more so than that adopted by their pagan predecessors.

But it is also true that their policy tended to isolate the Jews. We see them gradually pushed out of all the higher and lower echelons of public management. Whether there had ever been many Jewish officials is an open question. There have been Jewish senators, but never a Jewish consul or quaestor; the only Jewish provincial governors we know were renegades [469]. In the subaltern functions Jews were more numerous. The tendency of all the imperial decrees of the Christian period seems to have been to keep the two communities apart from each other, a policy that was doubtless inspired by the fear that Judaism might be contagious.

PART IV ASSESSMENT

1. Problems of the early Church

a. Internal problems

Let us recapitulate our findings so far and then try to come to an overall assessment. First of all, all generalizations in this field are dubious; the problem of the Jewish-Christian relationship needs a differentiated approach.

The Church of the first centuries was still a very young one, engaged in finding its definite form. Much had to be established : which books belonged to the canon of the New Testament, for instance. Theological tenets had to be defined, which caused problems with deviating sects, the largest of these being the Arians. The hierarchy had not yet acquired its definitive structure; a liturgy was being developed. A special problem was that of the faithful who had lapsed during the persecutions but wanted to be taken back into the fold. Finally, there was the problematic status of the judaizing Christians. True enough, the Church as such was 'judaizing' but the question was how much judaizing was to be allowed.

b. External problems

So much for the internal problems. But the Church had also to do with the outside world. The attitude of the pagan world was far from friendly which at irregular intervals led to bloody persecutions. During the first three centuries Christians could never feel safe. Then there were the Gnostics, no friends of the Christians and holding opinions of God, the Bible, and Christ, which were fundamentally different from those of the Church. I repeat that what pagans and Gnostics wrote about Jews and Judaism was on the whole far more hateful, insulting, and vitriolic than anything produced by a Christian author. The Fathers wrote innumerably more pages against the Gnostics than against the Jews, while we also possess several discussions with pagans. The impression that the Christians were the real enemies of Jewry in Late

Antiquity is wholly false. There was no persecution of Jews by Christians in this period. During the pagan period all the persecuting was done by the Empire. This also applies to the Jews who, apart from incidents in the first decades and in the peculiar circumstances of the Bar Kokhba revolt, did not harass the Christians.

2. The attitude of the Fathers regarding Jews and Judaism

The patterns in the attitude of the early Fathers with regard to Judaism are relatively uniform; the same topics, often expressed in almost identical terms, move from author to author [470]. But there are shades of meaning, differing according to the temperament of a specific author; they vary from the positive assessment by Aphrahat to the moderate utterances of a mild man like Clement of Alexandria to the diatribes of a fierce orator like John Chrysostom. What I read so often, that the early Church totally rejected Judaism and turned against, is not correct in this generalized form. All the Fathers were deeply convinced that Christianity had sprung from Judaism; they were grateful for the Jewish inheritance embodied in the Old and New Testaments from which profoundly Jewish books the whole Christian creed is born. This conviction made them sometimes defend Judaism against the Gnostics, the Marcionites, for instance, who would know nothing of the Old Testament.

It must be kept in mind that 'the Jews' in the writings of the Fathers were rarely, if ever, their contemporaries. Almost always the term refers to the historical Jews, those of the Old Testament and the time of Jesus [471]. If we want to be informed of the way of life and opinions of the Jewry of the second to fourth centuries, we would seek in vain in those bulky tomes. I wonder whether any of the Fathers was cognizant of the Talmud. If Jewish individuals appear in these works, anonymous as they almost always are, they are the teachers and advisers of the authors, who obviously appreciated them and admired their penetrating insight into the heart of the Old Testament.

The Fathers never speak of the Jews in racist terms. Neither do we find the denigrating and offensive labels attached to them by pagan authors nor do the Fathers believe the calumnies that were so readily swallowed even by intelligent and well-informed Romans. The Christian writers move about in the field of theology, and nowhere else. The tag is that 'mathematica mathematice scribuntur', that mathematics are described mathematically; likewise we may say that 'theologica theologice scribuntur'. As theologians the Fathers write theology and are not, or scarcely, interested in politics and social affairs. For a long time even philosophy remained a side-issue.

Speaking of the anti-Judaism of early Christian authors, we should never forget how difficult it was for them to define their position vis-à-vis Judaism with the unequivocalness the subject requires. Their attitude always remains somewhat ambivalent. It had to be made clear that Christians were not Jews, this also with an eye on faithful with judaizing tendencies; this was all the more urgent since not a few Christians practised a mixture of Judaism and Christianity. "We have originated from your midst", writes Tertullian, addressing pagans, "one becomes a Christian, one is not born as a Christian" [472]. 'Jewishness' is an ethnical concept, being a Christian is not.

On the one hand Christians knew perfectly well that the Church had her origin in Judaism and that she was 'Jewish' in many respects, for instance in her unconditional acceptance of the Old Testament. They were deeply convinced that their religion had originated from and was dependent on Judaism and the Old Testament. Christians too are children of Abraham. Our apologists found themselves often in a quandary when it came to defining their position vis-à-vis Judaism. For they also wanted to make it clear that the Church is not a branch of Judaism and that Christians are no Jews. The line these authors took was that the Jewish religion, venerable and valuable as it was, was nevertheless outdated and had become redundant. Now there was a new Israel and a new Covenant.

Tertullian for one saw himself obliged to steer a middle course between rejecting Judaism out of hand - which he was by no means prepared to do - and risk being accused of judaizing - which happened indeed. His predicament becomes evident where he speaks of Esau and Jacob, the twins in Rebecca's womb. "The Lord said to her : 'Two nations in your womb, two peoples going their own way from birth! One shall be stronger than the other; the older (Esau) shall be servant to the younger (Jacob)'" [473]. "The first and older nation, which is the Jewish one, must necessarily serve the younger, and the younger, which is the Christian, must lord it over the older" [474]. Of course, this is not phrased in a particularly amicable way, but the fact remains that the two 'nations' are brothers, and more than that, even twins.

3. The main points of the Jewish-Christian debate

With this in mind, we can state that the debate between Jews and Christians concentrated on two main points. On the Jewish side this was that the Church had abolished Mosaic Law, on the Christian side that the Jews were not prepared to accept that the Messiah had appeared in the person of Jesus of Nazareth. This Christian Messianic creed led to another controversial issue, namely, that this Jesus was the Son of God, the second person of the Holy Trinity. On the Jewish side this raised the anxious question whether perhaps the Christians were ditheists, that they venerated two gods. On the Christian side this tenet of the Sonship might lead, if driven to its ultimate consequences, to the accusation of 'deicide', of the murder of God. This accusation was in fact only rarely explicitly formulated, but it was doubtless implicitly present.

I feel that early Christian apologists found it hard to counter the Jewish reproach that the Church had abandoned Mosaic Law. Barnabas took the most radical way by declaring that the Law was all 'foolishness', but this simplistic solution was not sufficient to satisfy serious minds. To Irenaeus the Law was an educational device with only a temporary character. Now that Jesus Christ had come, the supreme teacher of mankind and a law onto himself, it had lost its validity.

Great problems ask for radical solutions, and Barnabas was ready to present one : there never had been a Covenant! God had been prepared to conclude an alliance with Israel, but when Moses was descending from the Sinai, he saw that the Israelites were adoring idols; he then shattered the two tables to the ground. And this meant that there would be no alliance, no Covenant [475]. The very welcome consequence was that there was also no Mosaic Law then, at least not a law that could claim general validity. Is there no law at all then? Of course there is; it is the Law of Jesus Christ that has been inscribed into the hearts of men long before Christ actually appeared [476].

A more subtle solution was to view the Jewish religion as a symbol for or a model of the more perfect religion that was still to come. This becomes apparent in the typological exegesis that so long was very popular among biblical scholars and preachers; this kind of exegesis implies that Old Testament figures must be taken as prefigurations of persons and events in the New Testament, for instance that the intended sacrifice of Isaac by his father Abraham foreshadowed the sacrificial death of Jesus on the cross. Melito of Sardes stated this with great precision. "All that has been said and all that has happened (i.e. in the Old Testament) is nothing ..., if it is separated from its symbolic significance and from the plan that was found in advance. All that occurs and all that is said participates of the symbol : the word of the symbolic significance, the event of the prefiguration, so that, just as the event is revealed by its prefiguration, the word is illuminated by its symbol".

Thinking of the Jewish religion, Melito also uses the word 'model' : Israel served as the model for the Church. "But when that for which the model was destined has been realized, that which presented the image of the future is destroyed, since it has become useless; it has ceded its image to that which really exists" [477]. Irenaeus takes the same line when he speaks of the story of Lot who slept with his daughters [478]. Bible-readers are sometimes somewhat offended that the Genesis author blames neither the father nor the daughters for this (the blame is, of course, built into the story itself). Irenaeus says that where God does not blame, we should not blame either. Instead, one should look for the typological meaning [479]; it is this meaning which lifts this story above the level of the purely incidental.

"Not only", concludes Taylor, "does this passage confirm that the references to Judaism had a symbolic meaning, but it testifies to the fact that the Church fathers adopted this symbolic approach in a deliberate and self-conscious meaning" [480]. It enabled them to take their distance from

Judaism, and in particular from the Law, and at the same time use the Old Testament as their goldmine.

The Fathers nowhere explained what they understood by 'the Law'; it would have saved a lot of misunderstandings had they done so. They did, of course, not reject the Ten Commandments and all the moral precepts that immediately followed from the Decalogue. But they saw no point in preserving the so-called 'oral law', the large collection of prescriptions and prohibitions, mainly of Pharasaic construction, and not to be found in the Old Testament. They also saw no use in a Christian world mainly of pagan provenance for the purity rules and food taboos that are inscribed in the books of the Pentateuch, Mosaic Law proper. Since Mosaic Law, its strict observance and its interpretation by the Rabbis, became the prop and mainstay of Jewish community life after the catastrophes, this rejection irritated the Jews immensely. But the Fathers replied that the Church did reject the Law only in its literal sense but kept the spirit, that of devotion, purity, chastity, liberality, love. In this sense, they felt, the Church remained tributary to Mosaic Law and true to its spirit.

That the Jews had not recognized Jesus as the Messiah and had even crucified him disappointed the Christians bitterly. The Jews had been the Messianic nation, but when the Messiah came, they defaulted. The Fathers found it really incomprehensible that the Jews had not understood what the prophets had foretold in no uncertain terms. This made them so angry that they sometimes become harsh and nasty. Their disappointment that the Jews had not come in en masse caused them to be unjust. When they went looking for an explanation, they could only conclude that the Jews, especially those of prophetic times, had become materialistic and worldly. The prophetic books offered them more than enough material for their opinions; the Fathers never tired of quoting their own prophets against the Jews.

4. The problem of judaizing

If this disaffection of the Jews was a source of disappointment in the Church, the status of the Judaizers was perhaps more important in determining the attitude of the Fathers. It is evident that with the term 'the Jews' they meant, more often than not, the ideological background of the Judaizers. The position these people occupied was very strong indeed, since the backdrop of Christianity was Judaism. The Fathers tried to weaken their position by cutting the ground from under their feet; the tactics they used was to lessen the impact Judaism still had by declaring it worthless and a thing of the past. The fact that Father after Father returned to the attack proves that judaizing did not easily go away. Even at the end of the fourth century John Chrysostom saw fit to mount a campaign against 'the Jews', not mincing his words, a campaign in which he constantly had the Judaizers in mind. That the same arguments were repeated over and over again is a clear indication that the faithful were not deeply impressed by what their pastors said.

But why did the Fathers, set their faces so sternly against judaizing, even to the point of disavowing the Judaistic roots of the Church? This was, I feel, a question of identity. The Church was 'Jewish' but not Jewish. She had this Judaistic background, and she readily acknowledged this. But she was neither a Jewish sect nor a branch of Judaism. The Judaizers, by blurring the distinctions and by wanting to belong to both camps at once, made the defining of the Christian identity more difficult that it needed to be. For centuries the Church wrestled with this problem till at last the habit of judaizing faded out and disappeared (or went underground).

The painful question is whether, with the cause, the consequences also disappeared, I mean the anti-Judaistic stance of the Church. This tendency, by prevailing for so long, became more or less constitutive for the Christian mentality. After centuries of arguing against judaizing tendencies (with its corrolary of polemizing against Judaism itself), it had become very hard, if not downright impossible, to conduct an irenic discussion with Judaism and to define without any bias or animosity the relations between the two religions. The Judaizers, as the disturbing factor, had made this impossible. The net result of the discussion, such as it was actually conducted, was that the Church had been manoeuvred (by the Judaizers) or had manoeuvred herself into a predicament out of which it was almost impossible to escape.

5. Was the Jewish-Christian relationship dualistic?

It will probably have struck the reader that I, throughout this long chapter, have studiously avoided to employ the terms 'dualism' and 'dualistic'. That I provided the chapter title 'Judaism and Christianity : a dualistic relationship?' with a question mark, signifies that I did not start from the premise, as many authors do, that the relation was indeed dualistic. No doubt, it was in many respects antagonistic which means that it was not uniformly peaceful and harmonious. Whether it was characterized by the unbridgeable oppositions of dualism, that I set out to examine, carefully, objectively, methodically, and in as unbiased a manner as possible.

Answering the climactic question whether or not the Jewish-Christian relationship in Late Antiquity was dualistic saddled me with considerable problems on which I have pondered deeply during the writing of this chapter. I think I had best start from my own definition of dualism such as I presented it in the Prefaces of volume after volume. We may speak of dualism when we are confronted by two fundamentally opposed poles (whether of conceptions, principles, systems, power blocks, groups of people, sects, or even worlds) without any intermediate terms between them. These opposites cannot be reduced to each other; in some cases they are not even dependent on each other. They are considered to be of a different quality - so much so that some of them are seen as distinctly inferior and hence must be neglected, repudiated or even destroyed. I add that I do not allow myself the escape road of stating that the relationship in question was, perhaps, partly dualistic. A relationship is either dualistic or it is not.

What makes the problem really complicated is that the Jewish-Christian relationship was not a simple thing, so much so that it will not do to speak of 'the Christians' and 'the Jews'. There are five strands in it : the relations between both population groups in these centuries on the level of daily life - the opinions of the Patres on the Jews of their own days - their arguing against 'the Jews' and 'Judaism' - the official ecclesiastical policy with regard to Jews - and the imperial policy regarding them since Constantine the Great.

Some of these points can be quickly disposed of. There existed no 'Jewish policy' formulated by the highest doctrinal office of the Church, from the Popes or, as we would say to-day, from 'the Vatican'. When the Council of Nicaea and some provincial synods took the matter up, it was to keep the Judaizers in check. With an exception made of the first decades of the Church during which the Jews behaved inimically towards Christians, things went smoothly enough between the two population groups on the social and personal level. True enough, towards the end of the fourth and during the fifth century there occurred acts of hooliganism against synagogues. Such acts will not have contributed to a reciprocally friendly atmosphere. On the other hand, no civil-war-like situations are reported. There seems to have been no Empire-wide drive to rob the Jews of their prayer-houses. We do not possess enough evidence to regard this kind of relationship as antagonistic, let alone as dualistic.

The attitude of the Fathers regarding, so to speak, their own Jews, their contemporaries and co-citizens, is almost entirely a blank; they were nearly totally unconcerned. In some of the rare cases that they mention them they are downright laudatory : Jews are assiduous Bible readers, display a deep understanding of the Old Testament, have a high morality.

The official policy of the Christian Emperors was and remained that Judaism was a religio licita entitled to protection by the authorities. This right was not always actualized. During the fifth century the Jews were being gradually ousted from all kinds of public functions. The rulers were clearly of the opinion that the Empire could not be truly 'Christian', if there were Jewish functionaries. Unpleasant and decidedly unchristian as this policy is, it did not lead to the formation of Jewish ghettoes. I see no reason for dubbing this policy as dualistic, since. quite apart from this, no other measures with regard to Jews or Judaism were involved. However, the situation was fraught with danger for Jewry. This socio-political antagonism could easily develop into dualism; the gradual exclusion of the Jews tended in this direction.

It is often stated that this policy of the Emperors was influenced or instigated by the Church. Now we saw that there were no official ecclesiastical pronouncements regarding Judaism to which the rulers might refer. Did the books of the Fathers have an influence on them? Politicians, practical men as they are, are not the greatest readers. Must we imagine that they, in their spare time, sat reading those voluminous tomes? On the whole we should not overestimate the effect of patristic writing on the general (Christian) populace. Not only are these texts often composed in sophisticated Latin or Greek, full of theological terms, but the degree of literacy among the whole population was rather low, perhaps not more than 10 %, higher in the towns than in the country.

6. Patristic neurosis

What now remains to be considered is the polemizing of the Fathers against 'Judaism' and 'the Jews'. Not without bewilderment I read, studied, analyzed, and pondered on the relevant texts. The Patres were, on the whole, well-educated, learned, intelligent, and benevolent men. But what on earth were they talking about? Certainly not about the biblical religion and people of Israel! They are fighting an hypothetical entity called by them 'Judaei' or 'Ioudaoi', artificially composed, mainly on the basis of the rebukes by the prophets. Often, when reading the Patres, I got the impression that they were conducting a donquixotic fight against windmills, against ghosts of their own making. There is something neurotic in this; it is a neurosis, in fact. I am not saying that the Fathers were abnormal people. By no means! But in this special respect they were surely unbalanced.

It is, of course, highly seductive to call their attitude dualistic, the more so because dualism, as I use to say, is, like beauty, in the beholder's eye. Their 'Jews' existed only 'in their eye' and had no basis in reality. But such a statement would not spell the solution of our problem. For those selfsame authors were perfectly aware that Christianity was not only dependent on but also tributary to Judaism in matters of understanding the Old Testament, of the main theological tenets, of the liturgy, of the hierarchy. In these things their attitude was just the opposite of dualism. How could it be otherwise in a community whose founder was a Jew? The Fathers could not reject Judaism without disavowing Jesus. Let us reach a conclusion. The attitude of the Fathers regarding Judaism and Jewry was not dualistic. There were far too many intermediate terms and connecting links between the two religions to allow us to speak of dualism.

Let us now try to establish what the causes were of the neurotic attitude of the Patres respecting Judaism and Jews. I believe there exist quite a number of causes. The first is the aggressiveness the Jews displayed against Christians during the first century A.D. Although there was no longer Jewish violence since the end of this century (with the exception of fatal incidents during the Bar Kokhba revolt in the period 131-135), a residual fear of it lingered on, a fear to which, for instance, Irenaeus gave expression as late as A.D. 170. The second factor is the disppointment (and irritation) felt by the Christian community over the fact that the Jews, instead of coming in en masse, had set their faces against the Church.

Possibly the fear would have died out and the disappointment have faded away (the non-conversion of the Jews having been accepted as a fait accompli), if there had not existed a third powerful factor, that of the judaizing of certain sections of the Christian fold. This wide-spread tendency to judaizing proved, to the dismay of the Fathers, that Judaism was still vital and attractive. They feared that the urge towards Judaism - exemplified by 'the synagogue' (hence the attacks on synagogues) - would be the channel along which Christians would slip away into the old religion.

But there is more to this. The Church of these centuries had to define her identity opposite paganism and the Gnosis. This was not so difficult since the difference with these two religions was great and clear-cut. But, as I wrote before, defining herself vis-à-vis Judaism was a far greater problem for the Church in view of the close kinship of the two religions. It was a work that should have been undertaken as a main task of theological scholarship in an irenic spirit, thoughtfully and caringly. However, the three factors I mentioned made this unworkable. Especially judaizing acted as a disturbing and destabilizing factor; judaizing Christians blurred the distinctions between the two religions. This made it extremely hard for the Church to find herself, so much so that it was all too easily lost sight of that the two religions had in common. This destabilization accounts for the neurosis.

7. A personal note

Just as I began this chapter with a personal note, I will end with one. If the Fathers were unjust towards Jews and Judaism, we should not be unjust with regard to them. They were saintly men, devout believers, convinced Christians, ready to die for their faith - Ignatius and Polycarp, Justin, probably Irenaeus too, and Cyprian suffered martyrdom, while Origen was cruelly tortured. Their combating Judaism and fighting judaizing formed only a small part of their activities; their theological and exegetical work covered far larger fields, while many of them were active as bishops, serving their flocks as good pastors and ably managing ecclesiastical affairs. But it is true that they did say things about Jews and Judaism that had better remained unsaid. This is their weak spot and this is where they failed, with consequences for the future.

In their zeal they were often blind, almost entirely forgetful of what Paul wrote to the Romans : that Judaism is the tree on which Christianity grows. The apostle did not say that the tree had been hewed down to make place for a new and better one. No, Christians are grafted upon the tree, and this means that they draw their vital sap from it. The Jewish-Christian relationship is not one of good neighbourhood, of ecumenism, of respecting and understanding each other. This relation is of an existential nature : Christianity cannot exist without Judaism.

It thrives on the metaphysical idea, and this idea it has from Israel, 'the only one of all ancient peoples that lived metaphysically' [481]. Israel was and is the guarantee of this idea. She was the only people in Antiquity that knew a transcendent God, a God who did not coincide with nature, who is not nature, who exists from eternity and does not need nature to exist.

She is also the soil on which the idea of a Messiah grew; she was and is God's envoy on earth, his messenger. In the words of Elisabeth Langgässer in her profound novel 'Die märkische Argonautenfahrt' (1950), she is "the object par excellence of the history of salvation, his (God's) bride, his womb, his sealed well, his cistern, his Ark of the Covenant; she, the only one, had to bring forth the only one, the Messiah". Israel is always present in the Church as a living force through her holy books and, above all, in Jesus Messiah who was a Jew.

Israel will accompany the Church throughout the ages; nobody can or will destroy her, no Haman, no Hitler. For the great event has still to come. Finally, is Paul's prophecy, when the mass of the heathen will have come in, Israel will enter too. There will be no longer any difference between Judaism and Christianity then; the two will be one. And then the end is there.

NOTES TO CHAPTER I

1. See Vol. IX, Ch. V, Part II.2.
2. Part I of Wistrich's book 'Antisemitism' is called 'From the cross to the swastika'.
3. Jules Isaac, Antisém. 15, expresses this sentiment in the most forceful terms. "Après enquête historique approfondie, je dis et je soutiens que le sort d'Israël n'a pris un caractère vraiment inhumain qu'à partir du IVe siècle après Jésus-Christ, avec l'avènement de l'Empire chrétien. Je dis et je soutiens que le sort d'Israël s'est terriblement aggravé dans l'Europe chrétienne, quand commença avec la première Croisade ce qu'on peut appeler l'ère de la Grande Chrétienté. Je dis et je soutiens que le racisme exterminateur de notre époque (i.e. the Holocaust), même s'il est dans son essence antichrétien, s'est développé en terre chrétienne, et qu'il a soigneusement recueilli l'héritage, le très douloureux héritage du christianisme." This sounds more like an indictment than an objective historical judgment. Isaac's statement is at variance with the conclusion of Léon Poliakov, Histoire I, 50/51, that for the first thousand years of Christianity one can hardly speak of Christian anti-Semitism. I heroically withstand the temptation to show that Adolf Hitler was as anti-Christian as imaginable and that he was not an anti-Semite in the ordinary sense of the word.
In his introduction to Ruether, Faith, Gregor Baum, writing as a Roman-Catholic priest, says this. "The Church has produced an abiding contempt among Christians for Jews and all things Jewish, a contempt that aided Hitler's purposes. The Church made the Jewish people a symbol of unredeemed humanity; it painted a picture of the Jews as a blind, stubborn, carnal, and perverse people, an image that was fundamental in Hitler's choice of the Jews as the scapegoat." I make two remarks. In Hitler's view the Jews did not have the function of 'the scapegoat'; to him they were something quite different. Secondly, if the allegedly wide-spread Christian anti-Semitism was so helpful, why then did he keep his real intentions with regard to the Jews so completely secret?
4. The Tablet (London), Jan. 21, 1995.

5. The Tablet (London), Febr. 4, 1995.
6. See for this subject Cohen, "Anti-Sem.' 43-47.
7. Sevenster, Roots 41 : "The term anti-Semitism is not old and was apparently first used by W. Mair who began the publication of his 'Zwangslose antisemitische Hefte' in 1880".
8. 1 Clem. 40:5.
9. The movie is in French, with Alain Delon and Jeanne Moreau as the main characters.
10. Rom. 10:12 and 11:17.
11. Horsley, Jesus and Jud. 57.
12. The term was also used for Pharisees.
13. See Vol. VII, Ch. IV.5g.
14. Flusser, Jesus and Judaism 88.
15. Jos., Ant. 20.9.1.
16. Jos., Ant. 13.10.6.
17. Flusser, Jesus and Judaism 97.
18. Neusner, Judaism 54/55.
19. Vol. VII, CH. V.
20. Neusner, Judaism 37.
21. They are regularly mentioned in Vol. XI, Ch. V, from Part III.4c, onward.
22. See Vol. VII, Ch. IV.4c.
23. Neusner, Judaism 38.
24. Vol. VII, Ch. IV.5h.
25. Acts 15:5.
26. Jo. 7:4.
27. Neusner, Judaism 30.
28. Neusner, Judaism 39.
29. Vol. VII, Ch. IV.5g.
30. Jo. 11:47-50.
31. Mt. 26:57.
32. Mt. 27:14.
33. Jo. 11:46 and 57.

34. Jo.18:12-14.
35. Jo. 18:31.
36. Acts 2:23.
37. Acts 3:17.
38. Mt. 16:11.
39. Mt. 23:1-4.
40. See for this subject also Vol. VII, Ch. IV.5g.
41. Mt. 13:53-56; Mc. 6:2-4; Lc. 4:20-30.
42. Mt. 26:59-67; Mc. 14:55-65; Lc. 22:66-71.
43. Jo. 19:7-12.
44. Lc. 23:1.
45. See Vol. XI, Ch. V.7b-c.
46. Contrary to the office of the High Priest, Jewish priesthood is hereditary (although priests were ordained). Priests are supposed to be descendants of Aaron. The word for this in Hebrew is 'kohen', plural 'kohanim'; all those male Jews who are called 'kohen', are allowed to exercize priestly functions. This applies to all the variations of the name 'kohen' : Cohen, Cohan, Cohn, Kahn, Kohn, Caen, even Coen, Kahan, Kagan, Kaganowitch, and numerous others in all kinds of languages. There exist families who have dropped the name 'cohen' in favour of another, a second one; for instance, the well-known Dutch family Belinfante is really a family Cohen Belinfante. Such a family too is priestly. Some 2 à 3 % of modern Jewry bears the name 'Cohen' or a variation of it. This does not mean that all those bearers of the priestly name really exercize their priestly functions. An example is my own professor of classical history in the University of Amsterdam, when I studied there, Dr. David Cohen; he was a non-practising Jew and never thought of acting as a priest. It does, however, not matter whether a 'kohen' is a believer or an oberver of the Law : priest he is. To keep the lineage pure, a priest may not marry a non-Jew, not even a proselyte. Priests no longer offer sacrifices, but they may recite the blessings and preside at ritual occasions, such as marriage and burial.
47. Neusner, Judaism 178/179, gives six reasons why the Pharisees, in contrast to other Jewish factions, survived the catastrophe. The most important, I believe, are : "They advanced a comprehensive program for the religious life to replace the sacrificial system"; 2. "They also had the confidence of large parts of the nation"; 3. "The Pharisees now vigorously pressed their earlier claims to represent the one legitimate authority for the interpretation of Judaism ... Now began the process by which they eventually came to constitute 'normative Judaism'.

48. Avery-Peck, Judaism 423.
49. See Vol. VII, Ch. VI.1b.
50. Avery-Peck, Judaism 411.
51. See Vol. VII, Ch. VI.1a-b.
52. Avery-Peck, Judaism 415.
53. See Vol. VII, Ch. VI.1.
54. Avery-Peck, Judaism 418.
55. Avery-Peck, Judaism 419.
56. Avery-Peck, Judaism 424.
57. This statement is repeated in Rom, 11:1 and in Gal. 1:13 and 2:15.
58. Gal. 2.
59. Vol. VII, Ch. IV.5k.
60. Jo. 18:31.
61. Jesus' harsh words : "You (the Jews) have the devil for your father", Jo. 8:44, have been explained as shorthand for Christian opposition to Judaism in the first and second centuries A.D. Rengstorf, Neue Test. 38, however, sees it as an ethical or theological expression meaning that a triumph over the devil would be necessary to make the Jews acknowledge the Messiah. John had not given up the Jews as hopeless. Jesus' words that "all those who believe in him will not be lost but will have eternal life", Jo. 3:16, also include the Jews; John does not consider it impossible that they will come to conversion.
62. Acts 6:7.
63. Axts 6:8-8:1.
64. See for this whole passage Vol. VII, Ch. IV.5l.
65. Acts 12:1-19.
66. Acts 18:1-7.
67. Acts 28:16-28. See also Vol. VII, Ch. IV.5l.
68. Here I am quoting myself verbatim from Vol. VII, p. 175.
69. The reader must forgive me for quoting myself again verbatim from Vol. VII, Ch. IV.5m.
70. See Matsunaga, Self-Ident., 355/356.
71. Matsunaga, Self-Ident. 356.
72. This is also the opinion of Rengstorf, Neue Test. 36 : "Insofern bildet die Einfügung der zitierten Bitte an das Achtzehngebet auf der

jüdischen Seite tatsächlich 'eines der Mittel zur völligen Scheidung der beiden Religionen'"; this author is quoting here I. Elbogen, Der jüdische Gottesidee in seiner geschichtlichen Entwicklung, Frankfurt a.M., 1931, p. 36. It should be noted that Kimelman in his study 'Birkat ha-Minim' (see Bibliography) comes to the conclusion that the prayer was not directed against Gentile Christians but against Jewish sectarians. These sectarians were Jewish Christians.

73. In his book 'History and Theology in the Fourth Gospel', Nashville, 1979, pp. 37-62, quoted by Matsunaga, Self-Ident. 358/359.

74. Goppelt, Christ. und Jud. 252.

75. Goppelt, Christ. und Jud. 259.

76. See for this subject Silver, Where Judaism differed (See Bibliography). This author goes much deeper into this subject than I can do here.

77. Acts 4:18.

78. Acts 5:40-42.

79. Just.Mart., Dial.Tryph. 10.3 and 32.1.

80. Simon, Verus Israel 190.

81. Acts 5:34-40.

82. Simon, Verus Israel 189.

83. Just., Dial. 48.1 and 49.1.

84. Simon, Verus Israel 196.

85. Scholem, Toward an Understanding 1.

86. Acts 10.

87. Acts 15:1-29. See also Vol. VII, Ch. IV.5j.

88. Acts 21:28.

89. See Vol. VII, Ch. VI.3a. Ziegler, Kampf 53 : "Nicht Jesus war der Gegner, sondern Paulus und seine Genossen und seine Nachfolger ... (73) dass das Judentum und seine Vertreter, gegen Jesus persönlich vorzugehen keinerlei Ursache hatten und es tatsächlich auch nicht taten. In dem Augenblick aber, in welchem Paulus die Befreiung vom Gesetze, von der Beschneidung und den Speisegesetzen aussprach, entbrannte sofort der Kampf".

90. This is what the Jewish author Silver, Where Judaism differed 4/5, has to say. "No special metaphysics, no unique 'knowledge' or secret gnosis which is requisite for salvation, no evangel of a miraculous scheme for salvation are offered by Judaism." This means that Judaism is essentially different both from the Gnosis and from Christianity. "Judaism is Torah - 'teaching' ... The term Halachah which the Rabbis employed for laws based on the Torah also means

the proper *way* (Silver's italics) in which a man should walk. Judaism's 'way' is designed to sustain and advance life, not to escape or transcend it. Its roots are set deep in the practical needs of man ... Judaism is a devout morality."

91. Adam Michnik, Poland and the Jews. New York Review of Books. May 30, 1991.

92. The real name of 'Jud Süss' was Joseph Ben Issachar Süsskind Oppenheimer, 1698 or 1699-2.IV.1738. While in prison in his last days, he refused to accept baptism to save his life. See the entries by Zvi Avneri s.v. 'Oppenheimer' in Enc.Jud. 12 (1971), 1428-1430, and by Theodor Kroner s.v. 'Oppenheimer' in Jew.Enc. 9 (1945), 415-419.

93. Deut. 22:8.

94. Schürer, Hist. III.1, 165/166. There were even Gentiles who took part in the sacrificial cult in the Temple of Jerusalem by offering sacrifices there, but "wished in no way to make thereby a confession of faith", Schürer, Hist. II, 309-313.

95. Harnack, Mission I. This is forcefully expressed in his introduction 1-3.

96. Harnack, Mission I, 77.

97. In his book of 1948 'Verus Israel' (see Bibliography).

98. Taylor, Anti-Judaism 3.

99. Taylor, Anti-Judaism 7 : "The consensus in support of Marcel Simon's thesis is indeed impressive".

100. Baron, Hist. I,135.

101. Feldman, Jewish Proselytism (see Bibliography).

102. Taylor, Anti-Jud. 5.

103. Acts 2:5-13.

104. Dio 67.14.68.

105. Emil G. Hirsch s.v. 'Proselyte', Jew.Enc. X (1945), 223.

106. EH/Ed. s.v. Proselytes', Enc.Jud. 13 (1971), 1185.

107. Simon, Verus Israel 274.

108. Simon, Verus Israel 278.

109. Bamberger, Proselytism 274, says that "the Pharisees and the Rabbis were eager for converts, highly successful in winning them, and friendly in their treatment of them", although he admits that not all the Rabbis were so favourably disposed, while (p. 277) "it seems probable that among the people as a whole there were certain prejudices against converts". The statements in the Talmud which

express hostility to proselytism are listed by him pp. 161-165. He lists all the cases of conversion to Judaism to be found in the Talmud in his Ch. XI. 45 cases in all are listed, but not one conversion was due to missionary activity on the Jewish side; these converts came to Judaism on their own initiative. Hence I do not understand Bamberger's conclusion that "the official leaders were eager to make converts and highly successful in achieving their aim" (p. 272).
Braude, Jew.Pros. 38, says that some of the disparaging rabbinic remarks about proselytizing are misunderstood; these Rabbis, he says, had nothing against converts, but only against unworthy converts. He comes to the conclusion (p.75) that "all the rabbis spoke enthusiastically of proselyting and idealized converts and their makers ... The Hadrianic and other persecutions did not dampen Jewish aspirations to win Gentiles to the faith of Israel". But somewhat surprisingly he then states that "there appears to be no evidence that Jews sent missionaries into partes infidelium to bring about mass conversions ... I am inclined to regard mass propaganda as a Christian invention".
More recently, Goodman, Jew.Pros., arrives at similar conclusions. With regard to the first century A.D. he explains "how unlikely the picture is of a Jewish mission to win converts" (p.71). And on p. 75 : "There is no good reason to suppose that any Jew would have seen value in seeking proselytes in the first century with an enthusiasm like that of the Christian apostles". With regard to the second and third centuries A.D. he states (p. 74) that "some Jews seem to have begun looking for converts in just the same way as they apparently were not doing in the first century", but he admits that the evidence, although extensive, is 'oblique'.

110. Mt. 23:15.
111. Simon, Verus Israel 278/279.
112. Taylor, Anti-Jud. 16.
113. Smallwood, Jews 129/130.
114. Smallwood, Jews 205/206.
115. Smallwood, Jews 130.
116. Smallwood, Jews 122.
117. Taylor, Anti-Jud. 4.
118. Taylor, Anti-Jud. 20/21.
119. Ruether, Faith 48-52. Her term 'Jewish Gnosticism' is invalidated by the 'diabolizing of the Jewish God". This is a contradiction in terms. Somebody who 'diabolizes' God cannot be called a Jew. Just as there was no Christian Gnosis - see Vol. IX, Ch. V, Part II -, there was no Jewish Gnosis.
120. Vol. VII, Ch. III.1c.

121. Vol. VII, Ch. III.1p.
122. Vol. VII, Ch. III.3.
123. Vol. VII, Ch. III.5d.
124. Vol. VIII, Ch. IV.13.
125. Vol. VIII, Ch. III.18c.
126. Vol. VIII, Ch. V.15.
127. Vol. VIII, Ch. VI.8c-d.
128. Vol. VIII, Ch. VII.4d.
129. Vol. IX, Ch. II.11.
130. Vol. IX, Ch. II.3d.
131. Vol. VIII, Ch. IX.3a.
132. Kirsopp Lake, Apost. Fathers I, 4.
133. Eus., HE 3.22.
134. The question what and who were meant by Ignatius when he spoke of Judaism and Judaizers is extensively treated by Barrett, Jews and Judaizers 221-244 (see Bibliography).
135. Ign., Magn. 2-7.
136. Ign., Magn. 4.
137. Ign., Magn. 7.2.
138. Ign., Magn. 11.
139. Simon, Verus Israel 311.
140. Ign., Magn. 8.1.
141. Ign., Magn. 10.3.
142. Ign., Magn. 9.1.
143. Ign., Magn. 10.2.
144. Rom. 11:16-24.
145. Ign., Magn. 10.3.
146. Ign., Magn. 8.2.
147. Ign., Phil. 6.1.
148. Ign., Phil. 9.
149. Kirsopp Lake, Apost. Fathers I, 307.
150. Kirsopp Lake, Apost. Fathers I, 337/338.

151. Simon, Verus Israel 91/92.
152. Barn., 2.
153. Barn. 4.6-8.
154. Barn. 5.1-2.
155. Barn. 9.
156. Barn. 10.2.
157. Barn. 18.1.
158. Barn. 20.
159. Simon, Verus Israel 92.
160. Williams, Bird's-eye view 14.
161. Diogn. 4.
162. PG 6. Paris, 1857.
163. 1Ap. 31.
164. 1Ap. 36.
165. 1Ap. 49.
166. PG 6. Paris, 1857.
167. Eus., HE 4.18.6.
168. Just., Dial. 10.2.
169. Just., Dial. 17.1.
170. Just., Dial. 16.4.
171. Tert., Scorpiace 10.4.
172. Taylor, Anti-Jud. 95.
173. Just., Dial. 12.
174. Just., Dial. 11.1.
175. Just., Dial. 29.2.
176. Just., Dial. 11.2.
177. Just., Dial. 11.5.
178. Just., Dial. 14.2.
179. Williams, Bird's-eye View 42.
180. Melito, Peri Pascha (see Bibliography). See Stuart G. Hall s.v. 'Melito von Sardes', Theol.Realenz. Bd. XXII, Lief. 2/3, 424-428. Berlin, 1992.
181. Taylor, Anti-Jud. 55.

213

182. Melito, Pascha 69.
183. This is exemplary for the feats he is performing, for 'pascha' is Hebrew, and 'paschein' is Greek.
184. Melito, Pascha 70.
185. Melito, Pascha 81.
186. Melito, Pascha 87.
187. Melito, Pascha 92.
188. Melito, Pascha 99/100.
189. Taylor, Anti-Jud. 63.
190. Melito, Pascha 94.
191. Melito, Pascha 75/76.
192. Rengstorf, Neue Test. 73 : "Mit Sicherheit wäre nichts verkehrter, als dem Bischof von Sardes einen platten und böswilligen Antisemitismus vorzuwerfen. Seine Schrift enthält nichts, was in diese Richtung weist. Die Juden, die er im Auge hat und anklagt, sind nicht die Juden seiner Zeit und vollends nicht die Juden seiner Diözese, sondern die Juden von damals, die Juden des ersten Karfreitags in Jerusalem".
193. Cfr. Ir., Adv.haer. 2, Praef. 2.
194. Ir., Adv.haer. 4.5 and 9.
195. Ir., Adv.haer. 4.21.1.
196. Ir., Adv.haer. 4.3.4.
197. Ir., Adv.haer. 4.21.3.
198. Taylor, Anti-Jud. 101. Although there were occasional inimical acts of Jews against Christians during the persecutions, we are not allowed to say that they collaborated with the pagans to harass the Christians. "The statement that the Jews were directly or indirectly responsible for the persecution which the Church endured in the early centuries is a commonplace among nearly all modern historians", writes James Parkes, Conflict 125, - a thesis that he rightly rejects. But when he says that allusions to Jewish enmity as found in Justin, Tertullian and Origen are 'based on theological exegesis and not on historical memory' (148), he is, in my opinion, going too far. The evidence presented in the Acts of Jewish inimical actions against Christians he consigns to the realm of legend (128) which seems to me a case of special pleading. He himself admits that the first decades of Christianity were "marked on the Jewish side by the official determination to oust the Christians from the shelter of the synagogue"; he adds that "we find in the documents considerable evidence of the bloodshed which such a situation (i.e. of Jewish-

Christian animosity) provoked" (149). But I do not know of a single case of Jewish blood having been shed by Christians in this period. Instead, there have been Christian victims in the age of the apostles and many more during the Bar Kokhba revolt. What I have in view is to make it understandable that Christians of the second century still had this at the back of their minds.

199. Ir., Adv.haer. 4.4.1.
200. A good survey of the 'Adversus Judaeos' genre and similar writings is to be found in Blumenkranz, Judenpredigt.
201. Adv.Jud. PL 4. Paris, 1844.
202. Pseudo-Cypr., Adv.Jud. 1.
203. Pseudo-Cypr., Adv.Jud. 7.
204. Pseudo-Cypr., Adv.Jud. 4.
205. Pseudo-Cypr., Adv.Jud. 7.
206. Pseudo-Cypr., Adv.Jud. 7.
207. Klijn, Na het Nieuwe Testament 90.
208. Eus., Chron. ad 169.
209. Theoph., Ad Autolyc. PG 6. Paris, 1857.
210. Theoph., Ad Autolyc. 3.9.
211. Theoph., Ad Autolyc. 3.20.
212. Theoph., Ad Autolyc, 3.24.
213. Theoph., Ad Autolyc. 3.18.
214. Theoph., Ad Autolyc. 3.25.
215. Theoph., Ad Autolyc. 3.20
216. Theoph., Ad Autolyc. 3.26.
217. Taylor, Anti-Jud. 62.
218. Min. Felix, Oct. 33.
219. Clem.Al., Strom. 1.11.2.
220. André Méhat s.v. 'Clemens von Alexandrien', Theol.Realenz. Bd. VIII. Berlin/New York, 1981, 101-113.
221. See Vol. VIII, Ch. I.1 and Vol. XI, Ch. V.6b.
222. Clem.Al., Strom. 1.21.4; See Vol. XI, Ch. V, Part IV.1o.
223. Clem.Al., Strom. 6.13.
224. Clem.Al., Strom. 1.15 and 17; Wilde. Treatment 171.

225. Clem.Al., Paed. 3.10.54.2; Strom. 1.19.93.1.
226. Clem.Al., Strom. 5.15; Wilde, Treatment 176.
227. Clem., Al., Strom. 5.14.107.1.
228. Clem.Al., Strom. 3.2.8.6.
229. Clem.Al., Strom. 1.5.28.3.
230. Clem.Al., Strom. 6.6.47.1.
231. G. Bardy s.v. 'Clément d'Alexandrie', Dict.Théol.Cath. 3, 164 (Paris, 1923).
232. Clem.Al., Paed. quoted by Taylor, Anti-Jud. 132.
233. Clem.Al., Strom. 2.9.
234. Schreckenberg, Texte 213, says that "es an antijüdischer Apologetik im engeren Sinne bei Klemens fast ganz fehlt ... Da fehlt jeder schrille Ton, wie denn Klement überhaupt zu den Autoren der alten Kirche zu zählen ist, die sich hinsichtlich des Verhältnisses zum Judentum am treuesten an die vom Neuen Testament gewiesenen Wege halten".
235. Clem.Al., Strom. 2.10.47.2.
236. Clem.Al., Strom.
237. Clem.Al., Strom. 2.5.21.
238. Clem.Al., Strom. 3.12.90.2.
239. Clem.Al., Strom. 6.7.59.2.
240. Clem.Al., Strom. 6.15.167.3.
241. Clem.Al.m Strom. 7.8.109.3.
242. A good survey of the 'Adversus Judaeos' genre and related writings is to be found in Blumenkranz, Judenpred. 9-58.
243. Blumenkranz, Patristik A, 86/87 : "Schon rein äusserlich ist bedeutungsvoll dass er im Kampf gegen die gnostischen Häretiker eine ganze Reihe von Streitschriften verfasst hat, gegen die Juden aber nur eine einzige ... Die Häretiker behandelt er mit beissendem Spott und höhnischer Verachtung, während er in der Auseinandersetzung mit den Juden sachlich bleibt. Besonders bedeutungsvoll ist bei einem Vergleich zwischen seiner antihäretischen und seiner antijüdischen Polemik, dass er bei seinen Angriffen gegen die das Alte Testament verwerfenden Gnostiker immer fast als Verteidiger von Juden und Judentum erscheint ... Verglichen mit den Beispielen antihäretischer Polemik, bleibt Tertullians antijüdische Polemik durchaus gemessen, ohne jede persönlich-feindliche Note, streng auf dem Boden einer **rein theologischen** (my emphasis) Gegnerschaft".
244. Taylor, Anti-Jud. 42, note 21.

245. Tert., Adv.Jud. 8.18.
246. Tert., De spect. 30.
247. Tert., Adv.Marc. 4.1.
248. Taylor, Anti-Jud. 174.
249. See Vol. IX, Ch. II.5.
250. Tert., Adv.Prax. 31.1-2.
251. Tert., Apol. 21.
252. Tert., De monog. 7.
253. Tert., De pudic. 6.
254. Aziza, Tertullien 62/63.
255. Tret., Apol. 16.3.
256. Tert., Adv.Jud. 2.12.14 and 3.1. See for Tacitus' calumnies Vol. XI, Part IV.2.d.
257. Tert., De pudic. 6.3-4.
258. Eus., Praep.Ev. 12.1.4; this somewhat free translation comes from Parkes, Conflict 118.
259. Parkes, Conflict 117.
260. Wilde, Treatment 183.
261. Trigg, Origen 133.
262. Eus., HE 6.30.
263. Bietenhard, Caesarea 32/33, note 1, enumerates twenty-one of such passages.
264. De Lange, Origen 26/27.
265. Orig., Contra Cels. 2.8 and 4.22.
266. Orig., Contra Cels. 3.1.
267. Taylor, Anti-Jud. 138.
268. Orig., Contra Cels. 3.75.
269. Orig., Contra Cels. 2.8.
270. Orig., Contra Cels. 5.32.
271. Orig., Contra Cels. 5.38 and 40.
272. Orig., Judicum 8.1.
273. Orig., Selecta in Ps. 126.
274. Orig., Hom. in Ps. 36.1.

275. Dt. 32:21.
276. Orig., Hom. in Ps. 36.1.
277. Rom. 11:28.
278. Orig., Comm. in Rom. 8.13.
279. Rom. 11:26; Orig., Comm. in Rom. 8:9. See Bietenhard, Caesarea, Ch. 8, Das Verständnis von Rom. 11 bei Origen.
280. Orig., Peri archoon 2.4.1.
281. Orig., Contra Cels. 5.43.
282. Orig., Contra Cels. 3.3.
283. Bietenhard, Caesarea, Ch. 7.
284. De Lange, Origen 66.
285. Orig., Contra Cels. 1.23 and 8.3.
286. De Lange, Origen 68.
287. De Lange, Origen 73.
288. Kötting, Patristik 145.
289. De Lange, Origen 86.
290. PG 10. Paris, 1857.
291. Wilde, Treatment 210.
292. Rowan Williams s.v. 'Methodius von Olympus', Theol.Realenz. Bd. XXII, Lief. 4/5, 680-684. Berlin, 1992.
293. Wilde, Treatment 210/211.
294. Methodius, Conv. 5.8, PG 18, Paris, 1857.
295. Methodius, Conv. 9.2. PG 18, Paris, 1857.
296. Methodius, Conv. 9.1.
297. See Vol. XI, Ch. VI, Part IV.12.
298. Wilde, Treatment 163.
299. Wilde, Treatment 162.
300. Hipp., In Deut. 25.
301. Wilde, Treatment 165.
302. Hipp., Adv.Jud. 10.
303. Quoted by Wilde, Treatment 166/167.
304. Wilde, Treatment 168.

305. Did., Introduction : "We ..., the twelve apostles of the only Son ..., have ratified this Didascalia". The book was originally written in Greek but we have only Syriac, Ethiopic, and Latin versions of it.
306. Parkes, Conflict 82.
307. F. Nau s.v. 'Didascalie des Apôtres', Dict.Théol.Cath. 4, 747 (Paris, 1924).
308. Did. 1.
309. Did. 2.
310. Did. 26.
311. Did. 21.
312. Did. 23.
313. Schreckenberg, Texte 216 : "Bei aller theologischen Strenge ist aber die Didaskalia weit entfernt von einer überheblichen Heilsgewißheit, die das jüdische Volk entweder als hoffnungslos verloren ignoriert oder als gottlosen, bösen Feind des Christentums betrachtet".
314. Wilde, Treatment 212.
315. Schreckenberg, Texte 213.
316. Cyprianus, De or. 13.
317. Vol. XI, Ch. VI, Part IV.13c.
318. Vol. XI, Ch. VI, Part IV.14c.
319. Cyprian, De or. 10.
320. Cyprianus, De bona pat. 19.
321. PG 4.
322. The canons are printed by Schreckenberg, Texts 248.
323. Vita Constantini. PG 20. Paris, 1857.
324. Schreckenberg, Texte 262; this theology is called 'subordinationism'.
325. Chronicorum libri duo. PG 19. Paris, 1857.
326. Historia ecclesiastica. PG 20. Paris, 1857.
327. Schreckenberg, Texte 263.
328. Or perhaps already in the very last phase of the persecutions.
329. PG 21. Paris, 1857.
330. PG 22. Paris, 1857.
331. Parkes, Conflict 161.
332. Gen. 10:25.

333. Praep.ev. 10.11.
334. Eus., Dem.ev. 1.6.
335. Eus., HE 1.4.6.
336. Eus., Praep.ev. 7.6.
337. Eus., Dem.ev. 2.3.20 and 23.
338. Eus., Praep.ev. 8.1.
339. Eus., Praep.ev. 7.6; Dem.ev. 1.2.
340. Eus., Dem.ev. 1.1.
341. Eus., Dem.ev. 1.1.
342. Parkes, Conflict 162.
343. Lact., Div. Inst. 4.20.
344. Schreckenberg, Texte 251.
345. Lact., Div.Inst. 4.18.
346. Schreckenberg, Texte 252/253.
347. Simon, Verus Israel 361, note 1.
348. Eus., Vita Constant. 3.18.
349. Simon, Verus Israel 361/362.
350. Schreckenberg, Texte 255.
351. PL 8. Paris, 1857.
352. Schreckenberg, Texte 256/257.
353. For Aphrahat's life see Neusner, Aphrahat 4-7.
354. Aphr., Hom. 1.19.
355. See Neusner, Aphrahat 19-30.
356. See Neusner, Aphrahat 68-76.
357. Neusner. Aphrahat 143-144, presents a summary of Aphrahat's critique of the Jews.
358. Williams, Adv.Jud. 102; idem Parkes, Conflict 276. Neusner, Aphrahat 127 : "Aphrahat ... had to confront the Judaic challenge for three reasons. First, he wrote for a relatively new Church-community, many of whose members could not have come from families Christian for more than three generations, and some of whom came from Judaism. Christianity in Babylonia, a church to which he addressed himself, was even more recent ... Second, the Christians were living in close contact with Jews loyal to the old covenant in pretty much the same formulation everyone knew from the Hebrew Scriptures. Third, to be

a Christian was a dangerous thing ... It ... is hardly surprising that the Christians had squarely to face the appeal of the Hebrew Scriptures as the Jews understood them".

359. Parkes, Conflict 277 : "On the whole he speaks without bitterness".
360. Neusner, Aphrahat 244.
361. Venantius Fortunatus (?), Vita Hil. 1.3.
362. Hil., Comm. in Ps. LI.6.
363. Hil., COmm. in Matt. 12.21-23.
364. Hil., Tract.myst. 1.4.
365. Hil., Tract.myst. 1.7.
366. Jo.Chrysost., Adv.Jud. 7.1.
367. Simon, Verus Israel 256 : "Le maître de l'imprécation anti-juive est sans conteste saint Jean Chrysostome".
368. I wholly agree with what Robert Wilken wrote (John Chrysost. 163) : "No matter how outraged Christians feel over the Christian record of dealings with the Jews, we have no license to judge the distant past on the basis of our present perceptions of events of more recent times".
369. Wilken, Chrysost. 107.
370. Jo.Chrysost. 7.1.
371. Wilken, John Chrysost. 107.
372. Wilken, John Chrysost. 123.
373. Wilken, John Chrysost. 125.
374. Parkes, Conflict 163.
375. Jean-Marie Leroux s.v. 'Johannes Chrysostomus', Theol.Realenz. 17, 125. Berlin/New York, 1988.
376. Jo.Chrysost., Adv.Jud. 1.2. PG 48. Paris, 1862.
377. Jo.Chrystost. Adv.Jud. 1.2.
378. Jer. 3:3.
379. Jo.Chrysost., Adv.Jud. 1.3.
380. Jo.Chrysost., Adv.Jud. 1.3.
381. Jer. 5:8.
382. Jo.Chrysost., Adv.Jud. 1.6.
383. Jo.Chrysost., Adv.Jud. 1.7.

384. Jo.Chrysost., Adv.Jud. 6.6.
385. Jo.Chrysost., Adv.Jud. 6.1.
386. Simon, Verus Israel 257.
387. Simon, Verus Israel 260 : "Une fois éteint le feu de son indignation, Chrysostome n'est peut-être pas dupe".
388. Parkes, Conflict 166.
389. Wilken, Chrysost. 62.
390. Wilken, Chrysost. 64/65.
391. Wilken, Chrysost. 65.
392. Jo.Chrysost., Adv.Jud. 1.3.
393. Jo.Chrysost., Adv.Jud. 7.1 : "The Jewish festivals are still with us; they even build their huts".
394. Jo.Chrysost., Adv.Jud. 1.1.
395. Jo.Chrysost., Adv.Jud. 4.3.
396. This text is to be found in PG 51, Paris, 1862, in a sermon entitled 'Si esurierit inimicus tuus, ciba illum' 3, one of the series 'Homiliae XXV in quaedam loca Novi Testamenti'; according to Wilken, Chrysost. 66, note 1, it rather belongs to the 'Homiliae XXXII in Epistolam ad Romanos', no. 12.20.3.
397. Jo.Chrysost., Adv.Jud. 2.3.
398. Jo.Chrysost., Adv.Jud. 3.3.
399. Jo.Chrysost., Adv.Jud. 3.5.
400. Jo.Chrysost., Adv.Jud. 4.4.
401. Jo.Chrysost., Adv.Jud. 1.1.
402. Wilken, Chrysost. 67 and note 3.
403. Jo.Chrysost., Adv.Jud. 8.4.
404. Schreckenberg, Texte 277/278.
405. Schreckenberg, Texte 313.
406. Ambr., Expositio. in Ps. CXVIII.31.
407. Blumenkranz, Judenpredigt 59 : "Die persönlichen Beziehungen Augustins zu den Juden scheinen äusserst oberflächlicher Natur gewesen zu sein."
408. A German translation of this 'Jewish sermon' is printed in Blumenkranz, Judenpredigt 89-110.
409. Aug., Ep. 196.39.

410. Blumenkranz, Judenpredigt 61 : "Noch zu Augustins Zeiten waren diese Judaizanten der verschiedensten Schattierungen in seinem Bereiche tätig und suchten Anhänger zu werben".
411. Blumenkranz, Judenpredigt 186-189.
412. Blumenkranz, Judenpredigt 211/212.
413. Schreckenberg, Texte 258, remarks that the term 'religio licita' is not an ancient juridical term; it is only to be found in modern authors.
414. Cod.Theod. 16.8.1.
415. Cod.Theod. 16.9.1.
416. Schreckenbrg, Texte 258.
417. Cod.Theod. 16.8.3.
418. See Vol. XI, Ch. V, Part IV.9d.
419. Schreckenberg, Texte 262.
420. Cod.Theod. 16.8.6, 13.VIII.339.
421. Cod.Theod. 16.8.7, 3.VII.357.
422. Cod.Theod. 7.8.2, between 368 and 372.
423. Cod.Theod. 3.1.5, in 384.
424. Cod. Theod. 3.7.2, 14.III.388.
425. Schreckenberg. Texte 301.
426. Ambr., Ep. 40.9.
427. Ambr., Ep. 40.18.
428. Ambr., Ep. 40.29.
429. This letter of Ambrose, no. 40, is, in fact, with no. 41, the only source for this affair.
430. Ambr., Ep. 40.31 and 33.
431. All this in Ambrose, Ep. 41.
432. Simon, Verus Israel 267.
433. Simon, Verus Israel 268.
434. Cod.Theod. 16.8.9.
435. Cod.Theod. 16.8.12.
436. Cod.Theod. 16.8.20.
437. Cod.Theod. 16.8.21; see Juster, Juifs I, 404, note 3.
438. Cod.Theod. 16.8.9 in 393; 16.8.13 in 397; 16.8.20 in 412.

439. The decree sealing this process is of 439, quoted Juster, Juifs II, 245, no. 2, see also 250-252.
440. Decree of 425, Juster, Juifs II, 263, no. 6.
441. Juster, Juifs I, 26/287.
442. Simon, Verus Israel 265.
443. Ambr., Ep. 40.23.
444. Severus Maj., Ep. de Jud.
445. Simon, Verus Israel 265.
446. Simon, Verus Israel 266.
447. Simon, Verus Israel 265.
448. Evagrius, HE 1.13.
449. Socrates, HE 7.13.
450. Socrates, HE 7.13.
451. Isaac, Genèse 188.
452. Cod.Theod. 16.8.22.
453. Juster, Juifs I, 469/470; the date of this law is uncertain.
454. Cod.Theod. 16.8.25.
455. Cod.Theod. 16.8.25.
456. Repetition of this injunction Cod.Theod. 16.8.26 and 27.
457. Juster, Juifs I,467.
458. Cod.Theod. 16.8.10.
459. Cod.Theod. 16.8.13.
460. Cod.Theod. 16.8.14.
461. Cod.Theod. 16.8.23.
462. See Vol. XI, Ch. V, Part III.9b.
463. Isaac, Genèse 177.
464. Isaac, Genèse 185.
465. Isaac, Genèse 185.
466. Cod. Theod. 16.8.18, 23.V.408.
467. Socrates, HE 67.13. The Jewish scholar L. Lucas, Zur Geschichte der Juden im IV. Jahrhundert, Berlin, 1909, p. 89, quoted by Isaac, Genèse 185, holds this story for false; Juster, Juifs II, 204 and Isaac l.c. find it doubtful, whereas Simon, Verus Israel 160, accepts it. I for

	one do not know why thoroughly inebriated hooligans could not commit such a deed.
468.	The fact that Pope Silvester I wrote an 'adversus Judaeos' is not relevant. Non-Catholics are inclined to believe that everything a Pope says is infallible truth and an authoritative doctrinal statement; howver, a booklet like this is no more than a private utterance without doctrinal status.
469.	Juster, Juifs II, 248/249.
470.	Parkes, Conflict 160 : "The endless repetition of the same epithets, the same charges and the same crimes can only be explained by ... theological and exegetical necessity".
471.	Parkes, Conflict 160 : "The phrase a Jew' or 'some Jews' is almost unknown in patristic literature.
472.	Tert., Apol. 18.4.
473.	Gen. 25:23.
474.	Tert., Adv.Jud. 1).
475.	Barn. 4.7-8, 14.1-3.
476.	Barn. 2.6, 4.8, 6.14. See Goppelt, Christ. und Jud. 216.
477.	Melito, Pascha 35-37.
478.	Gen. 19:30-38.
479.	Ir., Adv.haer. 4.31.1.
480.	Taylor, Anti-Jud. 168/169.
481.	Hermann Bahr in his novel 'Die Rotte Korahs'.

CHAPTER III

JUDAIZING AS A SEED OF DISRUPTION

1. Why this chapter

In the foregoing chapter the terms 'judaizing' and 'Judaizers' were frequently used; 'judaizing' was described as a disturbing and destabilizing factor that led to a Jewish-Christian relationship which carried in itself the germs of dualism. For this reason it seems useful to pay somewhat more attention to this phenomenon which sometimes appears as a hybrid of the two religions involved [1].

Yet another reason may be brought forward. Was judaizing a feature of the early Church alone? Did it disappear with the last Judaeo-Christians? Is it inconceivable that the judaizing urge surfaced now and then in later centuries?.

2. About terminology

It is absolutely necessary to be perfectly clear about the relevant terminology, for, as Georg Strecker writes, "the concept of Jewish Christianity is filled with different concepts in scholarship" [2]. Marcel Simon reduces the problem to its simplest dimension : "A Judaeo-Christian is someone who feels himself to be, who wants to be, and who in fact is, at home in the several manifestations of his religious life, at once Jewish and Christian" [3]. But he readily admits that it is not so simple as that. His definition immediately raises the question whether it was possible for a Christian (or a Jew) to have the best of both worlds.

The most current use of the term 'Jewish Christianity' is its application to those Christians who were born Jews and circumcized in case they were males. In the very first years of the Church there were none other than Jewish Christians; the whole community was 'judaeo-christian' then. As Judaeo-Christians we must also count their descendants, whether circumcized or not. As Segal remarks, Paul, although adressing himself mainly to Gentiles, was a Jewish Christian [4]. An important characteristic of this group was that it continued to observe the Law, although by no means always in the strictest literal sense. There were 'allegorizers' among them, people who "felt they were excused from observing the actual regulations, since they understood their inner meaning; they held that everything in the Law was said to convey some moral truth" [5].

3. The model community

The typical and original Jewish-Christian community was that of Jerusalem, under the leadership of James, a relative of Jesus, with which other communities in Galilee were affiliated. They were Christian to the extent that they recognized Jesus as the Messiah and probably even as the Son of God; they had themselves baptized and celebrated their own sacred meal, the Eucharist [6]. Apart from the fact that they were all born Jews, they were Jewish inasmuch as the males were circumcized, they went to the Temple to pray, they visited the synagogue on the Sabbath, and they observed the purity rules and the food taboos.

Another point in which the Jerusalemites agreed with the Jews is that they, like the Jews, "were not interested in missionizing among the Gentiles" [7]. Their attitude, however, was not so doctrinal or fundamentalistic as to make a compromise on the life style of heathen converts impossible. James and the other leaders of the Jerusalemite Church acquiesced in Paul's proposal that Gentile converts should not have to observe the Law [8]. That this Church did not think of herself as identical with Judaism appears also from the fact that she spoke of herself as an 'ecclesia' which signifies something different from the Jewish community.

It is hard to tell how long this Jerusalemite Christian community existed. Eusebius has it that, in the beginning of the Jewish War, it moved from the Holy City to Pella in the Transjordan [9]. If this is correct, it can only apply to part of the group, since this same author mentions fifteen bishops of Jerusalem after A.D. 70, all Jews [10]. The end must have come in 135, when Jerusalem was depopulated. Although small communities of Christian Jews may have subsisted for some time in Rome [11], in Egypt, and in Syria, their traces become ever vaguer, until they disappear altogether [12]. Some will have joined the Ebionites (about whom later on); others became hellenized [13]. Not enough Jews joined the Church after ca A.D. 100 to keep this earliest Christian group in force.

4. Messianic Jewish Christians

A second branch of Judaeo-Christianity is formed by those Jews who had become Christians but who had their reservations about the status of Jesus. They readily accepted the proposition that he was the Messiah but not that he was the Son of God. This kind of Judaeo-Christianity does not constitute a uniform group. There are Gnostics, Ebionites, and Elkasaites found among them. They all present forms of syncretism in which Judaism, Christianity, Gnosis, and Hellenism are mixed. It is impossible to view them as either Jewish orthodox or Christian orthodox. Daniélou believes that Simon the Magician was nurtured in this kind of milieu [14].

5. The Ebionites

In order to keep these, mainly heterodox streams apart, I think it is best to start with the Ebionites.

a. Their name

This appellation was, if not introduced, then at least used for the first time by Irenaeus [15]. It then became the generic name for Judaeo-Christians in Christian writings of the third and fourth centuries. They are sometimes also called 'Nazoraeans' according to Epiphanius, the term being derived from the hometown of Jesus, Nazareth [16]. Although the Jews used to speak of all Christians as 'Nazaraeans', Epiphanius applies it specifically to Jewish Christians [17] whom he dubs 'Nazoraeans' [18]. Ebionite and related sects were heterodox because, although they accepted Jesus as the Messiah, they did not believe he was the Son of God.

The name 'Ebionite' is not derived from a non-existent founder with the name of 'Ebion', as some Fathers believed [19], but from the Hebrew 'ebyon'. plural 'ebyonim' = the poor. This 'poor' is not to be taken in its social sense, as 'short of money', but spiritually, as 'poor in the relation to God', as pious, humble, and obedient. The fact that they gave themselves a specific name - one that implied a program - already points to their position of apartheid within the context of early Christianity. That it was a Hebrew name suggests that the Ebionite sect consisted of (baptized) Jews.

b. The Pseudo-Clementines, a source for Ebionism

The origin and development of the sect are hard to trace. We find references to it throughout patristic literature, the earliest in Justin the Martyr around A.D. 150, and continuing till in the fifth century [20]; other references are found in rabbinic literature [21]. It was the great merit of Hans Joachim Schoeps to have drawn our attention to an important, non-orthodox source, the so-called 'Pseudo-Clementines'. Schoeps did this in his book on Jewish Christianity - mainly Ebionism - which he prepared when he was an exile in Sweden during the Nazi period and which so far has not been replaced by a more recent work [22]. These Pseudo-Clementines are "a most precious source ..., the primitive substratum of which, such as it has been possible to reconstitute it under the reworkings it has undergone, present an indubitably Judaeo-Christian character" [23].

The original form of the Pseudo-Clementines - which is lost - was a novel [24] in the shape of a frame-story, originally a pagan romantic tale that later received a Christian content [25]. Its author is said to have been one Clement - Clemens Romanus -, a pagan, who fused with another Clement, a Christian of Jewish descent. The hero of the novel was the apostle Peter. The book was known in Rome in the second and third centuries. There exist two reworkings of this lost novel, the 'Clementine Homilies' and the 'Recognitions', both dating from the fourth century, according to Schoeps from the period after the Council of Nicaea. The final result was a compilation consisting, among other elements, of the so-called 'Testimonies of Peter' and the miracle stories of Simon the Magician.

c. The Jerusalemite community and Ebionism

According to Schoeps, we are entitled to see the ancestors of the Ebionites in those Christian Pharisees who advocated circumcision and the complete observance of Mosaic Law for Gentile converts [26]. The Ebionites later loved to appeal to James, the first bishop of Jerusalem, as the original spokesman for their ideas. They believed him to represent a, so to speak, fundamentalistic party that opposed Peter and Paul in matters of Mosaic Law. Paul relates how, to his indignation, Peter stopped having meals with Gentile Christians in Antioch, when "certain persons had come from James in Jerusalem" [27]. On the other hand, we know that James, as I have already written, accepted the decision of the Council of Jerusalem in A.D. 43/44. There can be no doubt that there were tensions in the Jerusalemite Church, but James was a strong personality and had the prestige of being a relative of Jesus; as Schoeps said, "he guaranteed and represented the unity of the community". It was only after his death that the tensions became manifest, and with this, writes Schoeps, the history of the Ebionite Church begins [28].

A few years later, in 66 or 67, followed the exodus of at least part of the Jerusalemite community (and other Christian groups in Palestine) to Pella in the Transjordan [29]. They took their tensions and the germ of Ebionism with them. According to Schoeps, in the next centuries Pella remained the spiritual capital of Ebionism [30].

d. Liturgy and organisation of the Ebionite Church

The Ebionite Church in Transjordan had her own bishop. She had furthermore a teacher college of seventy-two persons [31]. The Recognitiones say that these men had to be 'probati'; they were tested during an apprenticeship of six years. The candidate who was well trained was then ordained by the bishop; it is reported that during this ceremony the four elements, heaven, earth, water, air, were invoked. Out of the hands of the bishop the new teacher received the sacred books of the Ebionites (which were not the Bible), with the admonition not to show them to unauthorized persons. The correct use of these books was taught in secret sessions; the doctrine they contained was called the 'logos alêtheias', the 'word of truth' [32]. Enough to show that they distanced themselves from the orthodox Catholic community.

This same distance from the main Church can also be inferred from the fact that they called their prayer-houses 'synagogues' and the overseers 'archisynagogoi' [33]. Their eucharistic meal was also very different since they used bread and salt - "Peter broke the bread in the Eucharist and put salt on it" [34] - and water instead of wine - 'ordinary water', says Irenaeus deprecatingly [35]. Not unjustly Epiphanius remarks that this was 'an imitation of the holy mysteries of the Church' [36]. They seem to have celebrated it only once a year after the manner of the Jewish Passover [37]. They baptized their catechumens but circumcized the males too; they observed the Sabbath strictly and were on the whole extremely legalistic. This struck the Fathers as pure heresy; Jerome reproaches for not distinguishing 'the ceremony of the Law from the Gospel of Christ'; he adds that Ebionites only simulate being Christians [38]. Pseudo-Tertullian goes one step further by stating that they not only exclude the Gospel but, indeed, vindicate Judaism [39].

e. The Ebionites and the Old Testament

Ebionite legalism may lead us to the conclusion that these people stuck to the letter of the Old Testament, but this would not be correct. They had in common with other non-orthodox sects that their attitude to biblical texts was highly selective. It was their idea that the Torah had been handed down orally for a considerable time [40]. This enabled the devil to insert 'many lies about God into it' [41]. According to Epiphanius, the Ebionites "did not accept the whole Pentatech of Moses, but jettisoned some sayings." From the standpoint of this Father, the Ebionites found that the Bible was a fabrication and that all the stories concerning the Patriarchs were so many fictions. Although this was perhaps an exaggeration [42], it is true that the Ebionites were eclectic in their choice of Bible texts. For instance, all anthropomorphisms were considered wrong. The Bible translation (into Greek) by the Ebionite Symmachus, from about A.D. 200, contains many instances of rewording and reformulating [43]. They also expunged those passages that throw an unfavourable light on the great of the Old Testament, the stories, for example, that Noach got drunk and that Moses slew an Egyptian.

f. The dualistic Ebionite theology

Where the distance between the orthodox and the Ebionites grew greatest is in the fields of theology and Christology. It is sometimes asserted that the Ebionites recognized two Gods : one the highest God, and the second a lower one, the Demiurge, the creator of this world. We actually see Simon the Magician defending this thesis [44], but he is rebutted by Peter, the (Ebionite) spokesman in the Pseudo-Clementines, where Simon declares that goodness and justice are properties of the high God (and not of the Demiurge) [45]. Irenaeus states in as many words that the Ebionites recognize only one God [46]. On this point, therefore, they had no quarrel with the orthodox [47].

However, as in so many similar systems, the dualism starts one level lower. There are two principles in the world, a female and a male one, or, in Ebionite terminology, two aeons. The male aeon is that of the future, still invisible [48]. The present world, the cosmos, is the female aeon [49]. Together they form a sort of couple, a 'syzygia' [50]. That the female aeon is the 'syzygos' of the male one signifies that they have been created together, and as such they are both subject to the same high God [51]. Schoeps states correctly that the theory of the syzygia has as its consequence that "it shows the oppositions in the physical and moral world as ordained by God" [52]. We see the Ebionites at grips here with the same problem that haunted the Gnostics : how it is possible that there exist such imperfections in a world created by a just and good God? But whereas the Gnostics found the solution in the ditheism of the highest God and the Demiurge, the Ebionites posited the dualistic theory of the two aeons.

For dualistic it certainly was. The terms 'male-female' are not the only ones used to define the difference between the two aeons. Other terms are 'first and second' [53], heaven and earth, day and night, sun and moon, life and death [54], and, very telling, ignorance and knowledge ('gnoosis') [55]; it is the Ebionites who have the 'gnoosis' [56]. These terms distinguish the aeons as a superior and an inferior one [57]. And who would not think of the famous Pythagorean (and dualistic) list of opposites, as one reads that the upper world is 'right' and the lower one 'left' [58]; in this list too 'male and female'. 'Female' is identical with 'inferior'.

g. About Eve

Strecker is quite right when he writes that the opposites mentioned have many parallels in Gnostic literature, but not in rabbinic scripture [59] - and, let us add, neither in orthodox writings. Especially the male-female opposition was popular with the Gnostics. In Ebionite theology Eve, the female prototype and ancestress, is the mother of mankind, but she is less than Adam, who is the prototype of Christ. She is the moon whereas he is the sun. This is expressed in philosophical terms as 'ousia' and 'metousia', to be rendered as 'being' and 'sub-being', meaning that the female is the derived and dependent part of the couple in which the male is the original and autonomous principle.

Eve is called 'the first prophetess' [60], but it is a bad omen that it was she who gave her first-born the name of 'Cain' [61].

Although she is a prophetess, her doctrine does not illuminate mankind. Quite the contrary! As the doctrine of those 'from woman born', it is entirely human [62]. Those who adhere to it will always seek but will find nothing, until death overtakes them, for "from the beginning death lies in wait for blind people" [63]. It is Eve who seduces mankind to idolatry; she will be trusted because she is considered divine [64]. She prefers to parade as male in order to deceive people [65]; in doing this, writes Strecker, "she does all that false prophets do, present lies as truth" [66]. Here we encounter yet another opposition, that of the truth and the lie.

She deceives people by promising riches [67]. It was she who brought forth the kingdoms of this world, with all their wars and shedding of blood [68]. This anti-political teaching is an echo of that in the apocalypses. The opinion Ebionism has of the cosmos is entirely negative : "it pretends to have the gnoosis but was from the beginning destined for death" [69]. This negative viewpoint is identical with that of the Gnostics.

There is, as I said, yet another aeon, the future and still invisible one which is male. Its nature, its identity, is to be prophetic; "through it all the prophets appearing in the world speak, because they are sons of the coming aeon; they possess the knowledge (gnoosis) of the coming aeons" [70]. The two aeons are inimical to each other; the female one tries to smother the male aeon. "The female encircles with her own blood which is as red fire the white seed of the male ...; she enjoys the short blosoming of the flesh (the sexual act is meant - F.). Through short-lived pleasure she destroys the power of reason, seduces most people to adultery, and in this way robs them of the coming beautiful bridegroom" [71]. It is evident that we are sailing on Gnostic waters here : there is not only the opposition of two worlds, but also contempt of what is female, perceived as a great danger, and depreciation of sexuality which is seen as the opposite of spirituality.

Both aeons have their own children. "Because the present aeon is female, she gives birth to the lives ('psuchas') of her children" [72]. This must be seen as a purely natural event, for the word 'psuchê' does not denote the divine principle in man. The male aeon "will as a father receive his children" [73]; in other words, purely natural man must become a spiritual being. The sperma that is in man is the divine principle that will enable him to become spiritual. But the female aeon tries to prevent this. "She steals the spermata of the male and envelops them with her own carnal spermata" [74]. Here we have another Gnostic-dualistic opposition : that of matter and spirit. There are yet two other Gnostic elements : the idea that the divine principle is buried in matter (and has to be liberated), and the sexual imagery.

h. The situation of mankind

The Pseudo-Clementines take a sombre view of the situation of mankind. "The will of God has fallen into oblivion." Bad education leads to erroneous ideas. Habits like profligacy, unbelief, fornication, and others are so rampant that the world looks like a smoke-filled room; the eyes are infected, and blindness is the result. People are incapable of finding God [75]. Many, seeking a way out, accept an alien message (that of orthodox Christianity? - F.) which is equivalent to adultery; they will be banished from the realm of the bridegroom [76]. In spite of the general depravity there are still people who love the Truth and long for the light; they must pray, because they are incapable of seeing it themselves, that someone will come to open the door and let the light in [77]. Once again Gnostic dualism galore : the sparkle of Truth, utter helplessness, the opposition of light and dark, i.e. of heaven and earth.

j. The true prophet : Ebionite Christology

The true prophet will be the Saviour. "The man who alone is capable of illuminating the souls of men, so that they with their own eyes discover the road to eternal salvation, that man is called the true prophet" [78]. Who is he? Is he Jesus of Nazareth? He is not! He is no human being at all. He is Christ, the spiritual and eternal Christ, the ruler of the celestial world and created in the image of God [79]. He came to this world in the person of Adam; he is the Adam-Christ. Adam is the first man coming out of the hand of God; for this reason, he is in possession of the Holy Spirit of Christ. Adam did not fall; this is impossible. There is no forgiveness for those who believe this (i.e. for Jews and Christians) [80]. Need I argue that we are miles distant here from both Jewish and Christian orthodoxy?

After Adam humanity took the wrong course, twenty generations on end, since it took pleasure in bloody sacrifices. But Abraham was righteous. The true prophet appeared to him and taught him all he wanted to know, the science of divinity, the immortality of the soul, among other things. Another righteous man was Moses who gave his people the Law which, however, became a source of further corruption, and the people continued to sin. This is no wonder, since the Law is full of lies, inserted into it by the Evil one [81]. The text is constantly hinting at a secret knowledge that can only be divulged to the well-intentioned [82].

Christ, who had already manifested himself in Adam and Moses, finally appeared on earth to do away with all abuses, such as animal sacrifices, and to institute baptism with water. All those who are baptized will live in the perfect way and last forever, purified as they are, not by the blood of cattle but by wisdom; all others will be doomed [83]. This is decidely unorthodox, since in orthodox theology redemption is effectuated by the death on the cross of Jesus Christ.

k. The problem of Evil

Then there is the problem of Evil. Where, how did it originate? To answer this question, Ebionite theology resorted to the dualism of all dualisms, the theory of the two worlds. There are not two gods but there two realms, that of the Good and that of Evil. The fact that there was no Demiurge who created the cosmos and mankind could have as a consequence that it is God who created Evil. But the author will not have it so : the origin of Evil is to be found in the human will. Not a few people choose voluntarily for Evil. But God sealed the two worlds hermetically off from each other. The present world which is that of Evil is destined for the eternal fire [84].

Still the author is not quite sure of his case. Is the suspicion that God is, after all, the source of Evil, really allayed? But, he says, God has created everything in 'syzygies' or pairs of opposites that are constantly warring with each other; as a inevitable consequence, bad and good are also coupled [85]. He conveniently omits to explain why God has created a syzygy of good and evil. But he begs the question by stating that in the end all will be one again; the friction within the syzygies serves to further God's plans so that all oppositions will be resolved in the realm of eternal peace [86]. Finally, just as there are two worlds, there are two races of men, one good, one bad. God assigned to each of them its own king, the good rejoicing in good things, the wicked in malignity [87].

1. Was the Ebionite ideology Gnostic?

There can be not the slightest doubt that the Ebionite ideology of the Pseudo-Clementines was dualistic to the core. In my Volume VII I described it as Gnostic [88]. But Daniélou categorically states that it was not. "The Ebionites, although dualists, are no Gnostics." He distinguishes "between a fully Gnostic dualism and a gnosticizing dualism which is characterized by the idea that the creation is the work of an inferior Demiurge identified with Jahve". It is evident that in the Ebionite system God (Jahve) is not this inferior Demiurge [89]. But the question is what exactly is the hallmark of the Gnosis? Since there are definitely Gnostic systems that do not see Jahve as the Demiurge, we cannot consider the idea of a Demiurge as definitive. I myself have presented a twofold characteristic by which a system may be recognized as Gnostic [90]. This is that there are in every Gnostic system two dualisms, a horizontal one between worlds or realms, the other a vertical one between two races of men. Both these dualisms are an essential and fundamental part of the Ebionite ideology of the Pseudo-Clementines. If I am right in this, then Ebionism is a Gnostic system.

m. The spread of Ebionism

As I wrote above, the new centre of Ebionism after A.D. 70 became Pella in the Transjordan. This meant distancing itself, even geographically, from Judaism, since the new Jewish centre became Jamnia in Palestine. Pella kept its position for centuries to come; Schoeps dubs it 'the Jabne of Ebionism' [91]. From Pella during the next centuries Ebionism spread over the Transjordan region where already Jewish baptist sects existed [92]. Although there seems to have been an Ebionite community in Caesarea in Palestine, the great mass of these Jewish Christians, according to Schoeps, lived beyond the Jordan and had not much contact with the main Church [93]. They never called themselves 'Christians' [94].

Schoeps says that the Ebionite sect was active in the mission field. In the Pseudo-Clementines it is not Paul - the Ebionites are thoroughly anti-Pauline - but Peter who is the great apostle of the heathen. We see him rejoicing that Jesus' prophecy that many will come from east and west is being fulfilled; the masses of the heathen are coming in - into the Ebionite, Petrine, Church, of course [95]. Peter is credited with the foundation of many Ebionite communities. It will be evident that we have to do here with a missionary drive different from that of the main Church.

The Ebionite mission did not remain restricted to Jews (we may well ask whether many of them joined), but was mainly addressed to pagans. Schoeps goes so far as to state that, for a time, the whole of East Syria was Ebionite. There were radicals and moderates among them. The radicals insisted that non-Jewish converts had to accept the whole of Mosaic Law [96]. The moderate party found that circumcision was not unconditionally necessary : "even a non-circumcized person can be a true adorer of God" [97]. However, the converts were taught a 'lex vivendi' [98]; one was not 'illuminated' right from the start; the initiation seems to have progressed in three stages [99]. Do we have here the favourite three circles of esoteric groups?

What favoured the Ebionite mission was that it did not use the Aramaic language. like the Jews, but Greek [100]. On the other hand, they suffered from split offs; Epiphanius even called Ebionism 'polymorph' [101].

Many of the split offs have disappeared into nothingness. Schoeps thinks that the Ebionite Church had an existence of three-and-a-half centuries. Epiphanius mentions an Ebionite colony in Cyprus around 375 [102]. Augustine states that they still existed around 400 [103]. We have, however, a communication by Theodoretus, dating from ca. 450, that there were no longer Ebionites and even their name was forgotten [104]. During the first half of the fifth century the Ebionites must have disappeared from the ecclesiastical scene, at least in Syria, their 'homeland'. "We have no further reports of their physical presence", writes Schoeps [105]. But this does not mean that Ebionism had also disappeared as a theological or ideological 'presence'. It is highly probable that there was an Ebionite heritage to transmit to later generations.

n. The orthodox Church and Ebionism

The orthodox Church always remained averse from Ebionism. Some scholars believe that Jo. 10:16, "there are other sheep of mine, not belonging to this fold, whom I must bring in", refers to the Ebionites [106]. If this is correct, then the addition : "they too will listen to my voice", proved too optimistic. In the eyes of the Fathers Ebionism was 'a most criminal heresy'; what they had against it was that the Ebionites, who 'simulated being Christians', wanted to be and Jews and Christians, but were, in fact, neither [107]. The attitude of the Church respecting Ebionism was dualistic : it should simply not be there. For the Catholic Church, thinks Schoeps, Ebionism became the model for all later heresies, Arianism included [108].

o. Ebionism and Islam

It is a very important conclusion of Schoeps that Ebionism subsisted in Islam. "Jewish Christianity went under in the Christian Church but was conserved in Islam, reaching in some of its propelling impulses into our own days". This is, he says, 'a paradox of truly world-historical magnitude' [109]. But this is not the place to discuss this really fascinating proposition.

6. The Elkasaites

We stay nearer home with the baptist sect of the Elkasaites (Elkesaites, Elcesaites) [110]. I wrote already about them in my Volume IX [111] and must repeat myself somewhat in this context. We hear of this sect for the first time around A.D. 100; it was then situated on the Euphrates. Their name is derived from an hypothetical founder, called 'al-Khasyah', who in all probability is unhistorical. Later there was a certain Alcibiades who around 220 preached Elkasaite doctrine in Rome. It is a syncretistic religion in which Jewish, Christian, and Gnostic elements fused together.

A point in which they certainly did not concur with the Ebionites (nor, of course, with the orthodox Church) is that, although they used to refer to the Bible, they had a sacred book of their own, the 'Book of Elxai', that had been brought down from heaven by an angel. No more than fragments are left of it. But just as the Ebionites, the Elkasaites saw their teaching as a secret doctrine to be revealed only to an élite.

Another point of agreement between these two sects is that the Elkasaites too did not know of a Demiurge. But there is also no Trinity; they are not interested in Jesus of Nazareth. Instead, they too profess the 'Adam-Christ' who went through many manifestations, one of these being al-Khasiya or Elkesai or Elxai.

They purged the Old Testament of all passages referring to sacrifices, whether bloody or not. As one of the many baptist sects proliferating then between the Upper Jordan and the Lower Euphrates, they baptized by immersion in water and practiced many ablutions with water. When already baptized Christians came over, they had to be rebaptized. Mosaic Law, with circumcision, the Sabbath, and purifications, was of prime importance to them.

In many respects they agreed with the Ebionites, even with regard to horizontal dualism. For, according to their doctrine, there were two kings, the 'king of the future things' who is God, and the 'king of the present things'. This last king considers himself the ruler and possessor of the whole world. It was his aim to get the first king into his power. This smacks of dualism.

Very probably there was vertical dualism too, what with vegetarianism and the secret doctrine. It is not impossible that Elkasaite doctrine was one of the channels along which Gnostic-dualistic elements were transmitted to later periods. The Mughtasila sect, of which the prophet Mani was once a member [112], was related to it; Elkasaite-Mughtasila elements seeped through into Manichaeism.

7. The Judaizers

By far the largest group of those who, in some way or other, were harking back to Judaism or to important aspects of it, were the 'Judaizers'. By them we understand doctrinally orthodox Christians, most of them not Jewish by birth, who observed some or many Jewish customs. I frequently referred to them in the foregoing chapter. There existed many shades of judaizing, from accepting an invitation by Jewish neighbours to share in the Passover meal to the almost complete observance of Mosaic Law by the Ebionites (who, however, differed from ordinary Judaizers in important doctrinal respects). We have no idea how great a percentage of the Christians of these centuries was judaizing. It would have come in very handy if the ancients had had statistics based on questionnaires with questions like these : 'do you visit a synagogue on the Sabbath o every week o once a month o occasionally o never. But the ancients did not employ these useful instruments; we must satisfy ourselves with circumstantial evidence. The fact is that the Fathers never tired of warning and fulminating against judaizing which strongly suggests that Judaizers were numerous and omnipresent in the early Church. They formed a grey area, a shadow zone, a region of penumbra between Christianity and Judaism with which neither religion was happy.

An important question is whether judaizing tendencies had wholly disappeared by the end of Late Antiquity or whether they persisted into later times. It lasted centuries, for instance, before all dioceses had accepted the Christian Easter date as it was decreed by the Nicene Fathers in 325; this points in the direction of the second possibility. Another pointer is the conspicuous judaizing of the Carolingian Renaissance. In many respects the

Carolingian ruling class harked back to the Old Testament, in particular to the Pentateuch, as a source of law, and to the historical books like Joshua and Kings, because the kings of Israel were seen as the predecessors of the Carolingian princes. The Carolingian Empire was seen as the 'New Israel'; its kings and great gave themselves biblical nicknames such as David, Solomo, Aaron, Samuel. The episcopate compared itself to the priestly class of Israel; the bishops told the kings to read assiduously in the Books of Kings and the judges to study the Book of Judges [113]. A last instance. When Oliver Cromwell and his Puritans had established their absolute power over England in 1649, the strictest Sabbath-rest had to be observed by the whole population - a Sabbath-rest that was a copy of that prescribed by Mosaic Law. I feel it will be necessary to keep an eye on such tendencies, especially with regard to the question how they influenced Jewish-Christian relations.

NOTES TO CHAPTER II

1. Pritz, Nazarene 9 : "In the early centuries ther were many offshoot sects having some connections both to the New Testament and to Jewish thought".

2. Georg Strecker s.v. 'Judenchristentum', Theol.Realenz. 17 (1987), 310.

3. Simon, Problèmes 1. In : Aspects.

4. Segal, Jew.Christ. 326.

5. Segal, Jew.Christ. 327.

6. Munck, Primit.Jew.Christ. 83 : "The description of primitive Jewish Christianity shows how it differs from Judaism. It carries on missionary work among the Jews in Palestine, and assembles the baptized for special services and meals with celebration of Holy Communion, and has its own church charities ... Jesus, as the Lord of the Christians, makes them different from the Jews in every respect."

7. Munck, Prim.Jew.Christ. 84.

8. Acts 15. Brandon, Fall 126-154, has defended the thesis that there was an unbridgeable opposition between the Jamesian and Pauline positions; the opinion of James prevailed, according to him, until A.D. 70, after which that of Paul became predominant. Brandon made the fall of Jerusalem a decisive moment in the history of the early Church. Others have pointed out that James and Paul were not so far apart as

he contends. The compromise of the Council of Jerusalem, as described in Acts, was achieved without much difficulty.

9. Eus., HE 3.5.3.

10. Eus., HE 4.5.3.

11. The French scholar Stanislas Giet believes that there are traces of Judaeo-Christianity in the Pastor of Hermas. If this opinion is correct, then this would mean that there still were Jewish-born Christians in Rome in the middle of the second century. Giet's conclusion is that "the Pastor has ... its place in the history of Judaeo-Christianity". The fact itself does not seem doubtful. His opinion, however, is combated forcefully by Daniélou whose opinion is quoted in full by Giet, Courant 99-101. In view of the fact that indications for the continued existence of primitive = original Jewish Christianity are vague and scarce, I am in sympathy with the conclusion of the Danish scholar Munck, Prim.Jew.Christ. 91, that "primitive Jewish Christianity perished during the revolt of the Jews, and that the later movements known as Jewish-Christian, and more or less deserving the name, are a continuation of Gentile Christianity, which, intermingled with heretical, including Judaizing, elements, continues along heretical lines".

12. There may have been Jewish Christians in the Church of Rome, although a minority, until the end of the second century. At an early date already there were Jewish Christians in Egypt, one of them being the Apollos who is mentioned several times by Paul, see Vol. IX, Ch. V, Part I, 3f. According to Eus., HE 2.16, it was Mark who brought the Gospel to Alexandria. But when Segal writes that warnings by Clement of Alexandria (Eus. HE 6.13.3) and Origen (Comm. in Jo. 114) against judaizing "prove that Jewish Christianity was still a threat at the beginning of the third century", I don't go along with him. The term 'Judaizer' need not refer at all to Jewish born Christians. The sources we have make it extremely difficult to say something definite about Jewish Christians in Syria. According to Eus., HE 1.13, the Christian creed was brought to Edessa by a certain Addai, who arrived from Jerusalem and was in all probability a Jew. His name is an abbreviation of Adonya (Quispel, Évangile selon Thomas 37, note 1). The apocryphal Gospel of Thomas, dated by Quispel to ca. 146, is supposed to have been composed in a Jewish-Christian community at Edessa, see Segal, Jew.Christ. 336-339. The community at Edessa was characterized by strong ascetic tendencies; Quispel, Évangile 37 holds it for possible that this 'ascetic conception of Christian life' is (partly) due to the share of Judaeo-Christians coming from Palestine.

13. Daniélou, Théologie 19.

14. Daniélou, Théologie 18.

15. Ir., Adv.haer. 1.26.3.

16. Epiph., Pan. 29.6.5.

17. Epiph., Pan. 29.56.6.
18. Daniélou, Théologie 68, thinks that Ebionites and Nazoraeans were different groups.
19. Epiph., Pan. 1.30.1.
20. Schoeps, Theologie 14-21, Nachrichten über das ebionitische Christentum.
21. Schoeps, Theologie 21-25; on p. 21 he remarks that the Rabbis, as opponents of Ebionism, mainly used the weapon of ignoring.
22. Schoeps, Theologie (see Bibliography).
23. Simon, Problèmes 4.
24. Strecker, Juden-Christ. G Zur Entstehungsgeschichte des pseudoklementinischen Romans.
25. I am following Schoeps, Theol. pp. 37 sqq, here : "Eine ebionitische Quellenschrift in den Pseudoklementinen'.
26. Schoeps, Theologie 259; Acts 15:5.
27. Gal. 2:12.
28. Schoeps, Theologie 262.
29. Epiph., Pan. 1.29.7 and 30.2.
30. Schoeps, Theologie 273.
31. Recogn. 1.40.
32. Schoeps, Theologie 289-292.
33. Epiph., Pan. 1.30.18.2.
34. Hom. 14.1.4. The salt "symbolizes the incorruptibility of God's covenant with Israel", Segal, Jew.Christ. 346.
35. Ir., Adv.haer. 5.1.3.
36. Epiph., 1.30.16.1.
37. Schoeps, Theologie 292.
38. Hier., Ep. 112.13.
39. Pseudo-Tert., Adv.omnes haer. 3.
40. Hom. 3.47.1.
41. Hom. 2.38.1.
42. Schoeps, Theologie 149.
43. Schoeps, Theologie 170 171, presents a list of such passages. During the third century the Ebionites were often called Symmachians.

44. Hom. 4.13.
45. Recogn. 3.38.
46. Ir., Adv.haer. 1.26.2.
47. Schoeps, Theologie 16.2 : "Von dem charakterischen Hauptdualismus des wahren (sc. heidnischen) Gnosis - Weltschöpfer-höchster Gott - findet sich in den Klementinen nichts".
48. Hom. 2.15.2.
49. Hom. 2.15.3.
50. Hom. 2.15.2.
51. Hom. 3.22.1. See Strecker, Judenchrist. 155.
52. Schoeps, Theologie 162.
53. Hom. 3.23.1.
54. Hom. 2.15.1.
55. Hom. 2.15.2.
56. Hom. 2.15.5.
57. Hom. 2.16.1 states this in as many words.
58. Hom. 2.16.1.
59. Strecker, Judenchrist. 155.
60. Hom. 3.22.2.
61. Hom. 3.25.1; Gen. 4:1 does not say that Eve was the name-giver.
62. Hom. 3.22.2 and 23.2.
63. Hom. 3.24.3-4.
64. Hom. 3.24.1.
65. Hom. 3.23.2.
66. Strecker, Judenchrist. 157.
67. Hom. 3.23.4.
68. Hom. 3.24.2.
69. Hom. 11.18.2.
70. Hom. 2.15.3-4.
71. Hom. 3.27.2.
72. Hom. 2.15.3.
73. Hom. 2.15.3.

74. Hom, 3.23.3.
75. Hom. 1.18.1-3.
76. Hom. 3.28.1.
77. Hom. 1.18.4.
78. Hom. 1.19.1.
79. Recogn. 1.45.
80. Hom. 3.17.3-4.
81. Hom. 2.38.1.
82. Hom. 2.39.3-4.
83. Recogn. 1.39.2-3.
84. Bases on the summary in Neutest.Apokr. 159; see Hom. 3.33-38.
85. Hom. 2.15.1.
86. Based on the summary in Neutest.Apokr. 160.
87. Recogn. 3.52.4.
88. Vol. VII, Ch. II.5.
89. Daniélou, Judéo-Christ. 165. In the teeth of almost every other scholar and deviating from all handbooks, Schoeps, Theologie, Ch. IV, § 6, Die Gnosis des Ebionismus : der Kampf gegen den Marcionismus, defends the thesis that the Ebionists were no Gnostics, but, instead, their sharpest opponents. What they opposed was not the Gnosis as such, in its manifold manifestations, but the Marcionite theology. The controversial issue was, of course, that Marcion did away with Mosaic Law, in consequence of his wholesale rejection of the Old Testament, whereas the Ebionites remained attached to it. The guiding idea of Schoeps seems to be that, if a religious sect combats a Gnostic tenet or a Gnostic sect, it can not be Gnostic itself. But we know of many Gnostic sects inveighing against others. Schoeps presents five, in my opinion, not very convincing arguments why Ebionism should not be called Gnostic, but he overlooks the main characteristic, that of the double dualism. The term 'dualism' does not even appear in his disquisition.
90. See Vol. VIII, Preface 15.
91. Schoeps, Theologie 273.
92. Schoeps, Theologie 274.
93. Schoeps, Theologie 273/274.
94. Schoeps, Theologie 278.
95. Recogn. 4.4.

96. Tert., De praescr. 33.
97. Recogn. 5.34.2.
98. Recogn. 4.13.1.
99. Schoeps, Theologie 302.
100. Schoeps, Theologie 303.
101. Epiph., Pan. 1.30.14.
102. Schoeps, Theologie 304.
103. Aug., Contra Faust. 19.17.
104. Theodor., Comp.haer.fab. 2.11.
105. Schoeps, Theologie 305.
106. Schoeps, Theologie 320.
107. Hier., Ep. 112.13.
108. Schoeps, Theologie 324/325.
109. Schoeps, Theologie 342.
110. A critical review of all that the sources say of Elkasaites is to be found in Luttikhuizen, Revelation (see Bibliography).
111. Vol. IX, Ch. IV.5e.
112. See Vol. IX, Ch. IV.5e-f.
113. I owe this information to an essay by Mayke de Jong, Het rijk als huishouding, 43-45. De Jong refers to a book by R. Kottje, Studien zum Einfluss des Alten Testaments auf Recht und Liturgie des frühen Mittelalters (6. bis 8. Jahrhundert). Bonn, 1970.

BIBLIOGRAPHY

I ORIGINAL SOURCES

A COLLECTIONS

DIE GRIECHISCHEN CHRISTLICHEN SCHRIFSTELLER DER ERSTEN DREI JAHRHUNDERTE.

CODEX THEODOSIANUS. Ed. Thomas Wiedemann. London (1981).

CORPUS INSCRIPTIONUM LATINARUM. Vol. VI. Berlin, 1876 (quoted as CIL).

CORPUS SCRIPTORUM ECCLESIASTICORUM LATINORUM (CSEL).

THE APOSTOLIC FATHERS I and II. Ed. Kirsopp Lake. Loeb Classical Library 24 & 25. Cambridge (Mass.)/London, 1975 (1912 1) & 1970 (1913 1).

NEUTESTAMENTLICHE APOKRYPHEN. Herausg. Edgar Hennecke. Tübingen, 1924.

PATROLOGIA GRAECA (PG).

PATROLOGIA LATINA (PL).

B INDIVIDUAL AUTHORS

AELIUS LAMPRIDIUS
 Vita Elagabali.

AMBROSIUS
 1. Epistolae. PL 16. Paris, 1845.
 2. De officiis. PL 16 (1845).

AMMIANUS MARCELLINUS
Historiae. The Histories. Ed. J.C. Rolfe. 3 vols. Loeb Classical Library. Cambridge (Ms)/London.

APHRAHAT
Aphraat le Syrien, La version syrienne des oeuvres d' ... Ed. Guy Lafontaine. Corpus Scriptorum Christianorum Orientalium 382, 405, 406. Scriptores armeniaci 7, 9, 10. Louvain, 1977-1979.

APULEIUS
Apologia. Ed. Butler. Oxford, 1909.

ARNOBIUS
Adversus nationes. PL 5 (1844).

ATHANASIUS
Historia Arianorum.

ATHENAGORAS
Legatio pro Christianis. Ed. William R. Schroedel. Series : Early Christian Texts. Oxford, 1972.

AUGUSTINUS
1. De civitate Dei. City of God. Loeb Classical Library. Cambridge (Ms)/London, 1957-1972.
2. De consensu evangelistarum. PL, 32 (1845).
3. Contra Faustum Manichaeum. PL 42. Paris, 1861.
4. Epistola 196. PL 33. Paris, 1861.
5. In Psalmum CXVIII Expositio. PL 15. Paris, 1845.
6. Retractationes. PL 32 (1845).

AURELIUS VICTOR
Historiae abbreviatae. Livre des Césars. Ed. Pierre Dufaigne. Collection Budé. Paris, 1975.

BARNABAS
The Epistle of Barnabas. The Apostolic Fathers I. Ed. Kirsopp Lake. Loeb Classical Library 24. Cambridge (Ms)/London, 1975.

CICERO
1. De legibus. Ed. Clinton W. Keyes. Loeb Classical Library 213. Cambridge (Ms)/London, 1928.
2. De natura deorum. Ed. H. Rackham. Loeb Classical Library 268. Cambridge (Ms)/London, 1933.

CLEMENS OF ALEXANDRIA
1. Paedagogus. PG
2. Stromateis. Les Stromates. Texte et traduction de Marcel Casier et autres. Série : Sources chrétiennes 38, 278, 279. Paris, 1954-1981.

CLEMENS ROMANUS
1. The Epistles to the Corinthians. Apostolic Fathers I.
2. Paedagogus. PG 8. Paris, 1857.

CYPRIANUS
1. De bono patientiae. PG 4. Paris, 1844.
2. Epistulae. PL 4 (1844).
3. De Oratione Domenica. PG 4. Paris, 1844.
4. Testimonia adversus Judaeos. PG 4. Paris, 1844.

THE DIDASCALIA APOSTOLORUM IN SYRIAC. Ed. Arthur Vööbus. Corpus Scriptorum Christianorum Orientalium, Vols. 406, 407 and 408. Scriptores Syri T. 175, 176, 179 and 180. Louvain, 1979.

DIO CASSIUS
Roman History. 9 vols. Translated by Earnest Cary. Loeb Classical Library. Cambridge (Mass.)/London.

DIONYSIUS HALICARNENSIS
Roman Antiquities. Ed. Earnest Cary. Loeb Classical Library. Cambridge (Ms)/London, 1937-1950.

EPIPHANIUS
Panarion haeresium. Die griechischen christlichen Schrifsteller der ersten drei Jahrhunderte. Epiphanius I. Herausg. Karl Holl. Leipzig, 1915.

THE EPISTLE TO DIOGNETUS. The Apostolic Fathers II.

EUNAPIUS
The Lives of the Philosophers and Sophists. Ed. Wilmer Cave Wright. Loeb Classical Library 134. Cambridge (Ms)/London, 1922.

EUSEBIUS OF CAESAREA
1. Chronicorum libri duo. PG 19. Paris, 1857.
2. Demonstratio evangelica. PG 21. Paris, 1857.
3. Historia ecclesiastica (HE). Die griechischen christlichen Schriftsteller der ersten drei Jahrhunderte. Eusebius II.1. Herausgegeben von Eduard Schwartz. Leipzig, 1903.
4. De martyribus Palestinae. PG 20 (1845).
5. Praeparatio evangelica. PG 21. Paris, 1857.
6. De Vita Constantini. PG 20. Paris, 1857.

EUTYCHIUS
Annales. PG 111. Paris, 1863.

EVAGRIUS
Historia ecclesiastica. PG 86. Paris, 1865.

GALENUS
De differentia pulsuum. Opera omnia VIII. Ed. C.G. Kühn. Hildesheim, 1965 (photostatic reprint of edition Leipzig, 1824).

GREGORIUS NAZIANZUS
Orationes. PG 35 (1857) and 36 (1858).

HERMAS
Pastor. The Shepherd. The Apostolic Fathers II. Ed. Kirsopp Lake. Loeb Classical Library 25. Cambridge (Ms)/London, 1970.

HERODIANUS
Historia imperii. Ed. C.R. Whittaker. Loeb Classical Library. Cambridge (Ms)/London, 1970.

HIERONYMUS
1. Commentaria in Danielem. PL 25 (1845).
2. Epistolae. PL 22. Paris, 1845.

HILARIUS OF POITIERS
1. Commentarium in Mattaeum. PL 9. Paris, 1844.
2. Commentarium in Psalmos. PL 9. Paris, 1844.
3. Tractatus mysteriorum. Corpus Scriptorum Ecclesiasticorum Latinorum 65. Vienna/Liepzig, 1916.

HIPPOLYTUS
1. De Christo et Antichristo. PG 10 (1857).
2. Commentarium in Danielem. Hippolyte, Commentaire sur Daniel. Ed. Maurice Lefèvre. Sources chrétiennes 14. Paris, 1947.
3. Commentarium in Deuteronomium. Die griechischen christlichen Schriftsteller der ersten drei Jahrhunderte. Leipzig, 1897.
4. Refutatio omnium haeresium. Die griechischen christlichen Schriftsteller der ersten drei Jahrhunderte. Bd. 26. Hippolytus 2. Ed. Paul Wendland. Liepzog, 1916.
5. Adversus Judaeos. PG 10. Paris, 1857.

IGNATIUS OF ANTIOCH
1. Epistle to the Magnesians. The Apostolic Fathers I.
2. Epistle to the Philadelphians. The Apostolic Fathers I.

IRENAEUS OF LYONS
Adversus haereses. Contre les hérésies. Eds. Adelin Rousseau and Louis Doutreleau. Vol. 2 Textes latins et greces et traduction. Paris, 1982.

IULIUS CAPITOLINUS
Vita Marci Antonini Philosophi. The Scriptores Historiae Agustae I. Ed. David Magie. Loeb Classical Library 139. Cambridge (Ms)/London, 1922.

JOHANNES CHRYSOSTOMUS
 1. Adversus Judaeos. PG 48. Paris, 1862.
 2. 'Si esurierit inimicus tuus, ciba illum.' Homilia XXV in quaedam loca Novi Testamenti. PG 51. Paris, 1862.
 3. In Sanctum Babylum. PG 49/50. Paris, 1862.

JOSEPHUS, Flavius
 Jewish Antiquities. Ed. Ralph Marcus. Loeb Classical Library. London/Cambridge (Mass.), 1957 (1943 1).

JULIANUS APOSTATA
 1. Contra Galilaeos. Against the Galilaeans. The Works of the Emperor Julian. Ed. William Cave Wright. Loeb Classical Library 157. Cambridge (Ms)/London, 1961.
 2. Epistula ad Themistium.
 3. Misopogon.
 Juliani imperatoris quae supersunt praeter reliquios apud Cyrillum omnia. Rec. Fridericus Carolus Hertlein I. Lipsiae, 1875.
 4. Juliani imperatoris epistulae et leges. Ed. J. Bidez et F. Cumont. Collection Budé 50. Paris, 1922.

JUSTINUS MARTYR
 1. Apologia 1 and 2. PG 6. Paris, 1857.
 2. Dialogus cum Tryphone Judaeo. PG 6. Paris, 1857.

LACTANTIUS
 1. Divinae Institutiones. Corpus Scriptorum Ecclesiasticorum Latinorum 19. Prague/Vienna/Leipzig, 1890.
 2. De mortibus persecutorum. PL 7 (1844).

LIBANIUS
 Selected orations. Ed. A.F. Norman. 3 vols. Loeb Classical Library. Cambridge (Ms)/London.

LIVIUS
 Livy, History of Rome. 14 vols. Loeb Classical Library. Cambridge (Ms/London), 1919-1957.

LUCIANUS
 1. Alexander the False Prophet. Ed. A.M. Harmon. Loeb Classical Library 162. Cambridge (Ms)/London, 1925.
 2. The Passing of Peregrinus. Ed. A.M. Harmon. Loeb Classical Library 302. Cambridge (Ms)/London, 1955.

MARCUS AURELIUS
 The Communings with himself of --. Ed. C.R. Haines. Loeb Classical Library 58. Cambridge (Ms)/London, 1930.

MELITO OF SARDES
 Peri Pascha
 1a. On Pascha and Fragments. Ed. and transl. by Stuart George Hall. Oxford Early Christianity Texts. Oxford, 1979.
 1b. Sur la Pâque. Ed. and translated by Othmar Perler. Sources chrétiennes 123. Paris, 1966.

METHODIUS
 Convivium decem virginum. PG 18. Paris, 1857.

MINUCIUS FELIX
 Octavius. Translated by G.H. Rendall. Loeb Classical Library 250. Cambridge (Mass.)/London, 1931 4.

ORIGENES
 1. Commentarium in B. Pauli Apostoli Epistolam ad Romanos. PG 12. Paris, 1862.
 2. Contra Celsum. PG 11. Paris, 1857.
 3. In librum Judicum homilia. PG 12, Paris, 1862.
 4. Homiliae in Psalmos. PG 12. Paris, 1862.
 5. Peri archoon. PG 11. Paris, 1857.
 6. Selecta in Psalmos. PG 12. Paris, 1862.

PASSIO PERPETUAE ET FELICITATIS.
 The Passion of S. Perpetua. Newly edited from the mss. with an introduction and notes by J. Armitage Robinson. Nendeln (Liechtenstein), 1967 (photostatic reprint of the edition Cambridge, 1891).

PLINIUS
 Epistulae. Pliny the Younger, Letters II. Ed. Betty Radice. Loeb Classical Library 59. Cambridge (Ms)/London, 1969.

PLUTARCHUS
 On Superstition. Ed. Frank C. Babbitt. Loeb Classical Library 245. Cambridge (ms)/London, 1931.

PORPHYRIUS
 De abstinentia. Porphyre, De l'abstinence, T. II. Texte établi et traduit par Jean Bouffartique et Michel Patillon. Collection Budé. Paris, 1979.

PSEUDO-CLEMENS
 1. Homilien. Die griechischen christlichen Schriftsteller der ersten drei Jahrhunderte. Die Pseudoklementinen I. Herausg. Bernhard Rehm. Berlin, 1953.
 2a. Recognitiones. Neutestamentliche Apokryphen. Herausg. Edgar Hennecke. Tübingen, 1924.
 2b. Recognitionen in Rufins Übersetzung. Herausg. Bernhard Rehm. Berlin, 1965.

PSEUDO-CYPRIANUS
Adversus Judaeos. PL 4. Paris, 1844.

PSEUDO-TERTULLIANUS
Adversus omnes haereses. CSEL 47. Vienna/Leipzig, 1906.

RUFINUS
Historia ecclesiastica. PL 21. Paris, 1849.

SEVERUS MAJORICENSIS
Epistola de Judaeis. PL 20. Paris, 1845.

SEXTUS JULIUS AFRICANUS
The Fragments in PG 10. Paris, 1857.

SILVESTER I
The Fragments in PL 8. Paris, 1857.

SOCRATES
Historia ecclesiastica. PG 67. Paris, 1864.

SOZOMENOS
Historia ecclesiastica. Sozomenus, Kirchengeschichte. Ed. Joseph Bidez. Die christlichen griechischen Schriftsteller der ersten drei Jahrhunderte, Bd. 50. Berlin, 1960.

SPARTIANUS
Vita Severi. Ed. David Magie. The Scriptores Historiae Augustae. Loeb Classical Library 140. Cambridge (Ms)/London, 1924.

SUETONIUS
Claudius
Domitianus
Nero
Vespasianus
Lives of the Caesars. Loeb Classical Library 31. Ed. J.C. Rolfe. Cambridge (Mass.)/London, 1914.

SYMEON METAPHRASTA
Vita S. Symeonis Stylitae. PL 86. Paris, 1865.

TACITUS
1. Annales. The Annals. Ed. John Jackson. Loeb Classical Library 463-464. Cambridge (Ms)/London, 11931, 1937.
2. Historiae. The Histories. Ed. Clifford H. Moore. Loeb Classical Library 111 and 249. Cambridge (Ms)/London, 1925, 1931.

TERTULLIANUS
1. Apologeticus adversus gentes pro Christianis. PL 1. Paris, 1844.
2. Adversus Gnosticos Scorpiace. PL 1, Paris, 1844.
3. Adversus Judaeos. PL 1. Paris, 1844.
4. De idolatria. Tertulliani Opera Pars II. Corpus Scriptorum Christianorum, Pars Latina. Turnholti, 1954.
5. Contra Judaeos. PL 2. Paris, 1844.
6. Adversus Marcionem. Ed. and translated by Ernest Evans. Oxford, 1972.
7. De monogamia. PL 2. Paris, 1844.
8. Ad nationes. PL 2. Paris, 1844.
9. Adversus Praxeam. PL 2. Paris, 1844.
10. De prescriptionibus adversus haereticos. PL 1. Paris, 1844.
11. De pudicitia. PL 2. Paris, 1844.
12. De resurrectione carnis. PL 2. Paris, 1844.
13. Ad scapulum. Tertulliani Opera Pars II. Corpus Scriptorum Christianorum, Pars Latina. Turnholti, 1954.
14. De spectaculis. PL 1. Paris, 1844.

THEODORETUS
Haereticarum fabularum compendium. PG 83. Paris, 1864.

THEOPHILUS
Ad Autolycum. PG 6. Paris, 1857.

VENANTIUS FORTUNATUS (?)
Vita Hilarii. PL 9. Paris, 1844.

VERGILIUS
Aeneis. Virgil, The Aeneid. Ed. H.R. Fairclough. Loeb Classical Library 63-64. Cambridge (Ms)/London, 1934-1935.

II SECONDARY WORKS

A WORKS OF REFERENCE

DICTIONNAIRE DE THÉOLOGIE CATHOLIQUE.

ENCYCLOPAEDIA JUDAICA.

JEWISH ENCYCLOPEDIA.

PAULYS REAL-ENCYCLOPÄDIE DER CLASSISCHEN ALTERTUMSWISSENSCHAFT. Neue Bearbeitung von Georg Wissowa. Stuttgart (cited as PW).

THEOLOGISCHE REALENZYKLOPÄDIE.

B COLLECTIONS

ASPECTS DU JUDÉO-CHRISTIANISME. Colloque de Strasbourg, 23-25 avril 1965. Bibliothèque des Centres d'Études supérieures spécialisées. Paris, 1965.

AUFSTIEG UND NIEDERGANG DER RÖMISCHEN WELT. Geschichte und Kultur Roms im Spiegel der neueren Forschung. Berlin/New York.

BOUFFARTIQUE, Jean, Julien par Julien. L'empereur Julien. De l'histoire à la légende (331-1715). Études rassemblées par René Braun et Jean Richer. Tome I. Paris, 1978 (quoted as 'L'empereur Julien').

CAMBRIDGE ANCIENT HISTORY.

DAS FRÜHE CHRISTENTUM BIS ZUM ENDE DER VERFOLGUNGEN. Eine Dokumentation. Band 1, Die Christen im heidnischen Staat. Übersetzung der Texte von Peter Guyot. Auswahl und Kommentar von Richard Klein. Texte zur Forschung 60. Darmstadt, 1993.

EUSEBIUS, CHRISTIANITY, AND JUDAISM. Eds. Harold W. Attridge and Gohei Atta. Studia Post-Biblica 42. Leiden/New York/Köln, 1992.

HISTORY AND HATE. The Dimensions of Anti-Semitism. Ed. David Berger. Philadelphia, 1986.

JEWISH AND CHRISTIAN SELF-DEFINITION. II Aspects of Judaism in the Graeco-Roman period. Ed. E.P. Sanders. London, 1981.

JEWS, GREEKS AND CHRISTIANS. Religious Cultures in Late Antiquity. Eds. Robert Hamerton-kelty and Robin Scroggs. Leiden, 1976.

THE JEWS AMONG PAGANS AND CHRISTIANS IN THE ROMAN EMPIRE. Eds. Judith Lieu, John North and Tessa Rajak. London/New York (1992).

KIRCHE UND SYNAGOGE. Handbuch zur Geschichte von Juden und Christen. Darstellung mit Quellen. Herausg. Karl Heinrich Rengstorf und Siegfried von Korzfleisch. Bd. I. Stuttgart (1968).

SCHOLEM, Gershom, The Messianic Idea in Judaism and other Essays in Jewish Spirituality. New York (1978 4, 1971 1).

SCHRECKENBERG, Heinz, Die christlichen Adversus-Judaeos-Texte und ihr literarisches und historisches Umfeld (1.-11. Jh.). Europäische Hochschulschriften. Reihe XXIII Theologie, Bd. 172. Frankfurt am Main/Bern (1982).

STORIA DI ROMA. Bologna.

C MONOGRAPHS

ALLARD, Paul, Les dernières persécutions du troisième siècle (Gallus, Valérien, Aurélien). Paris, 1924 (quatrième édition, revue et augmentée, 1887)[1.]

AVERY-PECK, Alan, Judaism without the Temple : The Mishnah. In : Eusebius, Christianity, and Judaism.

AZIZA, Claude, Tertullien et le Judaisme. Publications de la Faculté des lettres et des sciences humaines de l'Université de Nice 16. 1977.

BAMBERGER, Bernard J., Proselytism in the Talmudic Period. Cincinnati, 1939.

BARON, Salo Wittmayer, A Social and Religious History of the Jews I. New York, 1937.

BARRETT, C.K., Jews and Judaizers in the Epistles of Ignatius. In : Jews, Greeks and Pagans.

BENKO, Stephen, Pagan Criticism of Christianity during the First Two Centuries. In : Aufstieg und Niedergang. 23.2 (1980).

BENGTSON, Hermann, Die Flavier. Vespasian, Titus, Domitian. Geschichte eines römischen Kaiserhauses. München (1979).

BIETENHARD, Hans, Caesarea, Origenes und die Juden. Franz Delitsch-Vorlesungen 1972. Stuttgart/Berlin/Köln/Mainz (1974).

BLUMENKRANZ, Bernhard
1. Die Judenpredigt Augustins. Ein Beitrag zur Geschichte jüdisch-christlichen Beziehungen in den ersten drei Jahrhunderten. Paris, 1978 (réimpression de la 1ère édition Bâle 1946).
2. Patristik und Frühmittelalter. A. Die Entwicklung im Westen zwischen 200 und 1200. In : Kirche und Synagoge I.

BRANDON, S.G.F., The Fall of Jerusalem and the Christian Church. London, 1951.

BRAUDE, William G., Jewish Proselyting in the First Three Centuries of the Common Era. The Age of the Tannaim and Amoraim. Providence, R.I., 1940.

BRAUN, René, Julien et le Christianisme. L'empereur Julien I.

BROWNING, Robert, The Emperor Julian. London, 1975.

COHEN, Straye D., The Problem of Definition. In : History and Hate.

COLIN, Jean, L'empire des Antonins et les martyrs gaulois de 177. Antiquitas. Reihe 1. Abhandlungen zur alten Geschichte, Bd. 10. Bonn, 1964.

DANIÉLOU, Jean
1. Judéo-Christianisme et Gnose. in : Aspects.
2. Théologie du Judéo-Christianisme. Bibliothèque de théologie. Histoire des doctrines chrétiennes avant Nicée. Tournai, 1958.

DAWSON, Christopher, The Making of Europe. An Introduction into the History of European Unity. London, 1946[7 (1932 1)].

FELDMAN, Louis, Jewish Proselytism. In : Eusebius, Christianity, and Judaism.

FREND, W.H.C., Martyrdom and Persecution in the Early Church. A study of the conflict from the Maccabees to Donatus. Oxford, 1965.

FREUDENBERGER, Rudolf, Das Verhalten der römischen Behörden gegen die Christen dargestellt am Brief des Plinius an Trajan und die Reskripten des Trajans und Hadrians. Münchener Beiträge zur Papyrusforschung und antiken Rechtsgeschichte. 52. Heft. München, 1967.

FLUSSER, David
1. Jesus and Judaism : Jewish Perspectives. In : Eusebius, Christianity, and Judaism.
2. Judaism and the Origin of Christianity. Jerusalem (1988).

GIET, Stanislas, Un courant judéo-chrétien à Rome au milieu du IIe siècle. In : Aspects du Judéo-Christ.

GOODMAN, Martin, Jewish Proselyting in the First Century. in : The Jews among Pagans and Christians.

GOPPELT, Leonhard, Christentum und Judentum im ersten und zweiten Jahrhundert. Ein Aufriss der Urgeschichte der Kirche. Beiträge zur christlichen Theologie. 2. Reihe. Wissenschaftliche Monographien, 55 Bd. Gütersloh (1954).

GRANT, Michael, Nero. London (1970).

GRANT, Robert M. Grant, Porphyry.

GRÉGOIRE, Henri, Les persécutions dans l'empire romain. Bruxelles, 1951.

HARNACK, Adolf von, Die Mission und Ausbreitung des Christentums in den ersten drei Jahrhunderten I. Leipzig, 1924 4 (1902 1).

HERMANN, Léon, Chrestos. Témoignages païens et juifs sur le Christianisme du premier siècle. Collection Latomus 109. Bruxelles, 1970.

HOENNICKE, Gustav, Das Judenchristentum im ersten und zweiten Jahrhundert. Berlin, 1908.

HORSLEY, Richard, Jesus and Judaism : Christian Perspectives. in : Eusebius, Christianity, and Judaism.

ISAAC, Jules
1. L'antisémitisme a-t-il des racines chrétiennes? Paris, 1960.
2. Genèse de l'antisémitisme. Essai historique. Paris (1956).

JONG, Mayke de, Het rijk als huishouding. Kanttekeningen bij de Karolingische wetgeving (The Empire as a Household. Notes to Carolingian legislation). Feit & Fictie, Jg. 2, no. 3 (autumn 1995).

JUSTER, Jean, Les Juifs dans l'Empire romain. Leur condition juridique, économique et sociale. Burt Franklin research and source work series. New York, 1914.

KARLHORST, Paul, Von Nero bis Konstantin dem Grossen. Politische und soziale Aspekte einer kirchengeschichtlichen Wende. Thesis Un. Frankfurt a.M., 1983.

KERESZTES, Paul, Rome and the Christian Church I. Aufstieg und Niedergang 23.1.

KIMELMAN, Reuven, Birkat Ha-Minim and the Lack of Evidence for an Anti-Christian Jewish Prayer in Late Antiquity. In : Jewish and Christian Self-Definition II.

KLIJN, A.J., Na het Nieuwe Testament. De christelijke literatuur uit de tweede eeuw (After the New Testament. Christian Literature of the Second Century). Baarn (NL), 1973.

KÖTTING, Bernhard, Patristik im Osten bis Justinian. In : Kirche und Synagoge I.

LANGE, Nicholas R.M. de, Origen and the Jews. Studies in Jewish-Christian relations in third-century Palestine. University of Cambridge Oriental Publications 25. Cambridge, 1978 (1976 1).

LUTTIKHUIZEN, Gerard P., The Revelation of Elchasai. Investigations into the Evidence for a Mesopotamian Jewish Apocalypse of the Second Century and its Reception by Judeo-Christian Prpagandists. Texte und Sudien zum Antiken Judentum. Tübingen, 1985.

MATSUNAGA, Kikuo, Christian Self-Identification and the Twelfth Benediction. In : Eusebius, Christianity, and Judaism.

MICHNIK, Adam, Poland and the Jews. The New York Review of Books, May 30, 1991.

MOLTHAGEN, Joachim, Der römische Staat und die Christen im zweiten und dritten Jahrhundert. Hypomnemata 28. Göttingen (1975², 1970¹).

MOMIGLIANO, Arturo, Nero. CAH X (1934).

MUNCK, Johannes, Primitive Jewish Christianity and later Jewish Christianity. in : Aspects du Judéo-Christ.

NEUSNER, Jacob
1. Aphrahat and Judaism. The Christian-Jewish argument in fourth-century Iran. Studia Post-Biblica Vol. XI. Leiden, 1971.
2. First-Century Judaism in Crisis. Yohanan ben Zakkai and the Renaissance of Torah. Nashville-New York (1975).

NOCK, A.D., Conversion. The Old and the New in Religion from Alexander the Great to Augustine of Hippo. Oxford, 1933.

PARKES, James, The Conflict of the Church and the Synagogue. A study in the origins of antisemitism. New York, 1974.

POLIAKOV, Léon, Histoire de l'antisémitisme I. Paris (1955).

PRITZ, Ray A., Nazarene Jewish Christianity. From the End of the New Testament Period until Its Disappearance in the Fourth Century. Studia Post-Biblic 37. Jerusalem/Leiden, 1988.

QUISPEL, Gilles, L'Évangile selon Thomas. In : Aspects du Judéo-Christ.

RAJAK, Tessa, The Jewish community and its boundaries. In : The Jews among Pagans and Christians.

RENGSTORF, Karl Heinrich, Das neue Testament und die nachapostolische Zeit. In : Kirche und Synagoge I.

RUETHER, Rosemary Radford, Faith and Fratricide. The Theological Roots of Anti-Semitism. New York (1979).

SCHOEPS, Hans-Joachim, Theologie und Geschichte des Judenchristentums. Tübingen, 1949.

SCHOLEM, Gershom, Toward an Understanding of the Messianic Idea in Judaism. In : The Messianic Idea.

SCHÜRER, Emil, The History of the Jewish people in the Age of Jesus Christ. Revised English version by Geza Vermes, Fergus Millar and Matthew Black. Edinburh, 1979 (first German edition 1885-1924).

SEGAL, Alan, Jewish Christianity. In : Eusebius, Christianity, and Judaism.

SEVENSTER, Jan N., The Roots of Pagan Anti-Semitism. 1975.

SILVER, Abba Hillel, Where Judaism differed. An Inquiry into Distinctiveness of Judaism. New York, 1956.

SIMON, Marcel,
1. Problèmes du Judéo-Christianisme. In : Aspects du Judéo-Christ.
2. Verus Israel. Étude sur les relations entre Chrétiens et Juifs dans l'Empire romain (135-425). Paris, 1948.

SMALLWOOD, E. Mary, The Jews in the Roman Empire. From Pompey to Diocletian. Studies in Judaism in Late Antiquity, Vol. 20. Leiden, 1976.

SORDI, Marta, Il Cristianesimo e Roma. Storia di Roma 9 (1965).

STRECKER, Georg, Das Juden-Christentum in den Pseudo-Klementinen. Texte und Untersuchungen zur altchristlichen Literatur Berlin, 1958.

STREETER, B.H., The Rise of Christianity. CAH XI (1936).

TAYLOR, Miriam S., Anti-Judaism and Early Christian Identity. A Critique of the Scholarly Consensus. Studia Post-Biblica 46. Leiden/New York/Köln, 1995.

TRIGG, Joseph Wilson, Origen. The Bible and Philosophy in the third-century Church. Atlanta (USA) (1983).

WILDE, Robert, The Treatment of the Jews in the Greek Christian Writers of the First Three Centuries. Diss. Washington D.C., 1949.

WILKEN, Robert L.,
1. The Christians as the Romans saw them. New Haven/London, 1984.
2. John Chrysostom and the Jews. Rhetoric and Reality in the late 4th Century. Series : The Transformation of the Classical Heritage Vol. IV. Berkeley (Los Angeles)/London (1983).

WILLIAMS, A. Lukyn, Adversus Judaeos. A Bird's-eye View of Christian Apologiae until the Renaissance. Cambridge, 1935.

WISTRICH, Robert, Antisemitism. The longest hatred. London, 1991.

ZIEGLER, Ignaz, Der Kampf zwischen Judentum und Christentum in den ersten drei christlichen Jahrhunderten. Berlin, 1907.

GENERAL INDEX

Aaron, 241
Abel, 38-39, 40, 141, 169
Abraham, 140, 143, 146, 148, 156, 163, 168, 194, 196, 235
Acts of the Apostles, 111, 112-114, 120
Adam, 232, 234-235
Addai (Adonya), Christian missionary, 242
Ahriman, 72
Ahura Mazda, 72
Alamanni, 73
Alcibiades, Elkasaite preacher, 239
Alexamenos, Christian Roman slave, 5
Alexander Severus, Roman Emperor, 55, 56
Alexandria, 2, 45, 53, 70, 147, 148, 152, 153, 186-187, 242
Algeria, 64
Allard, Paul, 62, 90, 93
Alps, 68
Ambrosius, bishop of Milan, 70, 90, 179-180, 180, 183-185, 185, 221, 222, 223
Ammianus Marcellinus, 77, 92, 93
Amsterdam, capital of the Netherlands, 120
Ananus, Jewish High Priest, 2
Anglosaxon, 171
Annas, Jewish High Priest, 105
Anterus, bishop of Rome, 57
Antichrist, 24, 32, 432
Anti-Judaism, 98
Antioch(ene), 1, 59, 64, 76, 132, 146, 169, 171, 172, 175, 177, 186, 229
Antiochus IV Epiphanes, 14
Antiquity, 98, 154, 171

Anti-Semitism, anti-Semites, anti-Semitic, 96, 97, 98, 99, 100, 109, 111, 114, 123, 130, 132, 171, 177, 178, 204
Antonini (Emperors), 49, 52
Antoninus Pius, Roman Emperor, 43, 50
Anulinus, proconsul of the province of North Africa, 68
Aphra(a)t(es), Christian author, 153, 168, 193, 219
Apion, a pagan author, 148
Apollinari(u)s, Christian apologist, 14, 145
Apollo, 68
Apollo oracle at Milete, 65
Apollos, a Christian, mentioned by Paul, 242
Apostles, 1, 27, 29, 159
Apuleius, Lucius, 7, 80
Arabs, 98
Aramaic, 237
Arcadius, Roman Emperor, 170
Archontics, Gnostic sect, 131
Arian(s), Arianism, 43, 70, 72, 74, 162, 165, 169, 170, 175, 179, 181, 192, 238
Aristo of Pella, Christian apologist, 145
Armenia, 170
Arnobius, pagan author, 16, 82
Asia, 33
Asia, Roman province, 49, 113
Asia Minor, 2, 63, 65, 71, 113, 119, 133, 134
Aspasius Paternus, proconsul of the province of Africa, 61
Assyrians, 39
Atarbius, governor of Syria, 77

Athanasius, bishop of Alexandria, 70, 91, 179
Athenagoras, Christian author, 9, 20, 31, 51, 81, 83, 85, 88
Athenians, 39
Athens, 73, 147
Augustine, Church Father, 14, 15, 16, 25, 33-41, 43, 82, 85, 86, 179, 180-181, 221, 222, 238, 246
Augustus, 32, 35
Aurelianus, Roman Emperor, 63
Auschwitz, 96, 98
Autolycus, a pagan, 146
Avery-Peck, Alan, 109, 207
Avneri, Zvi, 209
Aziza, Claude, 151, 216

Babylonia, 188, 219
Babylonian Captivity, 101, 107, 128
Babylonian Empire, 14
Bacchanalia, 19
Bacchic(s), pagan sect, 19
Bacchus, 19
Bahr, Hermann, 224
Bamberger, Bernard J., 209, 210
Bar Kokhba (revolt), 49, 107, 108, 138,, 190, 193, 202, 214
Bar Mitzva, 121
Barbelo-Gnosis, Gnostic sect, 131
Bardy, G., 215
Barnabas, Christian author, 135-136, 137, 195
Barnabas, Epistle of, 26, 84, 135-136, 212, 224
Baron, Salo Wittmayer, 209
Barrett, C.K., 211
Barsuma (Barsauma), a monk, 186
Basilidians, Gnostic sect, 131
Basilius the Great, Christian author, 179
Baum, Gregor, 204
Belinfante, Dutch Jewish family, 206
Bengtson, Hermann, 47, 87
Benjamin, tribe of, 110
Benko, Stephen, 3, 8, 12, 80, 81
Berlin, 97
Beth Din, Jewish Court of Justice, 114, 115
Bible, 108, 131, 157, 180, 192, 230, 231, 239
Bidez, Joseph, 93
Bietenhard, Hans, 156, 216, 217
Bithynia, 4, 65, 164, 177
Blandina, Christian martyr, 44
Blumenkranz, Bernhard, 181, 214, 221, 222
Book of Daniel, 14-15, 25, 26, 27, 41
Book of Joshua, 241
Book of Judges, 241
Books of Kings, 241
Book of Revelation, 24, 25, 27, 29, 41, 48
Bouffartique, Jean, 92
Brandon, S.G.F., 241
Braude, William G., 210
Braun, René, 93
Brown, Peter, 42, 86
Browning, Peter, 71, 77, 92, 93

Caecilianus, bishop of Carthage, 69
Caecilius, a Christian, 147
Caesar, Julius, 188
Caesarea, 59, 82, 113, 153, 162, 237
Caesarea Panias (Fenician town), 77, 93
Cain, 38-39, 40, 169, 233
Caiphas, Jewish High Priest, 105
Callistus (Calixtus) I, bishop of Rome, 52,, 157 56
Canaan, 146
Capitoline Hill, 59
Cappadocia(n), 57, 63, 71, 89
Caracalla, Roman Emperor, 52, 54
Carolingian, 240-241
Carthage, 34, 53, 59, 61, 62, 161
Catholic Letters, 110
Caucasus, 170
Celsus, pagan Roman author, 9-13, 13, 16, 17, 28, 154, 156
Celtic, Celts, 13, 17
Central Synagogue, New York, 122
Christ see Jesus Christ
Christian(s), Ch. I passim, Ch. II passim, 228, 229, 230, 235, 238,

265

239, 240, 241, 242
Christian Church see Roman-Catholic Church
Christianity, 2, 4, 8, 9, 10, 13, 16, 20, 28, 30, 32, 33, 35, 38, 40, 42, 45, 48, 53, 54, 56, 58, 62, 63, 64, 67, 68, 69, 70, 72, 74, 75, 77, 79, Ch. II passim, 227, 228, 234, 240
Church Fathers, 228, 238, 240
Church of Corinth, 132
Church of Magnesia, 133
Church of Rome, 132
Cicero, Marcus Tullius, 17, 18, 82, 83
Circumcision, 119, 135, 137, 138, 158, 168, 175, 182, 208, 229, 230, 237, 239
Claudius, Roman Emperor, 3
Clemens Romanus, supposed author of the Pseudo-Clementina, 229
Clement of Alexandria, 147-149, 193
Clement, First Letter of, 24, 48, 99, 132
Clement, Second Letter of, 26, 132
Clement of Alexandria, 53, 88, 214, 215, 242
Cohen, David, Dutch Jewish professor, 206
Cohen, Straye D., 205
Cohen Belinfante see Belinfante
Colin, Jean, 87
Cologne, 73
Comana town in Pontus, 170
Commodus, Roman Emperor, 9, 51, 52
Constantine I the Great, 38, 40, 43, 68-69, 70, 71, 162, 164, 165, 166, 167, 181, 199
Constantine II, 182
Constantinople, 71, 72, 73, 170
Constantius Chlorus, 66
Constantius II, 70, 71, 72, 73, 182
Corinth, 2, 113
Cornelius, bishop of Rome, 90
Cornelius, Roman centurion, 119
Council of Jerusalem, 229, 242
Council of Nicaea, 165-167, 168, 177, 229, 240
Crescens, Roman philosopher, 5

Crispus, son of Constantine the Great, 164
Crusade, First, 204
Cyprianus, Church Father, bishop of Carthage, 59, 61, 62-63, 90, 144, 149, 160-161, 178, 218
Cromwell, Oliver, 241
Cyprus, 2, 190, 238
Cyrene, Cyrenaica, 128, 190
Cyrillus of Jerusalem, Christian author, 179
Cyrillus, patriarch of Alexandria, 186-187

Damascus, 1
Damas, bishop of Magnesia, 133
Damasus I, bishop of Rome, 90
Daniel, 14
Daniélou, Jean, 227, 236, 242, 243, 245
Danish, 242
Danube, 73
David, 47, 104, 131, 146, 241
Dawson, Christian, 41, 42, 86
Dead Sea, 102
Decius, Roman Emperor, 57-60, 60, 61, 152. 160
Delon, Alain, 205
Demeter, 92
Dertona, Spanish town, 186
Deuteronomy, Book of, 155
Diaspora, 122, 126, 128, 188
Didache, 134, 137
Didascalia, 159-160, 218
Dio Casssius, 80, 87, 209
Diocletianus, 64-66
Diodorus of Tarsus, Christian author, 179
Diognetus see Letter o Diognetus
Dionysius, bishop of Alexandria, 87
Dionysius, bishop of Corinth, 27
Dionysius, bishop of Rome, 63
Dionysus Halicarnensis, 82
Docetists, heterodox sect, 133, 134
Domitia Longa, wife of Domitianus, 47
Domitianus, 4, 20, 24, 43, 47-48
Donatists, 188
Dualism, dualistic, 18, 22, 23, 24,

25, 27, 32, 33, 40, 78-79, 132, 150, 151, 199-201, 201-202, 225, 231-232, 234, 235, 236, 238, 239-240, 245
Dutch, 97, 206

Easter (date), 142, 165-166, 176, 240
Eber, ancestor of Abraham, 163
Ebionites, 227, 227-238, 239, 240, 243, 244, 245
Edessa, 242
Edomites (Idumaeans), 126
Egypt, 128, 139, 146, 190, 242
Egyptian(s), 11, 17, 39, 43, 58, 60, 66, 75, 77, 146, 148, 152, 166, 227, 231
Eidikios, prefect of Egypt, 77
Elagabalus, Roman Emperor, 55-56, 89
Elah-gabal, Syrian godhead, 55
Elbogen, I., 208
Eleusis, mysteries of, 73
Eliezer, a Rabbi, 127
Eliogagalum, temple in Rome, 55
Elkasaites (Elkesaites, Elcesaites), 227, 239-240, 246
Elvira, town in Spain, 161
England, English, 95, 241
Ephesus, 72, 112, 134, 138
Ephraim the Syrian, Christian author, 153, 179
Epicurean(ism), 9, 10
Epiphanius, 228, 230, 231, 237, 238, 243, 246
Esau, 144, 194
Essenes, Essenian(ism), 25, 100, 102, 107
Ethiopic, 218
Etruria, 60
Eucharist, 7, 9, 99, 133, 177, 226, 230, 241
Eudoxia, wife of the Emperor Arcadius, 170
Eunapius, Roman author, 92
Euphrates, 183, 239
Europe(an), 33, 96, 204
Eusebius of Caesarea, historian, 14, 47, 48, 53, 64, 66, 67, 68, 82, 84, 85, 86, 87, 88, 89, 90, 91, 92, 133, 138, 153, 162-164, 212, 214, 216, 219, 227, 242
Evagrius, Christan author, 223
Eve, 232-234, 244

Fabianus, bishop of Rome, 57, 58-59
Fabius, bishop of Antioch, 87
Father(s) of the Church, 102, 103, 109, 130, 134, 137, 149, 152, 154, 155, 156, 158, 164, 171, 179-181, 189, 190, 191, 193-204
Feldman, Louis, 79, 126, 209
Felicitas, Christian martyr, 53
Feuchtwanger, Lion, German author, 123-124
Firmilianus, Christian author, 57, 89
Fiscus judaicus, 48, 83
Flavia Domitilla, Roman matrona, 4-5, 48
Flavia Neapolis (Nablus), town in Samaria, 137
Flavius, bishop of Antioch, 170
Flavius Clemens, Roman consul, 4-5, 48, 126
Flusser, David, 101, 205
Forum in Rome, 54
Franks, 73
French, 99
Frend, W.H.C., 6, 19, 25, 46, 48, 50, 53, 60, 63, 64, 80, 83, 84, 86, 87, 88, 90, 91, 92
Freudenberger, Rudolf, 88
Fronto, M. Cornelius, Roman rhetor, 5-6
Fructuosus, bishop of Taragona, 62

Galenus, 8, 80
Galerius, Roman Emperor, 65, 66, 67
Galerius Maximus, proconsul of the province of Africa, 63
Galilaean(s), 75, 76, 77, 78, 79, 93, 102
Galilee, 102, 104
Gallienus, Roman Emperor, 61, 63
Gallus, Roman Emperor, 60, 71, 73

Gamaliel I, Jewish Rabbi, 117
Gamaliel II, Jewish Rabbi, 188
Gamaliel IV, Jewish patriarch, 187
Gaul, 62, 68
Genesis, 196
Gentile(s), 100, 103, 114, 119, 120, 139, 141, 148, 160, 163, 168, 170, 208, 209, 210, 226, 229, 242
German, 97, 99, 171
Germanic, 13, 17
Giet, Stanislas, 242
Gnosis, Gnostic(s), 95, 130-132, 136, 143, 146, 150, 152, 158, 176, 180, 192, 202, 208, 210, 215, 227, 232, 233, 234, 236, 239, 240, 245
Goethe, Johann Wolfgang, 93
Goodman, Martin, 210
Goppelt, Leonhard, 208, 224
Gordianus III, Roman Emperor, 57
Gospel of John, 21, 111-112, 113, 115-116
Gospel of Thomas, 242
Gospels, 96, 103, 105, 106, 111-112, 113, 138
Grant, Michael, 27, 82, 84
Greece, 2, 113, 119
Greek(s), 2, 11, 13, 19, 75, 119, 124, 130, 143, 146, 147, 148, 149, 157, 162, 163, 164, 167, 175, 201, 213, 218, 231, 237
Grégoire, Henri, 51 , 55, 66, 79, 88, 89, 91
Gregorius of Nazianze, Christian author, 92, 93, 179
Gregorius of Nyssa, Christian author, 179

Hadrianus, 46, 49, 50, 51, 67, 182
Haines, C.R., 80
Hall, Stuart G., 212
Haman, 294
Harnack, Adolf von, 125-126, 129, 209
Hebrew, 124, 151, 152, 153, 163-164, 213, 228
Hegesippus, Christian author, 47
Helena, mother of Constantine the Great, 167
Hellenism, Hellenistic, hellenized, 16, 103, 119, 145, 148, 175, 227
Hermann, Léon, 79
Hermas, Christian author, 25, 84, 136
Hermias, Christian apologist, 145
Hermon, Mount, 93
Herodes I the Great, 47, 188
Herodes Agrippa I, 113
Herodes Antipas I, 102
Herodians, 102, 126
Herodianus, Roman historian, 89
Hierax, a Christian scholar, 186
High Priest(s) (Jewish), 99, 100, 107, 109, 111, 112, 120, 134, 206
Hilarianus, procurator of the province of Africa, 53-54
Hilary of Poitiers, 168-169, 220
Hillel, a Rabbi, 153, 188
Hillel, school of, 101
Hippo, see of Augustine, 34, 40
Hippolytus, Church Father, 27-28, 28, 31, 56, 62, 84, 85, 88, 157-159, 217
Hirsch, Emil G., 209
Hitler, Adolf, 98, 120, 171, 204
Holocaust, 96, 98, 171, 204
Homer, 9
Horsley, Richard, 205

Idumaenas see Edomites
Ignatius of Antioch, Christian author and martyr, 132-134, 137, 203, 211
Imnestar, town in Syria, 190
Irenaeus of Lyons, Christian author, 30, 85, 143-144, 158, 195, 196, 202, 203, 213, 214, 224, 228, 230, 231, 243, 244
Isaac, Jewish patriarch, 141, 146, 156
Isaac, Jules, 187, 190, 204, 223
Isis, 75
Islam, 238
Israel, people of, 39, 40, 102, 110, 157, 159, 173, 195, 204, 241
Israelites, 40, 158
Italy, 19, 184

Jacob, patriarch, 124, 140, 141, 144, 146, 156, 194

James, first bishop of Jerusalem, 2-3, 226, 229, 241
James, brother of John, 113
Jamnia (Yavne), 114, 237
Japhet, son of Noah, 125
Jehuda, a Rabbi, 153
Jeremiah, 173
Jerome (Hieronymus), Church Father, 14, 82, 87, 153, 230, 243
Jerusalem, 1, 59, 105, 107, 108, 113, 114, 120, 126, 130, 144, 147, 148, 153, 165, 181, 188, 213, 226, 227, 229, 241
Jesus Christ, 1, 2, 3, 4, 5, 8, 9, 11, 12, 15, 16, 21, 22, 29, 31, 58, 61, 75, 77, 79, 97, 98, 100, 103-106, 111, 117-118, 120, 126, 133, 135, 139, 141, 142, 144, 148, 149, 150, 151, 153, 154, 156, 157, 158, 159, 161, 163, 165, 166, 169, 173, 180, 183, 192, 193, 195, 196, 201, 207, 208, 226, 228, 229, 234, 235, 239, 241, 242
Jewish War, 47, 227
Jews, Jewish, 1, 2, 3, 4, 11, 12, 14, 17, 19, 20, 22, 23, 39, 40, 47, 48, 53, 75, 79, 83, Ch. II passim, 226, 227, 228, 235, 237, 238, 239, 240, 241, 242
Job, 40
John, Gospel author, 48, 105, 111-112, 115-116, 116
John the Baptist, 79, 111
John Chrysostom (Johannes Chrysostomus), 141, 169-178, 193, 198, 220, 221
Jong, Mayke de, 246
Jordan, 239
Joseph, patriarch, 141
Joseph of Arimathea, member of the Sanhedrin, 112
Josephus, Flavius, 2, 79
Jud Süss, 123-124, 209
Judaea, Judaeans, 4, 14, 22, 23, 100, 102, 113, 128
Judah, patriarch, 140, 163
Judaism, 4, 5, 8, 11, 12, 13, 20, 48, 53, 54, Ch. II passim, 226, 227, 237, 240, 241

Judaeo-Christians see Judaizers
Judaizers, Judaizing, 110, 145, 159, 160, 162, 164, 166, 170, 175, 176-178, 178, 179, 180, 181, 189, 191, 192, 194, 197-198, 202, 222, Ch. III passim
Julianus Apostata, 43, 70, 70-78, 92, 93, 170, 181
Jupiter Capitolinus, 13, 55, 59, 75, 83
Juster, Jean, 187, 222, 223, 224
Justina, mother of Valentinianus II, 70
Justinus Martyr, Christian author, 9, 21, 31, 50, 52, 80, 85, 117, 137-141, 153, 158, 203, 208, 212, 213, 228

Kallinikon, village in Mesopotamia, 183-185
Karl Alexander, Duke of Württember, 123
Karlhorst, Paul, 27, 41, 44, 46, 84, 86, 87, 90
Keresztes, Paul, 87
Kimelman, Reuven, 208
Klijn, A.J., 145, 214
Kötting, Bernhard, 156, 217
Kottje, R., 246
Kroner, Theodor, 209
Kukusos, town in Armenia, 170

Lactantius, Caecilius Firmianus, Christian author, 3, 32-33, 64, 65, 80, 85, 91, 92, 164-165, 219
Lake, Kirsopp, 134, 135, 211
Lange, Nicholas R.M. de, 156, 157, 216, 217
Langgässer, Elisabeth, German novelist, 203
Laodicea, town in Phrygia, 178
Latin, 160, 164, 167, 168, 201, 218
Laurentius, Christian martyr, 62
Law of Moses, 48, 98, 101, 103, 104, 106, 116, 119, 120, 121-122, 125, 128, 130, 131, 138, 139, 144, 146, 148, 149, 151, 152, 154, 156, 157, 158, 159, 163, 164, 168, 169, 172, 195, 197, 206, 208, 226, 229, 230,

235, 237, 239, 240, 241, 245
Leonides, father of Origen, 53
Leroux, Jean-Marie, 220
Letter to Diognetus, 137
Letter to the Hebrews, 110
Letter of James, 110
Letter of John, 110
Letter of Jude, 110
Letters of Paul, 110, 113
Letter of Paul to the Romans, 110, 155, 203
Letters of Peter, 110
Letter to the Thessalonians, 29
Letter to Timothy, First, 23
Levites, 99, 107, 111
Libanius, pagan rhetor, 72, 78, 93, 94
Libyan, 157
Licinii, Roman clan, 60
Licinius, Roman Emperor, 69-70
Licinius Serenianus, governor of Cappadocia, 57
Livius, Titus, 82, 83
Losey, Joseph, film director, 99
Lot, 196
Lucas, I., 223
Lucianus, Greek satirist, 7-8, 80
Lucina, cemetery of -- in Rome, 62
Luke (Lucas), 15, 76, 98, 105, 113, 114
Luttikhuizen, Gerard P., 246
Lycia, 157
Lyons (Lugdunum), 44, 51, 87, 143

Maccabean brothers, 186
Macedonia, 2, 113, 119
Macedonian Empire, 14
Macrinius, Egyptian sorcerer, 60
Mair, W., 205
Magna Mater, 55
Magnesia, town in Asia Minor, 133
Magona, town in Minorca, 185
Mani, 240
Manichaeans, 188
Marcus Aurelius, 5, 7, 9, 32, 46, 51-52, 80
Marcia, wife of the Emperor Commodus, 52
Marcion, Gnostic prophet, 131-132, 135, 136, 146, 150, 152, 155, 245
Marcionite Church, Gnostic sect, 132, 245
Mark (Marcus), 105, 242
Martyn, J. Louis, 115, 208
Martyrdom of Polycarp, 136
Mary, mother of Jesus, 1, 98
Mass, Holy, 99, 120
Matsunaga, Kikuo, 115, 207
Matthew (Mattheus), 15, 76, 105
Maxentius, Roman Emperor, 68
Maximilianus, Christian conscript, 64
Maximinianus, Roman Emperor, 66
Maximinus Daja, Roman Emperor, 66-67
Maximinus Thrax, Roman Emperor, 43, 56-57, 57, 58, 158
Maximus, pagan philosopher, 72
Median Empire, 14
Méhat, André, 214
Melito, bishop of Sardes, 32, 51, 141-143, 146, 196, 212, 213, 224
Mesopotamia, 128, 183
Messiah, 2, 27, 79, 101, 104, 106, 110, 115, 116, 117, 118, 138, 142, 149, 150, 154, 155, 168, 180, 195, 197, 203, 204, 207, 226, 227, 228
Methodius, Christian author, 14, 157, 217
Michael, archangel, 25
Michnik, Adam, Polish author, 122-123, 209
Middle Ages, 98, 169
Middle Platonism, 137
Milan, 68, 70, 73, 179, 183, 184
Milete, 65
Miltiades, Christian apologist
Minucius Felix, Christian author, 5, 6, 80, 146-147, 214
Minucius Fundanus, proconsul the province of Asia, 49
Mishnah, 108-109, 121, 138, 153
Mithras, 72, 75
Molthagen, Joachim, 53, 54, 88, 89
Momigliano, Arturo, 46, 87
Montanists, heterodox sect, 150
Moreau, Jeanne, 205
Moses, 131, 135, 141, 146, 149,

156, 195, 231, 235
Mughtasila sect, 240
Munck, Johannes, 241, 242

Naissus (Nish) (Serbian town), 73
Nau, J., 218
Nazarenes, 79
Nazareth, 228
Nazism, Nazis, 96, 122, 183, 228
Nazoraeans, 243
Nebuchadnessar (Nabuchodonosor), 27
Neoplatonic, Neoplatonism, 71, 72, 75
Neopythagoreanism, 71
Netherlands, the, 171
Neusner, Jacob, 102, 103, 168, 205, 206, 219, 220
New Testament, 1, 9, 11, 15, 92, 98, 102, 110-114, 132, 143, 149, 150, 155, 158, 159, 165, 192, 193, 196, 235, 242
New York, 122
Nero, 3, 26, 43, 46, 48
Neronia, 26
Nicaea see Council of Nicaea
Nicodemus, a Pharisee, 111, 112
Nicomedia, capital of Bithynia, 65, 66, 71, 72, 164
Noach, 231
Nock, A.D., 21, 22, 83
North Africa(n), 32, 34, 40, 52, 54, 62, 64, 66, 147, 160, 164, 178, 180
Numa Pompilius, Roman king, 17
Numidia, 63

Octavius, a pagan, 149
Olck, 80
Old Testament, 9, 11, 92, 97, 99, 131, 132, 135, 136, 139, 140, 141, 142, 143, 149, 150, 152, 153, 155, 156, 158, 159, 162, 164, 165, 175, 193, 194, 196, 197, 200, 215, 231, 239, 241
Olympian deities, 16, 75
Olympus, town in Lycia, 157
Ophites, Ophitism, 131
Oppenheimer, Joseph Ben Issacher Süsskind = 'Jud Süss', 123-124, 209

Orestes, city prefect of Alexandria, 186
Origen, 10, 28, 31, 32, 53, 59, 79, 81, 84, 152-157, 157, 162, 213, 216, 217, 242

Paedagogicum, slave barracks in Rome, 5
Pagan(ism), 98, 103, 130, 146, 147, 148, 150, 152, 154, 155, 156, 176, 180, 181, 182, 183, 190, 191, 193, 197, 202, 213
Palatine hill, 5, 26, 55
Palestine, Palestinian, 1, 24, 63, 66, 74, 77, 82, 108, 128, 139, 153, 188, 190, 229, 237, 241, 242
Pandateria (island), 48
Pannonian, 58
Panthera, allegedly the father of Jesus, 11
Paris, 73, 99
Parkes, James, 153, 159, 163, 164, 172, 213, 216, 218, 219, 220, 222, 224
Parthians, 70, 77
Passover, 99, 120, 142, 145, 159-160, 162, 176, 177, 230, 240
Pastor of Hermas, 136, 242
Patmos (island), 48
Patriarchs of Israel, 163, 231
Patriarchs, Jewish, 188-189
Paul, apostle, 1, 2, 23, 29, 30, 31, 62, 98, 100, 103, 113-114, 119, 120, 133, 145, 155, 178, 203, 204, 208, 226, 229, 237, 241
Pella (town in the Transjordan), 227, 230, 237
Pentateuch, 197, 231, 241
Pentecost Day, 1
Pergamum, 8
Persephone, 92
Perpetua, Christian martyr, 53-54
Persia, Persian Empire, 14, 43, 64, 168
Peter, apostle, 1, 62, 105, 110, 113, 116, 119, 229, 230, 231, 237
Pharisee(s), Pharisaic, 1, 22, 79, 100, 110 101, 102, 103-106, 107-108, 108, 111, 112, 115, 116, 119,

120, 127, 197, 206, 209, 229
Philadelphia, town in Asia Minor, 133, 134
Philippus Arabs, Roman Emperor, 57, 58
Philo, 79
Phoenicia, 1, 13, 77
Pilate, Pontius, 2, 21, 105, 106, 112, 133
Pityus, town in Armenia, 170
Pius XI, Pope, 99
Pius XII, Pope, 96
Plato, 9, 137, 148, 156
Platonism, Platonist(s), 10, 164
Plinius, Gaius -- Caecilius Secundus, 4, 20, 86, 87
Plutarch, 18, 82
Poitiers, 168
Pole, 122
Poliakov, Léon, 204
Polycarpus, bishop of Smyrna, 5, 133, 203
Pons Milvius, battle of, 68
Pontianus, bishop of Rome, 56, 158
Pontus, 57. 170
Pope(s), 120, 185, 190, 200, 224
Porphyry, 13-17, 82
Praetor, 19
Pritz, Ray A., 241, 242
Proselytes, proselytism, proselytizing, 1, 48, 123-130, 182, 209-210
Protestantism, 97
Pseudo-Clementina, 131, 228-229, 231, 234, 236, 237
Pseudo-Tertullian, 230, 243
Ptolemaic, 128
Punic, 40
Purim Feast, 190
Puritans (English), 241
Pythagorean, 232

Quartodecimans, 142, 166
Quinta, Christian martyr, 45
Quispel, Gispel, 242
Qumran, 102, 107

Rebecca, 194
Reformation, 120

Remus, 39
Rengstorf, Heinrich, 207, 213
Revelation of John, 110
Revius, Jacob, Dutch poet, 97
Rhône, 45
Roman(s), Ch. I passim, 100, 101, 103, 104, 105, 107, 113, 116, 122, 128, 130, 133, 15, 183, 175, 179, 194
Roman-Catholic Church, Roman-Catholics, 1, 2, 9, 15, 21, 25, 26, 28, 29, 40, 41, 43, 44, 52, 56, 59, 65, 69, 70, 74, Ch. II passim, 225, 230, 237, 238, 239
Roman Empire, 1, 2, 8, 13, 14, 17, 20, 21, 22, 23, 24, 25, 26, 27, 28, 29, 30, 31, 32, 33, 34-41, 41, 42, 44, 45, 51, 58, 59, 60, 61, 63, 68, 69, 72, 110, 127, 143, 152, 155, 181-191, 189, 190, 191, 200
Rome (city), 2, 3, 4, 19, 26, 27, 29, 39, 55, 56, 59, 68, 113, 134, 138, 149, 152, 172, 185, 227, 229, 239, 240, 242
Romulus, 17, 39
Ruether, Rosemary, 130, 204, 210
Rufinus, Christian author, 94
Rusticus, Q. Iunius, praefectus urbis in Rome, 52, 138, 144

Sabbath, 75, 111, 120, 121, 125, 133, 137, 138, 156, 163, 166, 168, 175, 176, 178, 185, 186, 226, 230, 239, 240, 241
Sadducees, 100, 101, 102, 103, 106, 107
Saint Peter in Rome, 120
Samaria, 1, 113, 137
Samaritans, 55, 111, 188
Samuel, 241
Sanhedrin, 2, 104-106, 112, 113, 114, 116, 117, 118
Sardes, town in Asia Minor, 141, 142, 143
Sardinia, 52, 56, 158
Satan, 24, 28, 32, 120, 160
Saturnilos, Gnostic prophet, 131
Saul see Paul
Scaliger, Giulio Cesare, 2

Scandinavia, 171
Schäfke, Werner, 86
Schoeps, Hans Joachim, 228, 229, 230,, 245 232, 237, 238, 243, 244, 246
Scholem, Gershom, 118, 208
Schreckenberg, Heinz, 160, 165, 167, 181, 182, 215, 218, 219, 221, 222
Schürer, Emil, 209
Scillium (North African town), 52
Scribes, 100, 101
Scyths, 28
Segal, Alan, 226, 241, 242, 243
Seleucid, 14, 128
Sem, son of Noah, 125
Semite(s), 55, 98, 99, 100
Senate, Roman, 19, 47, 54
Seneca, 79
Septimius Severus, Roman Emperor, 43, 52-53, 54
Septuagint, 124
Serapis, 75
Serbia, 73
Sethian, Gnostic sect, 131
Sevenster, Jan N., 205
Severi (Emperors), 52-54, 58
Severus Majoricensis, 223
Sextus Julius Africanus, Christian author, 157
Sexuality, 233, 234
Shammai, school of, Shammaites, 101, 102
Shebbes-goy, 121
Sibylline Books, 33
Silver, Abba Hillel, 208, 209
Silvester I, bishop of Rome, 165, 167, 224
Simeon the Stylites, 186
Simon, Marcel, 117, 118, 126, 127, 129, 135, 166, 184, 185, 208, 209, 210, 211, 212, 219, 220, 221, 222, 223 , 225, 241, 243
Simon the Magician, 131, 227, 229, 231
Sinai, Mount, 195
Sixtus II, bishop of Rome, 52
Smallwood, Mary, 128, 129, 210
Smyrna, 5, 59, 133, 134

Socrates, the sage, 73, 148
Socrates, the historian, 186, 190, 223
Sodomites, 131
Sofar Award, 122
Solomo, 131, 241
Solomo's porch in the Jerusalem Temple, 112
Sordi, Marta, 21, 22, 55, 83, 88, 89
Soter, bishop of Rome, 27
Sozomenos, Christian historian, 92, 93, 94
Spain, Spanish, 62, 161, 162
Spartianus, Roman historian, 88
Stephen, the first Christian martyr, 113
Stoa, Stoic, 9, 169
Strecker, Georg, 225, 232, 233, 241, 243, 244
Stuttgart, 124
Suetonius, Tranquillius, 3, 79, 80, 84, 87
Sweden, 228
Switzerland, 97
Symmachians, 244
Symmachus, an Ebionite, 231
Synod of Carthage, 178
Synod of Elvira, 161-162
Synod of Laodicea, 178
Syria(n), Syriac, 14, 55, 58, 63, 77, 132, 167, 168, 169, 190, 218, 227, 237, 238, 242

Tabernacles, Feast of the, 120, 176
Tacitus, Publius Cornelius, 3-4, 46, 47, 80, 87, 216
Talmud, 108, 120, 127, 193, 209, 210
Tannaim, 107, 108
Tarphon, a Rabbi, 138
Tarsicius, Christian martyr, 90
Tarragona, 62
Tatianus, Christian author, 145
Taylor, Miriam, 126, 129, 144, 146, 150, 154, 196, 209, 210, 212, 213, 214, 215, 216, 224
Temple of Concordia in Rome, 35
Temple of Jerusalem, 100, 102, 103, 107, 108, 109, 111, 112, 113, 114,

116, 120, 147, 151, 160, 181, 209, 226
Tertullianus, 22, 30-31, 32, 33, 44, 48, 49, 80, 83, 85, 86, 87, 88, 89, 92, 139, 149-152, 194, 212, 213, 215, 216, 224, 246
Teveste (Tebessa) (North African town), 64
Theodoretus, Church Father, 93, 94, 238, 246
Theodosius I the Great, 38, 40, 182, 183-185, 188
Theodosius II, Roman Emperor, 186, 187, 188, 189, 190
Theophilus, Christian apologist, 145-146, 214
Thracian, 56
Tiber, 68
Tiberias, town in Palestine, 188
Tiberius, 151
Tigris, 168
Titus, 47, 130
Torah, 106, 108, 208, 231
Traianus, 4, 20, 43, 49, 50, 57, 67
Tralles, town in Asia Minor, 134
Transjordan, 227, 230, 237
Treves (Trier), 164
Trigg, Joseph Wilson, 153, 216
Troy, 39
Troyes, 62
Tryphon, a Jew, 117, 118, 138-140
Tyrus, 13, 66, 152

Urbicus, city prefect of Rome, 50

Vagany, L., 82
Valens, Roman Emperor, 43, 70
Valentinians, Gnostic sect, 131
Valentinianus I, Roman Emperor, 182
Valentinianus II, Roman Emperor, 70 Valerianus, Roman Emperor, 50, 60-63, 160
Valerius Maximus, prefect of Rome, 60
Vandals, 34
Varius Avitus (= Elagabalus), 55
Vatican, 120
Vatican Hill, 62

Venantius Fortunatus, 220
Vespasianus, 47, 48, 126
Vergilius (Virgil), Publius -- Maro, 35, 85
Via Appia, 62
Via Cornelia, 62
Via Ostiensis, 62
Victor, Aurelius, Roman historian, 90

Wilde, Robert, 153, 157, 158, 214, 215, 216, 217, 218
Wilken, Robert, 8, 15, 80, 81, 82, 171, 220, 221
Williams, A.L., 136, 140, 168, 212, 219
Williams, Rowan, 217
Wistrich, Robert S., 204
Württemberg, Duchy of, 123

Yom Kippur, 120
York, 66, 68

Zealot(s), 22, 100, 102, 107
Zeno of Verona, Christian author, 179
Zephyrinus, bishop of Rome, 90
Zeus, 66, 76
Ziegler, Ignaz, 208